Mercer Commentary on the Bible

Volume 8

General Epistles and Revelation

Mercer University Press

Mercer Dictionary of the Bible
July 1990; 5th and corrected printing July 1997

Mercer Dictionary of the Bible Course Syllabi
July 1990

Mercer Commentary on the Bible
November 1994

Cover illustration: *The Four Horsemen of the Apocalypse* by Jacob von Steinle (Austrian, 1810–1886). "And I saw, and behold, a white horse. . . . another horse, bright red. . . . behold, a black horse. . . . and, behold, a pale horse" (Revelation 6:1-8 RSV).

Mercer Commentary on the Bible

Volume 8

General Epistles and Revelation

GENERAL EDITORS
Watson E. Mills, Richard F. Wilson

ASSOCIATE EDITORS
Roger A. Bullard, Walter Harrelson, Edgar V. McKnight

MERCER UNIVERSITY PRESS EDITOR
Edmon L. Rowell, Jr.

WITH MEMBERS OF THE
National Association of Baptist Professors of Religion

MERCER UNIVERSITY PRESS
March 2000

ISBN 0-86554-513-8 MUP/P140

Mercer Commentary on the Bible: General Epistles and Revelation
Volume 8 of an 8-volume perfect-bound reissue of
the *Mercer Commentary on the Bible* (©1995)
with articles from the *Mercer Dictionary of the Bible* (1990, 1997)

Printed in the United States of America
First printing, March 2000

The paper used in this publication meets the minimum requirements
of the American National Standard for Information Sciences—
Permanence of Paper for Printed Library Materials, ANSI Z39.48-1984.

Library of Congress Cataloging-in-Publication Data

Mercer commentary on the Bible.
Volume 8. General Epistles and Revelation /
general editors, Watson E. Mills and Richard F. Wilson;
associate editors, Walter Harrelson . . . [et al.].
pp. cm.
1. Bible—commentaries. I. Mills, Watson Early. II. Mercer University Press.
III. National Association of Baptist Professors of Religion.

CIP data available from the Library of Congress.

Contents

Commentaries (from the *Mercer Commentary on the Bible*)

Preface

From the *Mercer Commentary on the Bible* (MCB), this volume includes the commentaries on the so-called General Epistles (here including Hebrews) and on the Book of Revelation. Appropriate articles from the *Mercer Dictionary of the Bible* (MDB) make up the introduction section which precedes the commentaries. This MCB/MDB fascicle is for use in the classroom and for any other setting where study focuses on these New Testament writings and where a convenient introduction text is desired. This is number 8 in the series of MCB/MDB portions or fascicles.

1. Pentateuch/Torah (Genesis–Deuteronomy)	Isbn 0-86554-506-5 P133
2. History of Israel (Joshua–Esther)	Isbn 0-86554-507-3 P134
3. (Wisdom) Writings (Job–Song of Songs)	Isbn 0-86554-508-1 P135
4. Prophets (Isaiah–Malachi)	Isbn 0-86554-509-X P136
5. Deuterocanonicals/Apocrypha	Isbn 0-86554-510-3 P137
6. Gospels (Matthew–John)	Isbn 0-86554-511-1 P138
7. Acts and Pauline Writings (Acts–Philemon)	Isbn 0-86554-512-X P139
8. Epistles and Revelation (Heb–Rev)	**Isbn 0-86554-513-8 P140**

That these divisions—and their titles—are arbitrary is obvious. These divisions originate in the classroom as convenient and provisionally appropriate blocks of text for focused study during a semester- or quarter-long course of study. Other divisions are possible, even desirable (combining Acts with the Gospels, for example, rather than with Paul), but the present divisions seem appropriate for most users. (For comparison, we may note, for example, the contents of volume 12 of the *New Interpreter's Bible* [1998]—Hebrews–Revelation.)

Regarding the use of this and other MCB/MDB portions, please note the following.

A bracketed, flush-right entry at the head of each MDB article and MCB commentary indicates the original page number(s): for example, "Hebrews [MCB 1267-81]"; "Symbol [MDB 865-67]." The text from both MDB and MCB is *essentially* that of the original, differing only in format: here the text is redesigned to fit a 6x9-inch page (the page size of both MDB and MCB is 7x10 inches). Also, we have taken advantage of the opportunity of this fascicle reprint to make some corrections and minor revisions.

References to other MDB articles are indicated by small caps. In addition, the "See also" sections at the end of the MDB articles indicate other articles that are appropriate for further study.

MDB has introductory articles for every book of the Bible, including those routinely referred to as apocryphal and/or deuterocanonical. For this volume the appropriate introductory articles are reprinted here, but MCB does *not* include small-caps references to these MDB introduction articles unless reference is made to a specific statement in the article. For other fascicles in this series, it is assumed the reader is aware of these MDB introductory articles and will refer to them in MDB as needed.

Notice that small caps are used also for BCE and CE, for certain texts and versions (LXX, KJV, NRSV), and for the tetragrammaton YHWH.

For abbreviations, see the lists in either MDB or MCB. Regarding the editors and contributors, please see both MDB and MCB. The *Course Syllabi* handbook has a complete listing of original MDB articles (pp. 73-80). MDB includes a complete listing of articles arranged by contributor (pp. 989-93).

We intend that these texts be available, appropriate, and helpful for Bible students both in and out of the classroom and indeed for anyone seeking guidance in uncovering the abundant wealth of the Scriptures. Your critical response to these and other texts from Mercer University Press is welcome and encouraged.

March 2000 — *Edmon L. Rowell, Jr.*
Macon, Georgia USA — Mercer University Press

Introduction

Of Apocalypses, Numbers, and Eschatons

Apocalyptic Literature [MDB 36-38]

•**Apocalyptic Literature.** [uh-pok'uh-lip"tik] The adjective "apocalyptic" refers to a field of literature that includes a GENRE of literature called apocalypses (in the Bible the books of DANIEL and REVELATION qualify) as well as other types of literature (e.g., certain letters or the WAR SCROLL from Qumran) whose subject matter closely resembles that of the apocalypses. The noun "apocalypse" comes from the Greek word ἀποκάλυψις, which means "revelation." An apocalypse is thus a book that reveals hidden information. To describe the nature of that information is to describe the genre itself.

Description of an Apocalypse. Scholars have typically listed a number of characteristics belonging to apocalypses. In terms of literary characteristics, we may mention the prevalence of visions and auditions, the revelation of secrets, and the activity of a celestial being to interpret the vision. Apocalypses are often pseudonymous, i.e., they are written under the name of a worthy past figure. Often the name of the figure will give the reader insight into the contents of the apocalypse. For example, 4 EZRA utilizes the Jewish tradition that EZRA copied the whole OT by having him receive numerous "secret" works for the last days. 2 BARUCH deals with the destruction of the second TEMPLE in 70 CE through the eyes of JEREMIAH's scribe, who witnessed the destruction of the first temple in 586 BCE. Apocalypses employ coded speech, in which numbers, animals, and unusual natural occurrences take on special meanings. The images of the apocalyptic literature are reused by later writers, so that meanings are piled on top of one another. Also, apocalypses employ much hortatory or paranetic material, instructing persons how to live on the basis of the secrets revealed to them. Finally, apocalypses employ narration, which identifies the seer, his state of mind, his reactions, and any final instructions about preserving the revelation.

Themes characteristic of apocalypses are numerous. One such element is the periodization of history, in which the vicissitudes of national life are arranged according to a definite model (see the bright and dark waters of *2 Baruch*). However history is presented, the time of the actual author of the apocalypse is depicted as the last, bitter days of this age, with the age to come already casting its influence over those who have insight. Much of the "prediction" in an apocalypse is actually "prophecy after the fact," a review of the time between the alleged author and the time of the actual author. This practice gives apocalypses the appearance of determinism, but apocalypses presume that individuals have the full right to choose, and they hold people accountable for their choices.

Apocalyptic ESCHATOLOGY tends toward DUALISM. It envisions two aeons, this age and the age to come. This age is speeding toward an imminent end, often including cosmic upheavals. The periodization of history allows those in the know to read the signs of the coming eschaton or end. That eschaton will be marked by the reversal of the sociological status quo, with the righteous triumphing. This reversal will be brought about by God's activity, either directly or through his MESSIAH. Judgment will properly compensate good and evil people. Often the seer will tour HEAVEN and/or HELL. God's rival, SATAN, will be defeated. The entire cosmos might be renewed. The righteous will enjoy an eschatological banquet. Often the nations, perhaps after being purged, will be allowed to join in. Finally, apocalypses develop systems of angelology, demonology, COSMOLOGY, ASTROLOGY, and even botany.

By no means are all of these characteristics unique to apocalypses. Nor does the listing of them adequately define an apocalypse. Some scholars, therefore, have attempted to reduce the list of characteristics to one essential characteristic. That one characteristic might be the apocalyptic view of history, or the failure of apocalyptic to translate its picture of the future into historical, political terms, or the emphasis on visions and wisdom. None of these suggestions has won widespread acceptance. A new definition for an apocalypse has emerged which defines the genre in terms of structure, content, and function.

" 'Apocalypse' is a genre of revelatory literature with a narrative framework, in which a revelation is mediated by an otherworldly being to a human recipient, disclosing a transient reality which is both temporal, insofar as it envisages eschatological salvation, and spatial, insofar as it involves another, supernatural world" (J. J. Collins, 9), "intended to interpret present, earthly circumstances in light of the supernatural world and of the future, and to influence both the understanding and the behavior of the audience by means of divine authority" (A. Y. Collins, "Introduction," 7).

Types of Apocalypses. This definition lends itself to designing a typology of apocalypses. Apocalypses, both Jewish and Christian, can be distinguished on the basis of the presence or absence of an otherworldly journey (*Semeia* 14:30-44, 70-95). Type I apocalypses will be those lacking such a journey, while type II apocalypses will describe an otherworldly tour. Each type manifests three subtypes: (a) apocalypses with a historical review, (b) apocalypses with a cosmic and/or political eschatology, and (c) apocalypses with only a personal eschatology. There are no Jewish examples of type Ib and Ic, and no Christian example of type IIa. A list of apocalypses written between the mid-second century BCE and the late third century CE follows, classified by type.

Type Ia. Apocalypses with a historical review and no otherworldly journey. Jewish: Daniel (7–12); the "Animal Apocalypse" of 1 ENOCH 87–90; the "Apocalypse of Weeks" (1 Enoch 93; 91:12-17); JUBILEES 23; *4 Ezra*; and *2 Baruch*. Christian: LADDER OF JACOB.

Type Ib. Apocalypses with a cosmic and/or political eschatology and no otherworldly journey. Jewish: none extant. Christian: Revelation; the APOCALYPSE OF PETER; the SHEPHERD OF HERMAS; the *Book of Elchasai*; the *Apocalypse of St. John the Theologian*; and the *Testament of the Lord* 1:1-14.

Type Ic. Apocalypses with only personal eschatology and no otherworldly journey. Jewish: none extant. Christian: *5 Ezra* (2 Esdr 1–2) 2:42-48; the TESTAMENT OF ISAAC 2–3a; the TESTAMENT OF JACOB 1–3a; the *Questions of Bartholomew*; and the *Book of the Resurrection of Jesus Christ* by Bartholomew the Apostle 8b–14a.

Type IIa. Apocalypses with a historical review and an otherworldly journey. Jewish: the APOCALYPSE OF ABRAHAM. Christian: none extant.

Type IIb. Apocalypses with cosmic and/or political eschatology and an otherworldly journey. Jewish: *1 Enoch* 1–36; the *Book of the Heavenly Luminaries* (*1 Enoch* 72–82); the *Similitudes of Enoch* (*1 Enoch* 37–71); 2 ENOCH (or Slavonic Enoch); and the *Testament of Levi* 2–5. Christian: the ASCENSION OF ISAIAH 6–11; the APOCALYPSE OF PAUL; *4 Ezra*; and the *Apocalypse of the Virgin Mary*.

Type IIc. Apocalypses with only personal eschatology and an otherworldly journey. Jewish: 3 BARUCH; the *Testament of Abraham*; and the APOCALYPSE OF ZEPHANIAH. Christian: the *Testament of Isaiah* 5–6; the *Testament of Jacob* 5; the *Story of Zosimus*; the *Apocalypse of the Holy Mother of God concerning the Punishments*; the APOCALYPSE OF JAMES, the Brother of the Lord; the *Mysteries of St. John the Apostle and the Holy Virgin*; and *Book of the Resurrection of Jesus Christ* (by Bartholomew the Apostle) 17b–19b; and the APOCALYPSE OF SEDRACH.

Origin of Apocalyptic Thinking. The question of the origin of apocalyptic has drawn much attention from scholars. Opinions can be reviewed under three main headings.

Many, perhaps most, scholars (e.g., R. H. Charles, H. H. Rowley, D. S. Russell) have argued that apocalyptic literature is a child of prophecy. Postexilic, eschatological prophecy in the OT seems to provide a natural link between the classical, preexilic prophets and apocalypses (see below), so scholars point to texts like Ezek 38–39, Isa 24–27, 34–35, 56–66, Joel, and Zech 9–14 as the seedbed for apocalyptic thinking.

Not all scholars, however, agree with this view. An alternative was proposed by Gerhard von Rad, who argued that the essence of apocalyptic literature was its deterministic view of history, a view unaffected by the prophetic conception built on reciting the creeds about God's mighty deeds, and derived from WISDOM LITERATURE.

Still others saw apocalyptic literature as the child of foreign influences. Usually characteristics like dualism caused scholars (e.g., Wilhelm Bousset) to point to Zoroastrianism as the most likely source of influence, but T. Francis Glasson and Franz Boll looked toward Greece and Rudolf Otto thought pre-Hindu Aryan thinking had made an impact.

All of these views build on a degree of evidence, so where did apocalyptic thinking originate? Recently, biblical scholars have looked to the disciplines of anthropology and sociology to help answer this question. Scholars in those disciplines indicate that apocalyptic thinking arises in societies or subcultures of a society which experience relative deprivation, i.e., when the reality of their lives becomes too far separated negatively from their hopes and aspirations. Hence, external attacks or persecutions, as well as internal disarray that threatens a group's internalized system of assumptions, values, and commitments, threatens the group's self-identity, and challenges its worldview and its perception of moral order, may cause some members of a society to break with its leaders and their program and formulate a new program. The Book of Daniel gives evidence of just such a break.

Daniel contains stories about Jews living in foreign courts and remaining faithful to Judaism. Such stories would be told by people attempting to cope with life and work in a foreign court. Apocalyptic thought could develop among such people, however, if their expectations were not met. In the same way, priests out of power or prophets conscious of the discrepancy between prophetic expectations for the restoration and the realities of the postexilic period began to think in an apocalyptic fashion. The time when the pressures reached a climax in ancient Israel seems to have been the period of persecution under Antiochus Epiphanes, and apocalyptic thought gave birth to the genre of apocalypses as the authors' vehicles for expressing their hopes.

The insight that apocalyptic literature arises from groups experiencing at least relative deprivation may explain why apocalyptic did not develop among some Jews. PHILO and the author of 4 MACCABEES were quite at home in the dominant Greek culture and needed only to defend their worldview and sense of moral order, which they did in Greek terms. Likewise, the SADDUCEES constituted a priestly collaborationist group, standing far from apocalypticism. By contrast, the impotent priests at Qumran became somewhat apocalyptic in their thought.

There were, of course, antecedents in the OT for apocalypses. The visions of Zech 1–6 anticipate the characteristic report of visions with an interpreting ANGEL. Further, texts like Ezek 38–39, Isa 24–27, 34–35, 56–66, Joel, and Zech 9–14 developed eschatological thinking, providing later apocalyptic literature with such themes as the imminent inbreak of the KINGDOM OF GOD, judgment, the return of the exiles, protection of God's people, an eschatological banquet, the defeat and/or conversion of the nations, paradisiacal living conditions, natural disorders heralding the end, and salvation to the faithful.

Related Literature. Apocalyptic thinking also emerged in literature other than apocalypses. Scholars often cite the TESTAMENTS OF THE TWELVE PATRIARCHS (esp. the *Testaments of Levi*, *Dan*, and *Judah*) and the SIBYLLINE ORACLES as books containing apocalyptic thinking. Among the DEAD SEA SCROLLS a number of the sectarian works, especially the *War Scroll*, share a thought world very similar at least to that of the apocalypses. New Testament scholars speak of Mark 13 and its parallels as the synoptic apocalypse, thought the material occurs within the genre of gospel and takes the *form* of a farewell discourse. The eschatology of Paul, particularly in 1 Thess 4, resembles apocalyptic eschatology in terms of its expectation of the imminent return of the Messiah and the end of this age. Further, Ernst Käsemann argued that behind the Gospel of Matthew stood, among others, an apocalyptic group that generated a type of legal saying of Jesus in which the protasis is conditional, but the apodosis is apodictic (e.g., Matt 5:23-24), and a set of sayings by Jesus summarizing who he was in the form "I am come . . . " (e.g., Matt 10:34-35). According to Käsemann the Gospel of Matthew preserves the compulsion of early, apocalyptic preachers to make known the secret things of the Lord.

Summary. Apocalyptic literature includes both apocalypses and other genres that exhibit a distinctive worldview and eschatology. This worldview involves a multi-storied universe, with earth, heaven, and hell. It involves further a view of history that is divided into periods. That history is leading humankind nowhere, and must soon be brought to an end by God himself. The end time will be characterized by cosmic disorders, social class reversal, and warfare; in short, the *status quo* will be reversed and the apocalyptic group will receive its due recompense. The people by whom and for whom apocalyptic literature is written perceived themselves to be deprived of that recompense in this age. They designed the literary genre called apocalypse to convey their message of eschatological reversal. Specifically, an apocalypse exhibits a narrative structure within which an otherworldly being conveys a revelation of eschatological salvation and a supernatural world.

See also DANIEL; REVELATION.

Bibliography. G. Allan, "A Theology of Millenarianism: The Irvingite Movement as an Illustration," *BJS* 25 (1974): 296-310; R. H. Charles, *A Critical History of the Doctrine of the Future Life*; A. Y. Collins, "The Early Christian Apocalypses," *Semeia* 14 (1979): 61-121; idem, "Introduction: Early Christian Apocalypticism," *Semeia* 36 (1986): 1-11; J. J. Collins, "Introduction: Towards the Morphology of a Genre" and "The Jewish Apocalypses," *Semeia* 14 (1979): 1-59; T. F. Glasson, *Greek Influences in Eschatology*; P. D. Hanson, *The Dawn of Apocalyptic*; E. Käsemann, "The Beginnings of Christian Theology," *JTC* 6 (1969): 17-46; R. Otto, *The Kingdom of God and the Son of Man*; O. Plöger, *Theocracy and Eschatology*; G. von Rad, *Old Testament Theology*; H. H. Rowley, *The Relevance of Apocalyptic*; D. S. Russell, *The Method and Message of Apocalyptic*; W. Schmithals, *The Apocalyptic Movement*; P. Vielhauer, *New Testament Apocrypha*; R. D. Wilson, "From Prophecy to Apocalyptic: Reflections on the Shape of Israelite Religion," *Semeia* 21 (1981): 79-95; P. Worsley, *The Trumpet Shall Sound.*

—PAUL L. REDDITT

•**Apocalypticism.** *See* APOCALYPTIC LITERATURE; ESCHATOLOGY IN THE NEW TESTAMENT; ESCHATOLOGY IN THE OLD TESTAMENT.

Epistle/Letter [MDB 258]

•**Epistle/Letter.** Epistles and letters are written messages to individuals or groups separated from their authors by distance or special circumstances. In antiquity letter writing was a well-established mode of communication and assumed many forms ranging from simple personal addresses to elaborate literary masterpieces. Epicurus, Seneca, and Cicero used the epistolary medium for discourse on moral, ethical, and philosophical questions.

In the early church the letter became the most prominent means of elaborating on matters of theology and Christian conduct. Out of twenty-seven NT works, twenty-one are letters, and two of the remaining ones (Acts and Revelation) contain letters. The practice of writing letters was widely continued in primitive Christianity by bishops and influential church leaders such as Clement of Rome, Polycarp, and Ignatius. Thus there came into existence a new epistolary genre called encyclical letters which were meant to convey doctrinal decisions affecting the whole church.

Adolf Deissmann distinguished between "letter" and "epistle." Letters, he suggested, are a private, nonliterary means of communication; epistles are artistic compositions intended for public dissemination. According to such a definition, Paul's writings were not meant to be literary compositions but simple letters not intended for large audiences. Yet many of Paul's letters, even the very personal Letter to Philemon, were in fact written to be shared with the larger community. Most modern scholars refer to NT written communications as "letters" rather than "epistles." The RSV, for example, never mentions the term "epistle."

NT letters, however, have been elevated by the early church to a level of spiritual eminence which places them in a unique category eluding traditional definitions. Their permanent use in the church as inspired texts gives them a quality and meaning never shared by other epistolary documents.

The NT contains several different types of letters. There are general letters (to churches) and pastoral letters (to individuals). The general Letters of Paul tend to deal with larger doctrinal issues affecting the community as a whole. The Pastoral Letters (1-2 Timothy, Titus), whose authorship is contested, belong to the second generation of Christians. They take the form of private communications to Paul's associates. Early Christians regarded the Catholic Letters (James, 1-2 Peter, 1-2-3 John, Jude) as universal and more complete in their teaching. They are encyclical in character, and are often contrasted with Paul's more personal and more local letters. Hebrews is sometimes considered a letter but would qualify more as a treatise containing a long sustained argument in favor of the preeminence of Christianity over Judaism.

NT writers could not foresee that their letters would be collected into a body of canonical literature. Paul's open discussions of scandals and misconduct suggest he meant to keep a large portion of his writings private. At the same time, the direct nature of the letters attests to their reliability and makes them indispensable for an appreciation of the apostolic age. It is thus understandable that the early church elevated them to the dignity of canonical status.

See also GENERAL LETTERS; LETTERS/INSCRIPTIONS; PASTORAL EPISTLES; PAUL; WRITING SYSTEMS.

Bibliography. A. Deissmann, *Light from the Ancient East*; W. G. Doty, *Letters in Primitive Christianity*; S. K. Stowers, *Letter Writing in Greco-Roman Antiquity*.

—PAUL CIHOLAS

Eschatology in the New Testament [MDB 259-60]

•**Eschatology in the New Testament.** [es'kuh-tol"uh-jee] "Eschatology" is from a combination of two Gk. words: "the last thing" (ἔσχατον) and "teaching," or "word" (λόγος). Eschatology became a technical term in German (and subsequently English-speaking) dogmatic theology during the 1800s, referring to doctrine or teaching about the final things that included DEATH, RESURRECTION, the PAROUSIA (second coming), JUDGMENT, the MILLENNIUM, ETERNAL LIFE, HEAVEN, and HELL. When defined in these terms eschatology can be thought of only in relation to the future and otherworldly matters.

Examination of the books of the Bible, however, shows that this understanding is an oversimplification, for certain biblical materials commonly referred to as eschatological are at least as concerned with present existence as they are with the future. Moreover, even when defined strictly in terms of the future, a dogmatic approach to biblical eschatology has problems, for there is no single biblical point of view on the future. For example, some authors are concerned with the future of earthly life, while others seem interested in a world and time beyond the human realm. Indeed the biblical authors show a remarkable variety of thinking in this area. Thus, biblical eschatology is complex, and the study of it is complicated.

Scholars have, however, found ways of talking about the diverse eschatological thinking of the biblical authors and have coined a number of phrases that describe the complex biblical materials. Thus one reads about (1) prophetic versus apocalyptic eschatology, (2) individual versus national eschatology, (3) individual versus general or universal eschatology, (4) consistent versus realized eschatology, and (5) consistent or realized versus inaugurated eschatology. These phrases are not without liabilities, for frequently the eschatology of a biblical author will not fit neatly into any one category, rather it will be characterized by elements of more than one of these descriptions. But, if these categories are understood as general descriptions that must be nuanced appropriately for each specific biblical author, rather than as absolute and exclusive summaries, they are helpful in understanding the thoughts of the biblical authors about the future/end.

In general, prior to the Babylonian Exile, the prophets of Israel were not interested in individual and otherworldly matters. Instead, preexilic prophets thought, spoke, and wrote of the future of the nation in history. For these biblical authors, the future was the time in which the judgment of God on Israel and its enemies would come about in this world. Therefore divine judgment did not mean the end of the world, but a dramatic alteration of the current patterns of life. God would crush Israel's enemies, or the enemies would execute God's judgment on a sinful Israel (e.g., Isa 1–39; Hosea; Amos; Micah). During the Exile, through the encounter of Israel's religious thought with that of the Babylonians, a less historically bound form of eschatology evolved, normally called apocalyptic eschatology. The outlook of apocalyptic eschatology is universal rather than national in orientation. In this pattern of thought God acts directly, intervening in history and judging the world in order to bring the current course of history to an end. Beyond this act of judgment lies a new, radically transformed world order (e.g., Isa 40–66, esp. 56–66; Dan 7). In the late pre-Christian period both traditional prophetic eschatology and the newer apocalyptic eschatology informed the outlook of the Jewish people, but the literary sources show that an apocalyptic point of view became increasingly popular.

In the writings of the NT one finds many examples of the apocalyptic pattern of eschatological thought (Matt 25; Mark 13; 1 Cor 7:29-31). Around the turn of the twentieth century, Albert Schweitzer argued that the eschatological teaching of Jesus was apocalyptic in character: the whole life, work, and especially teaching of Jesus was a declaration of a future but imminent act of God that would end the present age through judgment and issue in a new era (the KINGDOM OF GOD) where God's will would be done. Schweitzer maintained that Jesus' whole ministry could only be understood as "consistently eschatological" in this apocalyptic sense. Schweitzer's interpretation was opposed by C. H. Dodd who contended that Jesus' teaching and ministry was to be understood in terms of "realized eschatology." Dodd saw the Kingdom of God as already present in Jesus' own ministry, not as a future entity. Other NT scholars have moved to a position between these options, called "inaugurated eschatology," that understands the teaching and ministry of Jesus to possess characteristics of both "consistent" and "realized" eschatologies. Thus, the Kingdom of God is present in the life and work of Jesus, but its fulfillment still lies in the future; and so, one can speak of the "already" and the "not yet" of the Kingdom.

Much of contemporary NT scholarship focuses on the significance of eschatology for the interpretation of various NT writings. Scholars agree on the importance of this subject for accurate interpretation, but the nature of the eschatology of the NT writings is a point of extensive debate. The Book of Revelation is an obvious center of such study, but the Letters of Paul are also scrutinized in terms of eschatology and, to a lesser degree, the remaining books of the NT are presently being interpreted in this way.

See also APOCALYPTIC LITERATURE; DEATH; ESCHATOLOGY IN THE OT; ETERNAL LIFE; HEAVEN; HELL; JUDGMENT, DAY OF; KINGDOM OF GOD; MESSIAH/CHRIST; MILLENNIUM; PAROUSIA/SECOND COMING; RESURRECTION IN THE NT; RESURRECTION IN THE OT; SATAN IN THE NT; SATAN IN THE OT; SON OF MAN.

Bibliography. J. Bright, *A History of Israel* and *The Kingdom of God*; C. H. Dodd, *The Parables of the Kingdom*, rev. ed.; P. D. Hanson, *The Dawn of Apocalyptic*, rev. ed.; N. Perrin, *The Kingdom of God in the Teaching of Jesus*; F. Richter, *Die Lehre von den letzen Dingen*; J. A. T. Robinson, *In the End, God . . .*; A. Schweitzer, *The Quest of the Historical Jesus*; G. von Rad, *The Message of the Prophets*.

—MARION L. SOARDS

General Letters [MDB 320-21]

•**General Letters.** Contemporary scholars routinely designate seven letters as General (or Catholic) Letters: James; 1 and 2 Peter; 1, 2, and 3 John; and Jude. Others argue for only five letters: James; 1 and 2 Peter; Jude; and Hebrews—adding

Hebrews because of similarities to the others and placing the "letters of John" in the Johannine corpus. Continuing debate about what constitutes a "general epistle" reflects the troubled history of these Letters.

Eusebius is the first to apply the term "catholic epistles" (ca. 324) to a collection of letters: James, Jude, 2 Peter, and 2 and 3 John, which he also designated as "disputed letters," i.e., not having universal acceptance in the church. As the process of formation of a NT canon drew to a close, 1 Peter and 1 John were added to the Catholic Epistles corpus as evidenced by Athanasius's so-called Festal Letter of 367 (Hebrews is designated a Pauline work).

Clearly the designation "Catholic" or "General" Letters is a flexible one, although there are certain elements common among the letters of the corpus. First John and Hebrews (if included in the corpus) lack mention of intended readers but have epistolary closings. Third John is directed to a person, Gaius, while the remaining letters have vaguely defined audiences: a single congregation for 2 John and community clusters in James, Peter, and Jude. While the audiences may be elusive, one infers that they share a common commitment to a distinctly Jewish-Christian heritage—especially the audiences for James, Peter, Jude, and Hebrews—over against the assumed gentile heritage which underlies the Pauline corpus. Thus the General Letters provide a necessary perspective on the diversity of the early church. Such are the internal commonalities of these letters.

Externally, at least two additional shared characteristics may be noted. During the formation of a NT canon only 1 Peter and 1 John among the General Letters escaped dispute. Reasons for hesitancy in accepting the remaining letters are manifold, yet one issue seems dominant, that of apostolic authorship. James, Jude, and 2 Peter are linked in that Jude draws authority from James (Jude 1:1) and content from 2 Peter. Second and 3 John are written by "the elder" and reflect themes found in the Fourth Gospel and 1 John (undisputed works) as well as in the Book of Revelation. Clear apostolic authority was lacking in the five disputed letters, according to the judgment of the early church. The inclusion in the canon of the General Letters, however, is a forceful statement of the conviction of the early church that these works are an authentic, authoritative expression of Christian faith.

See also EPISTLE/LETTER; HEBREWS, LETTER TO THE; JAMES, LETTER OF; JOHN, GOSPEL AND LETTERS OF; JUDE, LETTER OF; PETER, LETTERS OF.

—RICHARD F. WILSON

Gnosticism [MDB 333-35]

•**Gnosticism.** [nos"tuh-siz'uhm] The word Gnosticism derives from the Gk. noun γνῶσις (*gnosis*), knowledge. The term is used by modern scholars to designate a series of diverse religious movements in the first three centuries CE. In antiquity the groups so identified designated themselves, and were designated by others, with other names. Some scholars find enough in common among these groups to argue that they should be described as "the Gnostic religion." Others have classified the early movements into types of religiophilosophical systems, e.g., Syrian gnosis,

Marcionite Christianity, Valentinianism, the Basilidian movement. On this model the numerous distinct groups, such as the Cainites, Peratae, Barbelo-Gnostics, the Sethians, and the Borborites, to name only a few described in the later Church Fathers, are seen as arising out of the earlier systems.

The movements can be grouped under the rubric "Gnosticism" because they do make certain common assumptions. Essentially the groups are anticosmic, or world-rejecting. While they describe it differently, the CREATION of the world is portrayed in negative terms as driving from an error-prone creator. Hence the highest spiritual reality had nothing to do with the creation of the world, for creation was EVIL in its origins. Therefore the world holds humanity trapped in ignorance of its higher spiritual possibilities. Only an emissary sent by the higher spiritual reality into the world can bring the special gnosis that illuminates and liberates. These elements—evil creation, enslavement in the world, emissary from beyond the world, and special knowledge that illuminates—are expressed in the Gnostic movements in a variety of ways. The reader of the original sources may expect to encounter a bewildering array of actors and mythologoumena in the various expressions of this drama of SALVATION.

Extant Original Sources. The ancient sources for these Gnostic movements are of three kinds: (1) patristic reports refuting Christian-Gnostic heretics; (2) original Gnostic writings discovered before 1945; and (3) the NAG HAMMADI codices.

(1) In their treatment of Gnosticism the church fathers concern themselves exclusively with refuting Gnostic heresies that influenced Christian churches. As far as the church fathers are concerned Gnosticism is a Christian heresy. The major sources for the patristic reports are Irenaeus of Lyons (second century CE), *Unmasking and Refutation of the False Gnosis* (*Adversus haereses*); Clement of Alexandria (second and third centuries CE), *Miscellanies* (*Stromata*) and *Excerpts from Theodotus* (*Excerpta ex Theodoto*); Hippolytus of Rome (second and third centuries CE), *Refutation of All Heresies* (*Refutatio omnium haeresium*); Tertullian (second and third centuries CE), *Against Marcion* (*Adversus Marcionem*), *Against Valentinus* (*Adversus Valentinianos*), *The Prescription against Heretics* (*De praescriptione haereticorum*), *Scorpiace* ("a remedy for the scorpion's sting" of the Gnostic heresy); Origen (third century CE), *Commentary on John* (*Commentarii in Johannis Evangelium*). *Against Celsus* (*Contra Celsum*); Epiphanius of Salamis (fourth century CE), *Medicine Box* (*Panarion*).

These polemical works are also important because, in some instances, they contain quotations from the writings of the Gnostics, such as in the case of Valentinus, Heracleon, Basilides, Isidore, and others.

(2) Until the end of the eighteenth century, all that could be known of Gnosticism came from brief quotations from certain Gnostic writings and the extensive polemical reports refuting these movements by their opponents, the church fathers. A modern understanding of the nature of these movements was shaped by their highly polemical reports. Toward the end of the eighteenth century in separate

discoveries three ancient codices, containing original Gnostic writings in the Coptic language, were announced.

The Askew Codex was acquired by the British Museum in 1785. It contains four books, the second of which bears a title inserted into the text at a later time: the *Second Book of the* PISTIS SOPHIA. On the basis of that insertion the entire codex has been known by that title. The text, dated to the third century CE takes the form of a dialogue between Jesus and his disciples in which Jesus communicates arcane, speculative instruction in response to the disciples questions.

The Bruce Codex was discovered in Upper Egypt in 1769, but not published until 1892. The manuscript contains two Gnostic treatises: the TWO BOOKS OF JEU and the "Untitled Text." The *Two Books of Jeu* are dialogues between the "Living Jesus" and his disciples in which Jesus instructs them in esoteric, arcane gnosis. The "Untitled Text" is a highly speculative religiophilosophical treatise in which Christian elements seem superficial.

The Berlin Codex, discovered in 1896, was not published in its entirety until 1955. The codex has been dated to the fifth century CE, though the actual composition of the text would have been earlier. It contains four separate writings: the GOSPEL OF MARY, the APOCRYPHON OF JOHN, the SOPHIA OF JESUS CHRIST, and the ACT OF PETER. The first three writings are clearly Gnostic in character. They constitute dialogues between the resurrected Christ and his disciples in which Jesus provides esoteric teaching in response to the disciples' questions. The *ActPet* is not explicitly Gnostic but describes the healing ministry of Peter and holds forth a message of asceticism and self-control.

Most of the material in these three ancient books has been regularly understood to reflect a stage of decline in the vitality and influence of Gnosticism.

(3) The situation with original source material changed in 1945 with the discovery of the Nag Hammadi library. In the library there are fifty-two separate treatises, forty-one of which are known only from the Nag Hammadi texts. The manuscripts were manufactured in the middle of the fourth century CE, but the texts date from an earlier period. These texts reflect a variety of traditions. A number of texts provide us with instances of non-Christian varieties of Gnosticism, i.e., texts whose narratives betray no evidence of influence from Christian traditions: the APOCALYPSE OF ADAM, the PARAPHRASE OF SHEM, and EUGNOSTOS. Some texts, such as the APOCRYPHON OF JAMES and the TEACHINGS OF SILVANUS, appear to be Christian texts influenced by Gnosticism. Other texts stand in a more Neoplatonic tradition than in a Jewish-Christian tradition, such as ALLOGENES and the THREE STELES OF SETH. In certain other cases, some texts were originally composed as non-Christian texts, but later they were Christianized in an attempt to claim them for use in a Christian-Gnostic context, such as the GOSPEL OF THE EGYPTIANS, the *Sophia of Jesus Christ*, and the TRIMORPHIC PROTENNOIA. Still other texts are associated with Valentinus, such as a VALENTINIAN EXPOSITION; and still others are associated with Greek wisdom literature, such as the SENTENCES OF SEXTUS. A number of texts derive from the Hermetic corpus, such as the DISCOURSE ON THE EIGHTH AND NINTH, and ASCLEPIUS. In short, the texts reflect a

wide variety of tradition types originally written at different times from different parts of the ancient world.

The Problem of the Sources. There is significant lack of agreement between the polemical reports of the church fathers about the Gnostics and the Gnostic writings of the Nag Hammadi library. The most extensive and close agreement appears between the report of Irenaeus, *AdvHaer* 1.29 and the *ApJohn.* There is also the problem that the church fathers separate Gnostic groups into clearly defined sects on the basis of specific teachers and distinctive teaching, but in the Nag Hammadi library one finds side by side in one tractate distinctive teachings that the church fathers attributed to different teachers and sects. While one may sort some of the Nag Hammadi tractates in terms of the sects identified in the reports of the fathers (e.g., Valentinian and Sethian), most of the writings in the library do not fit into the categories of the fathers.

Recent evaluation of the reports of the church fathers concludes that the fathers did not have independent knowledge of most sects, but depended upon the reports of Irenaeus and then upon one another for their information. Where they do appear to have independent knowledge, they frequently do not agree in their description of the same sect.

The Problem of Gnostic Origins. The debate about where and when Gnosticism began is a modern problem. Until the end of the nineteenth century Gnosticism was thought to have been a product of Christian heresy. The early church fathers traced its origins to SIMON MAGUS (Acts 8:9-24) who was acclaimed as the "Great Power" of God. It was from Simon that all heresies originated (Iren., *AdvHaer* 1.29). Gnosticism's rapid growth in the ancient world was encouraged by an early Christian fascination with Greek philosophy and mythology. This view of Gnostic origins remained the consensus until the beginning of the twentieth century. The classic statement was made by Adolf Harnack who described Gnosticism as the "acute Hellenization of Christianity." Harnack argued that certain early Christians were led into Gnosticism when they rejected the OT and their Jewish roots, and turned to Platonic DUALISM.

Near the beginning of the twentieth century, scholars of the history of religions (*Religionsgeschichtliche Schule*), working with the polemical reports of the church fathers argued that evidence pointed toward a non-Christian origin for Gnosticism in the East, in Iranian, Persian, and Mandaean thought.

Near the middle of the twentieth century Hans Jonas, following up on these insights, argued that Gnosticism was produced in late antiquity as the result of a blending of eastern mysticism (a belief in ASTROLOGY, fatalism, and MAGIC) with Greek thought. Hence there was no one single point of beginning, rather Gnosticism derived from the mood or attitude of late antiquity, and it simultaneously emerged in different forms throughout the ancient world.

Others have found the origins of Gnosticism in a kind of radical Judaism. Some argue that it arose among Jewish apocalyptic groups who expected the immediate appearing of the KINGDOM OF GOD. When the TEMPLE at Jerusalem was destroyed in

70 CE, and the kingdom failed to appear, these sectarian Jews rejected their traditional faith and apocalyptic hopes. It was out of such a shaking of the foundations of faith that Gnosticism emerged. Others argue that Gnosticism derived from the challenge to God's character due to the presence of evil in the world. By definition a righteous God could not be associated with the disorder and evil that one observes in the created order. Such Jews gave up the traditional Jewish view of the goodness of creation and its later corruption through the sin of ADAM and EVE. They rejected the benevolence of the creator and developed out of their traditional faith an anti-cosmic religion of transcendental gnosis.

One problem that has continued to influence the scholarly discussion has been the date of the primary Gnostic sources, principally the texts discovered at Nag Hammadi. Virtually all documents date from the second century CE and later. Some have argued that you can find evidence of Gnosticism reflected in the NT. For example, the opponents that Paul debated in 1 Corinthians have been described as Gnostic (cf. 1 Cor 2:14–3:1), and the "Christ Hymn" in Phil 2:5-11 has also been described as an independent piece of tradition quoted by Paul, but deriving originally from Gnostic thought. Scholars who find evidence of Gnosticism in the NT argue that the clearly defined Gnostic groups of the second century would have required a certain amount of lead time in the first century CE and earlier to have become so distinctive and widespread in the second century. Further they point out that the church fathers—and Paul—were only concerned to refute heresy in Christian churches. They would have had no interest in non-Christian varieties of Gnosticism that did not impact Christian churches. Hence one could expect Gnosticism in its non-Christian forms to be earlier than the second century CE. Other scholars, however, take a position of "No texts; no history!" These scholars argue that Gnostic motifs appearing in both the NT and the DEAD SEA SCROLLS simply are not evidence of a fully developed Gnosticism. Gnostic "features" are not sufficient evidence to conclude that there were gnostic groups in the first century. Hence, Gnosticism is not a pre-Christian phenomenon.

The Nag Hammadi library, however, has provided clear evidence of a non-Christian variety of Gnosticism. Such non-Christian Gnostic texts as the *ApocAdam*, the *ParaphShem*, the *StelesSeth*, and *Eugnos* conclusively demonstrate the existence of non-Christian Gnosticism. Hence, while there may currently exist no Gnostic text that can conclusively be dated into the first century CE so as to allow an argument for pre-Christian Gnosticism in a temporal sense, there is ample evidence for a "pre-Christian" Gnosticism in a logical sequential sense. Indeed one of these non-Christian Gnostic texts exists both in its non-Christian form (*Eugnos*) and in a later Christianized form (*SophJC*). The Nag Hammadi library may be expected to produce further helpful insights into the problem of Gnostic origins.

Principal Gnostic Systems of the Second Century. Since the time of Irenaeus it has been customary to distinguish sects within Gnosticism on the basis of Gnostic teachers and their distinctive teaching. While the Nag Hammadi library raises serious questions about this procedure, it remains the most convenient way to synthesize the material in a brief way.

MARCION and the Marcionite movement are not usually included as a Gnostic sect, but because they share certain features with Gnostic sects, they should be mentioned. Marcion (ca. 150 CE), excommunicated by the church at Rome, founded his own church. His movement proved to be a serious competitor to orthodoxy, and survived well past the fourth century CE. The teaching of Marcion is characterized by his absolute rejection of the Jewish roots of Christianity, i.e., he rejected the creator God of Judaism and the OT. He described the creator God of Jewish faith as a just and righteous God, but who cannot be characterized as merciful and good. On the other hand, Jesus Christ reveals a merciful God of love. So far as we know, Marcion was the first to establish a NT CANON of scripture. It contained an abbreviated form of the Gospel of Luke and ten Pauline letters.

Basilides, who was active in Alexandria during the first half of the second century CE, is the earliest of the Christian Gnostic theologians of that century. All that remains of his considerable literary activity are a few fragmentary quotations preserved in the polemical reports of the church fathers. Among his lost writings are a gospel and an exegesis of the gospel in twenty-four books. It is reported that he was a disciple of Glaucias, who was described as "the interpreter of Peter." His work was continued by his pupil Isidore, of whom also only a few fragments remain. Basilides' movement continued into the fourth century. It is difficult to describe the Basilidean system since the two major descriptions of his thought by Irenaeus and Hippolytus are irreconcilable.

The principle difference between the system of Hippolytus and that of Irenaeus is in the conscious rejection of emanation by the system in Hippolytus. According to Hippolytus, Basilides viewed the systems of emanation with their theory of devolution as crude and ineffective. Further, it was the very nature of all existence to strive to rise to the better. No creature would be so unintelligent as to descend. Thus, according to Hippolytus the entire thrust of Basilides' system is upward.

Quotations from the writings of Basilides and Isidore contain only allusions to a cosmogonic system. In these fragments the teaching of Basilides and Isidore deal primarily with ethics.

Valentinus, mid-second century CE, was the most influential and creative of the Gnostic teachers of his time. The movement he began at Rome survived into the fifth century. His followers claimed that he was a disciple of Theudas, who was described as a disciple of Paul. Until the discovery of the Nag Hammadi library only a few sources for our knowledge of the teaching of Valentinus existed. The patristic sources deal primarily with Valentinianism in its later forms, which they describe as an elaborate system of emanation. For the thought of Valentinus himself we are dependent upon fragmentary quotations preserved in Clement of Alexandria and Hippolytus. The GOSPEL OF TRUTH, a Nag Hammadi text, has been described as a writing of Valentinus. There are also extant excerpts from the writings of some of the disciples of Valentinus: Ptolemaeus, Heracleon, Marcus, and Theodotus. The following Nag Hammadi writings have been identified as belonging to the Valentinian movement: PRAYER OF THE APOSTLE PAUL; TREATISE ON THE RESURRECTION; TRIPARTITE TRACTATE; GOSPEL OF PHILIP; FIRST APOCALYPSE OF JAMES; INTERPRETATION OF KNOWLEDGE; and A VALENTINIAN EXPOSITION.

See also HERMETIC LITERATURE; MARCION; NAG HAMMADI.

Bibliography. (Studies). W. Bousset, *Kyrios Christos: A History of the Belief in Christ from the Beginnings of Christianity to Irenaeus*; C. W. Hedrick and R. Hodgson, Jr., eds., *Nag Hammadi, Gnosticism, and Early Christianity*; H. Jonas, *The Gnostic Religion. The Message of the Alien God and the Beginnings of Christianity*; B. Layton, ed., *The Rediscovery of Gnosticism. Proceedings of the International Conference on Gnosticism at Yale, . . . 1978*; K. Rudolph, *Gnosis. The Nature and History of Gnosticism*; D. Scholer, *Nag Hammadi Bibliography 1948-1969*, updated annually in *NovT* beginning with vol. 13 (1971); R. McL. Wilson, *Gnosis and the New Testament*; F. Wisse, "The Nag Hammadi Library and the Heresiologists," *VC* 25(1971) 205-23.

(Texts). H. W. Attridge, ed., *Nag Hammadi Codex I (The Jung Codex)* (*NHS* 22-23), 1985; A. Böhlig, and F. Wisse, eds., *Nag Hammadi Codices III,2 and IV,2: The Gospel of the Egyptians* (*NHS* 4), 1975; S. Emmel, ed., *Nag Hammadi Codex III, 5. The Dialogue of the Savior* (*NHS* 26), 1984; W. Foerster, ed., *Gnosis: A Selection of Gnostic Texts*; R. Haardt, *Gnosis. Character and Testimony*; B. Layton, *The Gnostic Scriptures*; D. Parrott, ed., *Nag Hammadi Codices V,2-5 and VI with Papyrus Berolinensis 8502, 1 and 4* (*NHS* 11), 1979; J. M. Robinson, ed., *The Nag Hammadi Library in English*; C. Schmidt and V. MacDermot, eds., *Pistis Sophia* (*NHS* 9), 1978, and *The Books of Jeu and the Untitled Text in the Bruce Codex* (*NHS* 13), 1978.

—CHARLES W. HEDRICK

Millennium [MDB 576-77]

•**Millennium.** [muh-len'ee-uhm] From a combination of two Latin words: *mille*, "thousand," and *annus*, "year." Millennium designates a period of 1,000 years. Specifically in relation to the Bible, millennium names the 1,000 years mentioned in Rev 20:1-10, esp. vv. 2-6, when SATAN is bound and shut up in "the pit," a time during which the resurrected martyred (Christian) saints reign with Christ before the final onslaught of Satan and, then, the final judgment.

Historically Christians have been divided sharply about the interpretation of this 1,000-year period, taking one of three basic positions.

(1) *Premillennialists* maintain that the 1,000 years is a literal time between the second coming of Christ and the final judgment. This group subdivides further into two schools of thought: *historical premillennialists* understand the millennium as a historical extension of the work of Christ in history, a phase between the era of the church and the full form of the KINGDOM OF GOD; *dispensationalists* regard the millennium as a distinct period, not a phase in the ongoing work of God in history, wherein all unrealized OT prophecies to Israel will be perfectly fulfilled.

(2) *Postmillennialists* contend the 1,000-year period is a literal time in history prior to the coming of Christ, as yet not realized, when the proclamation of the gospel will be exceptionally well received.

(3) *Amillennialists* interpret the millennium as a literary device typical of apocalyptic writings (such literature influenced the writing of the Book of Revelation). As such a literary convention, the millennium is interpreted as a symbol of the church's growing faith. The binding of Satan that takes place in relationship to the millennium is also understood as a literary device symbolizing the triumphant work of Christ during his ministry and passion and in his death and resurrection.

Three further observations are necessary in relation to a consideration of the millennium. First, the only passage in the Bible that makes explicit mention of the millennium is Rev 20:1-10.

Second, it is probably true that the idea of a 1,000-year reign of Christ as presented in Rev 20 is a development of the basic OT prophetic notion of a future messianic era, but the use of prophetic passages from the OT in developing millennarian doctrine is illegitimate; for, in fact, the passages cited have nothing to do with a 1,000-year reign, but rather anticipate the (first) coming of the Messiah and/or the ultimate consummation of the work of God in the Christ in the age to come, i.e., in the full and final form of the Kingdom of God. In other words, the OT has no concern with the idea of a millennium.

Third, most millennarian teaching shows no interest in or knowledge of the historical context in which, and in relation to which, the Book of Revelation was written. This disregard for the historical situation of John of Patmos and of his readers routinely leads to serious misinterpretation of the passage in Rev 20. The author of Revelation plainly states that the events to which he refers "must soon take place" (Rev 1:1). He addresses lukewarm Christians (Rev 3:1, 15-16) in an atmosphere of persecution (Rev 1:9; 2:2, 9, 13, 19) clearly issuing admonition and encouragement (Rev 1–3). The content and imagery of the whole book relate to the purposes established in the early chapters of the work. Understood in this manner, the millennium is a promise of Christ's steadfastness and an example of the security believers have, despite adversity, through their faith in Christ.

Whether the millennium is understood as a symbol or as a precise period of future time is not so much decided by a careful reading of the text as it is by the attitudes and methods of study that one brings to the text. Moreover, no matter what interpretation one chooses to defend, one must realize that Rev 20 is concerned to portray Christ and his victory, in which the faithful believers have a share, not to communicate special information that puts the readers in a privileged postition if the millennium is correctly understood.

See also APOCALYPTIC LITERATURE; ESCHATOLOGY OF THE NEW TESTAMENT; ESCHATOLOGY OF THE OLD TESTAMENT; KINGDOM OF GOD; MESSIAH/CHRIST; MESSIAH/MESSIANISM; REVELATION, BOOK OF; SATAN IN THE NEW TESTAMENT; SATAN IN THE OLD TESTAMENT.

Bibliography. G. R. Beasley-Murray, *The Book of Revelation*; G. B. Caird, *The Revelation of St. John the Divine*; S. J. Case, *The Millennial Hope*; N. Cohn, *The Pursuit of the Millennium*, rev. and expanded ed.; A. Y. Collins, *The Apocalypse*; F. Stagg, *New Testament Theology*.

—MARION L. SOARDS

Numbers/Numerology [MDB 621-22]

•**Numbers/Numerology.** A *number* is the name of a quantity. A *numeral* is a symbol for a number. *Numerology* is the symbolic use of numbers for esoteric knowledge. In the Bible, numbers are used to quantify, and they are used to symbolize a nonquantifiable figure. A mediating, rhetorical usage of numbers may also be observed in which quantification is present, but more important purposes lie in the numbers' ideological significance.

Numbers and Arithmetic. Ancient peoples used various ways to represent quantities. Numbers were written as words; the acrophonic variant of this system was to represent the number by the phonetic symbol for the initial sound of the number word. Numerals were also used, or number values were assigned to letters of the alphabet. These systems were used side by side. At Ugarit, for example, administrative and economic documents used numerals, while words were used in literary documents.

Hieratic (Egyptian) numerical symbols on ostraca from Samaria, Arad, and elsewhere demonstrate preexilic Israelite use of numerals. If Israelite writers followed the convention known from Ugarit, the absence of numerals in the OT may indicate that materials which appear to be administrative documents were preserved as literary documents. Maccabean coins are the earliest evidence for Jewish use of the alphabetic system. The acrophonic system is nowhere in evidence in the Bible.

The OT preserves examples of basic arithmetic operations such as addition (Gen 5), subtraction (Gen 18:28), multiplication (Lev 25:8), and division (Exod 21:35). In addition, Israel used simple fractions such as 1/2 (Num 15:9), 1/3 (Num 15:6), 1/4 (Lev 23:13), 1/5 (Lev 6:5 [Heb 5:24]), 1/6 (Ezek 4:11), 1/10 (Num 28:5), 2/10 (Num 15:6), 3/10 (Num 15:9), 1/50 (Num 31:30), 1/100 (Neh 5:11), and 1/500 (Num 31:28). Clearly, numbers are used in the Bible to quantify. In such cases, the biblical writers certainly intended to represent some exact quantity. Historical judgment must, of course, be exercised as to the accuracy of such quantifications.

Numbers and Rhetoric. Numbers may also be used rhetorically. The final tally of Job's possessions (42:12) bespeaks more than mere quantification. Taken with the figures for length of life in 42:16, they are more than an "audit." They indicate that the restoration was a double portion of new life (cf. Pss 90:10; 128:6).

The common sequence x/x+1 is more concerned with emphasis than counting. Often this pattern does make the figures "come out right" (cf. Prov 30:15-31), but this is not always obvious (cf. Job 5:19; 33:14, 29). Other times, the pattern may be used for stylistic reasons alone (e.g., Amos 1:3–2:16).

Many interpreters argue that certain numbers carry meanings beyond quantity. The number SEVEN signifies completeness and perfection. Others that may mean more than mere quantity are *ten*, TWELVE, *forty*, and *seventy*. No single rule can be given for such significance-laden numbers. Each case must be weighed on its own merits.

The number *ten* derives its comprehensive significance from the ten fingers. Its pedagogical value is obvious from the fact that the TEN COMMANDMENTS (Exod 34:28) can be counted in various ways, but that however they are counted, Jewish, Roman Catholic, and Protestant traditions always come out to ten. Job uses the number *ten* comprehensively, not quantitatively, to refer to his friends' tenfold reproach (Job 19:3).

Whatever its prehistory, the biblical importance of the number *twelve* derives from its usage in the expression "the twelve tribes of Israel"; it is often noted that the tribes named are more than twelve, but that the various lists are adjusted to make them "come out right" to the number *twelve*. (Judg 5 is exceptional in this regard.) Similar observations could be made about the NT lists of the twelve disciples/apostles (cf. Matt 10:1-4 and par.). Acts 1:15-26 indicates that the number itself was felt to be significant. It came to indicate the whole people of God as summed up in their leaders.

The numbers *forty* and *seventy* may often be round numbers. The rains of Noah's flood fall for forty days and nights (Gen 7:12); the wilderness and wanderings are forty years (Deut 1:3); Moses spends forty days on the mountain (Exod 24:18); Elijah and Jesus fast for forty days (1 Kgs 19:8; Matt 4:2); and the Ninevites are given forty days to repent (Jonah 3:4). *Seventy* is the traditional number for a group of the elders of Israel (Exod 24:1; Num 11:16), the number of rulers' "sons" (Judg 9:2; 2 Kgs 10:1), and the number of years of Israel's punishment at the hands of Babylon (Jer 25:11). In terms of people, *seventy* probably refers to "a larger group of people taken as a whole" (Fensham). Dan 9:2 and 24 show that the number *seventy*, if taken as a precise quantification of years, demands reinterpretation.

Numbers and Esoterica. Although numerological senses have been suggested for John 21:11 and Gen 14:14, the only clear use of numbers to refer to something esoteric is the well-known 666 of Rev 13:18. This is the sum of numerical values assigned to the letters of a human name. Nero is the most likely of the countless suggestions. The Hebrew transcription of the Greek form of his name, which would give the value of 666, is attested in a scroll from Murabba'at; moreover, the Hebrew transcription of the Latin form of his name would explain the variant reading of 616 in some manuscripts.

Otherwise, various systems of interpretation find remarkable numerical relationships in the biblical text. Such numerical relationships are taken to be mathematical evidence of the rationality of scriptural teachings (Philo). Others argue that the striking numerical phenomena which they see in the biblical text constitute mathematical proof of the inspiration of scripture (Lucas and Washburn, or Luna). All such speculative systems stand under the ancient observation of Iamblichus regarding such numerological speculations, which the Greeks called *geometria*: "in this way we could easily transform anything into any number, by dividing or adding or multiplying" (cited by Sambursky).

See also SEVEN, THE; TWELVE, THE.

Bibliography. Y. Aharoni, "The Use of Hieratic Numerals in Hebrew Ostraca and the Shekel Weights" *BASOR* 184 (1966): 13-19; J. J. Davis, *Biblical Numerology*; F. C. Fensham, "Numeral Seventy in the Old Testament and the Family of Jerubbaal, Ahab, Panammuwa and Athirat." *PEQ* 109 (1977): 113-15; D. R. Hillers, "Revelation 13:18 and the Scrolls from Murabba'at." *BASOR* 170 (1963): 65; J. Lucas and D. Washburn. *Theomatics: God's Best Kept Secret Revealed*; M. Luna, *The Number 7 in the Bible: Thousands of Amazing Facts concerning the Sacred Number: A Scientific Demonstration of Divine Inspiration of the Bible*; H. R. Moehiring, "Arithmology as an Exegetical Tool in the Writings of Philo of Alexandria," *SBLASP* 13 (1978): 191-227; O. Neugebauer, *The Exact Sciences in Antiquity*, 2nd ed.; S. Sambursky, "On the Origin and Significance of the Term Gematria," *JJS* 29 (1978): 35-38; W. H. Shea, "Date and Significance of the Samaria Ostraca," *IEJ* 27 (1977): 16-27.

—JOHN KEATING WILES

Persecution in the New Testament [MDB 668]

•**Persecution in the New Testament.** Political and religious persecution was a reality in the ancient world. The history of the Jewish nation is characterized by persecution in various forms. By the first century CE. Palestine was occupied by the Romans whose presence had alleviated some forms of oppression but added others. Christianity was born into an atmosphere of oppression and persecution.

Traditionally, those who have addressed the subject of persecution during the NT era have paid careful attention to the official persecutions of Christians under PAUL, HEROD, Nero, Domitian, and Trajan. More recent evaluations of the religious and political atmosphere within the Greco-Roman world have questioned the severity (and sometimes the reality) of such persecutions, especially those of Nero and Domitian. Much of the evidence of oppression during NT times comes from Christian writings; very little corroborating evidence can be found in non-Christian sources. Religious persecution of Christians was a reality, however, and took both official and unofficial forms.

The narratives of the NT portray early conflict between Christians and the Jewish authorities. Jesus' conflict with the Jewish authorities led to his CRUCIFIXION. The Gospels certainly place the blame for that crucifixion at the feet of the Jews, even though they are also quite clear that the Roman government actually executed Jesus. In Acts, the Jewish persecution of Christianity intensified. Paul is introduced during Stephen's martyrdom (Acts 7:58). Stephen's death inaugurated a systematic oppression of Palestinian Christians, and Paul led the fight to stamp out "the Way" (Acts 8:1).

Acts also narrates the official persecution of Christian leaders in Jerusalem by Herod Agrippa (Acts 12:1-5). Peter was imprisoned; James was executed. Herod may well have been acting on his own, though he imprisoned Peter because he wanted to please the Jews, which implies some Jewish influence in the ongoing official persecution of Christians (Acts 12:3). The Fourth Gospel also indicates that Christians had been forced out of the synagogues, a less drastic, but every bit as official, form of religious persecution (John 9).

Acts is less clear about official Roman persecution of Christians elsewhere in the empire. That Christians were affected by Claudius's edict which expelled Jews from Rome in 49 CE is very possible (Acts 18:2). This persecution should not be construed as official persecution of Christians. Claudius's edict concerned the Jewish inhabitants of Rome; persons such as Aquila and Priscilla were forced to leave Rome because they were Jewish, not because they were Christian. Acts seems to have gone to great lengths to argue for a harmonious relationship between the government and the church. This apologetic purpose seems to have been aimed as much at convincing the church that the government was helpful to the Christian mission as it was aimed at convincing the government that the church could be trusted to uphold the laws of society.

Ecclesiastical tradition has long claimed that the martyrdom of Peter and Paul in Rome took place during a period of intense persecution of Christians by Nero. The Roman historian Tacitus also mentioned Nero's persecution of Roman Christians following the fire of 64 CE. Quite likely the Christian population of Rome, not well received in Roman society because of its dislike of the Roman lifestyle, was used by Nero as a scapegoat. Nero was himself blamed for the fire which left many homeless; perhaps he blamed the fire on the Christians to quell the rumors of his own guilt. This persecution was probably limited to the area of Rome itself.

Many have proposed an official persecution during the reign of Domitian (cf. *1 Clem* 1). Such a proposal is usually part of the solution to the dating of the Book of Revelation. Once again, the historical evidence indicates a more local persecution which resulted in the imprisonment of John, rather than an organized pogrom against believers in the empire. In fact, the clearest record of any official persecution of Christians for their faith came during the reign of Trajan (98–117 CE), as both the Christian bishop IGNATIUS of Antioch and a Roman official (Pliny the Younger) wrote about an official attempt to discourage the practice of Christianity.

More common was an unofficial type of persecution (Heb 10:32ff.; 1 Pet 3:13ff.). The exclusive nature of Christianity invited problems with the surrounding society. Christians increasingly found themselves in conflict with the Jewish community, as the church desired or was forced to establish a separate identity from the synagogue. Anti-Semitism was a first-century reality, and often the survival of the church outside of Palestine demanded such separation. Christians were also reluctant to become involved in the social activities of Greco-Roman cities, many of which had strong pagan religious overtones. For that reason, they were considered antisocial, a charge which could very easily be construed as anticivil as well.

Another subtle form of unofficial persecution was economic deprivation. In a world which boasted of upward social and economic mobility, many Christians were unable to succeed economically because of the political and religious nature of business. All aspects of Greco-Roman social life were strongly connected to pagan worship practices. In addition, the Christians considered coins which bore the image of the emperor to be idolatrous; therefore, engaging in commerce was often difficult. Furthermore, refusal to worship according to the imperial cult separated Christians from society and earned them the distrust of other citizens who were vitally concerned with the imperial religion which was woven into the fabric of the empire.

The persecutions of Christians by Jewish and Roman officials have been the focus of much scholarly attention. While one can see evidence of such persecution, one must admit the relative lack of proof that such persecutions were pervasive. First-century persecution of Christianity was often unofficial, and the NT epistles stress the need for Christians to maintain their reputation as valuable members of society, even in the face of such persecution.

See also ANTI-JUDAISM IN THE NT; CRUCIFIXION; HEROD; PAUL; PETER, LETTERS OF; RELIGIONS, HELLENISTIC AND ROMAN.

Bibliography. F. W. Beare, "Persecution," *IDB*; A. Y. Collins, *Crisis and Catharsis: The Power of the Apocalypse*; J. H. Elliott, *A Home for the Homeless: A Sociological Exegesis of 1 Peter*; B. Reicke, *The New Testament Era*; P. W. Walaskay, *"And So We Came to Rome": The Political Perspective of St. Luke.*

STEVEN SHEELEY

Suffering in the New Testament [MDB 860]

•**Suffering in the New Testament.** By combining the images of the Messiah and the suffering servant, the Gospels set forth suffering as a divine necessity and the essence of the Messiah's mission (Matt 16:21; 17:12; Mark 8:31; Luke 9:22; John 3:14; 12:32). Three times Jesus received the title Messiah—in the temptation, upon Peter's confession at Caesarea Philippi, and at the trial/execution, and each time Jesus freely (John 10:15-18) set aside other ways of redemption for the way of suffering—"The Son of man must suffer." The power of Jesus' miracles to relieve suffering reinforced the call that disciples do the same (Luke 10:30-37). However, Jesus prevented the removal of suffering from himself.

The distress and trouble which overcame Jesus in Jerusalem (Mark 14:33) was climaxed by his feeling of abandonment on the cross where Jesus questioned, "My God, my God! Why hast Thou forsaken me?" (Mark 15:34; Matt 27:46). Yet, at the cross, where Jesus most pointedly joined us in our suffering, Jesus exhibited what suffering really means. Jesus was able to be open to God, even while the evil worked its dreadful suffering: "Father, into thy hands I commit my spirit" (Luke 23:46). Jesus also refused to place a wall between himself and other persons: "Father, forgive them; for they know not what they do" (Luke 23:34). Jesus counseled a similar suffering for the disciples: "If they persecuted me, they will persecute you" (John 15:20). The fellowship of Jesus and the disciples is set precisely through suffering: "If any man would come after me, let him deny himself and take up his cross and follow me" (Mark 8:34; Matt 10:38; 16:24; Luke 9:23; 14:27).

Paul sees the whole creation as groaning in travail toward fulfillment. God shares in that process and pain: "In Christ God was reconciling the world to himself" (2 Cor 5:19; cf. Phil 2). Persons also share in the process: to live in Christ is to suffer with Christ (2 Tim 2:11; Rom 8:17; Gal 2:20). In Colossians, human suffering is seen as involved in the work of the Messiah: "Now I rejoice in my sufferings for your sake, and in my flesh I complete what is lacking in Christ's afflictions" (Col 1:24).

First Peter, Hebrews, and Revelation grow out of the experience of suffering, and in all three books hope appears over against suffering. Suffering is the gateway to new life in Christ: "For to this you have been called, because Christ also suffered for you, leaving you an example, that you should follow in his steps" (1 Pet 2:21). Hebrews understands that suffering conditions life and obedience (12:7-11); it even conditioned the obedience of Jesus who was made perfect through suffering (2:10; cf. Phil 2:8) and "for the joy that was set before him endured the cross" (12:2).

The NT as a whole modifies six OT ideas: (1) suffering disciplines character (Jas 1:2-4; 1 Pet 1:7; Heb 2:10; Rev 19-21); (2) it awakens hope (Rom 8:18; 2 Cor 4:17; John 14; 1 Cor 15); (3) it provides knowledge (Matt 11:29; Phil 3:8-11; Luke 15:11-32); (4) sin brings suffering (Luke 13:1-5; Rom 1:18-3:20); (5) suffering is sacrificial (Phil 2:5-8; Col 1:24; 2 Cor 4:8-12); and (6) it tests faith (1 Pet 1:3-7; 2 Cor 4:9-11). The NT also witnesses to a suffering God who, as Creator/Sustainer, suffers with persons (John 5:17; Acts 17:27-28); as Redeemer, suffers for us (Phil 2:5-11; 2 Cor 8:9; Heb 2:17-18; Rom 5:6-10); and, as Sanctifier, suffers in us (2 Cor 3:17-18; 1 Cor 6:11; Eph 4:22-24).

See also SEVEN WORDS FROM THE CROSS; SUFFERING IN THE OT.

Bibliography. G. A. Buttrick, *God, Pain, and Evil*; E. S. Gerstenberger and W. Schrage, *Suffering*; H. W. Robinson, *Suffering: Human and Divine*.

—FRANK LOUIS MAULDIN

Symbol [MDB 865-67]

•**Symbol.** A symbol is a representation of a transcendent and invisible reality by means of an image borrowed from the sensuous and visible. Symbol differs from metaphor and analogy by the fact that the reality to which it points is not available for rational recognition. Thus a symbol points to a hidden and mysterious reality and is held to be analogous to it, yet the presence of such analogy is given in the experience of that reality and results from intuitive insight.

In the light of this definition, we may immediately affirm that symbols belong to the realms of art and religion. Symbols are attempts to interpret and make intelligible that which transcends sense experience, thus they belong especially to the religious sphere and the understanding of the sacred. They are given in the divine-human encounter in which divine REVELATION takes place. They point, as signs do, but they do more than a sign, they enable the recipient to participate in the mysterious depth to which they point. This means that all symbols have a double intentionality. They have a literal and evident meaning, for they refer to what can be sensuously observed, an object in this worldly environment. But they also have a second meaning which points beyond this first meaning to one that is analogous to the literal meaning and yet belongs to the realm of the sacred and transcendent. As such, symbols participate in that which they represent and penetrate into its depth. They are indeed inexhaustible and continually furnish new insights into the divine reality. Unlike images and signs, they participate in the sacred reality which they represent and are the accompaniment of all revelation.

Because they convey meaning and are vehicles of the divine revelation, symbols belong to the realm of words and communication. Symbolism takes form under human discourse as it is confronted by a revelatory depth in reality. It is therefore the natural accompaniment of an understanding of God which regards God as one who communicates and discloses the divine self in the divine word. God's word, God's self-giving, is communicated through the human words of those chosen to be the media of God's self-disclosure. Thus, in biblical thought, a primary symbol is the WORD OF GOD. God has no body, no mouth. In transcendent majesty and infinite being God is beyond all such literal descriptions, yet words become a symbol for divine self-giving and revelation.

For the Hebrew mind, a word was something objective that embodied the intention of the one who uttered it. Hence a word of blessing or of curse carried such content in itself. When received by the one to whom it was addressed, it proceeded to accomplish, in that person's being, the purpose for which it had been uttered. Thus JACOB having received Isaac's word of blessing, was not about to give it back, nor could Isaac revoke it, for already that blessing was taking effect in Jacob's life. So, too, by analogy with God's word; it could not return void, but would accomplish that to which it had been sent (Isa 55:11). It was pregnant with the divine intention, and was a projection of God's own presence into the realm that God had created and sustained. Word becomes a symbol for God's self-disclosure.

The Heb. term for "word," *dābār*, could be rendered "deed" as well as "word." Thus God's word could be both utterance and act. Hence we have a symbolism of action as well as a symbolism of words in biblical thought. In the biblical record we find symbolic acts especially in cultic celebration, as well as symbolic descriptions of God and of God's saving acts for the people of Israel.

Symbolic Presentation of God and the Divine Activity. In Hebrew thought the name of a person was an extension of that person's own being. It represented the person; to give someone your name was to give yourself. The possession of a name meant the possession of the authority and power of the person. When MOSES asked for the name of the God addressing him, he sought to possess divine authority and presence, just as a prophet speaking in the name of the Lord would be indwelt by the divine spirit and have the divine authority in the utterance (Exod 3:13-15; Gen 17:1ff.; Jer 11:21; Deut 18:20). Thus the divine name was a symbol for the very presence of God. To trust in God is to trust in God's holy name (Isa 50:10; Ps 33:21); to pray is to invoke the name (Gen 12:8; 1 Kgs 18:24). The TEMPLE of SOLOMON is the place where that name has been set (1 Kgs 8:29). Thus the divine name is a symbol for God's presence.

When we turn to the nature of God, we find an emphasis on God's personal being. Descriptions of human personal being become symbolic of God. God is personal, although the divine transcendent greatness means that the analogical aspect of the symbolism is stretched to its limits. God is infinite personal being, but the disclosure of the divine self is compatible with our own finite personal being, so the Bible speaks of God's will and purpose, of God's love and wrath. The divine revelation comes through the personal mediation of prophets, priests, and the wise, and provides a link between human personal being and the divine being such that love can be symbolic of the divine nature. Hence the Bible can describe God as loving Israel with an everlasting love (Jer 31:3). God's love is elective and creative, choosing Israel and creating it (Deut 7:7; Hos 11:1-4; Isa 41:8). This love is merciful and redemptive, a disclosure that reaches its OT climax in Hosea's prophetic words (11:7-9; 14:4). This love is directed especially on Israel, but is to reach through them to all nations. The symbolic and analogical nature of such love is brought out in the NT testimony, where the Greek word *agapē* is used only of God's love, especially as it is incarnated in Jesus Christ. Indeed, in the NT, God *is* love, the kind of love revealed in Jesus Christ (1 John 4:8). This divine kind of love is celebrated in the hymn of 1 Cor 13.

Family imagery is particularly suited to the expression of God's character. God is portrayed as husband of the bride Israel (Hos 1–3; Jer 2), or father of Israel (Jer 3:4, 19; Isa 63:16; 64:8) or of all persons (Mal 2:10), or displays the qualities of mother or midwife (Ps 103:15—where the analogy is with the father, but the quality mentioned is motherly compassion; Ezek 16; Isa 42:14-15) in the OT. In the NT, Jesus' use of the term "father" for God connotes a most intimate association between himself and the "heavenly father" or the "father in heaven." Throughout the letters and the rest of the NT, God is described as father of all humankind, and some references to God the Spirit or to the Holy Spirit also carry the associations with the mother that appear in the OT.

There are also particular symbolic uses of various human bodily aspects. Thus although God may not be literally pictured in bodily form, the Bible can speak of God's face, hand, arm, and nostrils. Ps 18 includes many bodily parts in its description, and the prophet of the Exile frequently uses corporeal members in picturing God's activity (Isa 40:10-11; 42:13-14). Isaiah opens his prophetic mission with a vision of God seated on a throne (Isa 6). We find references to God's face, back, and hand in Exod 33:19-23. In such cases, the words are not used in the physical sense but symbolically. The face is symbolic of God's presence, as Exod 33:14 makes clear (the word for "face" is translated "presence" in RSV). Sincere worshipers seek God's face and presence (Pss 24:6; 27:8). When God's face is hidden, the divine presence is withdrawn. The right hand of God symbolizes victory (Exod 15:6); both hands, creative power (Ps 119:73); and the arm, helping power (Isa 52:10). God's nostrils represent judgment (Ps 18:15), and their blast, deliverance at the sea (Exod 15:8).

Prophetic Use of Symbolism. For the prophets the word of the LORD could be act as well as utterance. So we find the prophets performing symbolic acts to bring the divine message to their hearers. Isaiah proclaimed the imminent Assyrian captivity of Egypt and Ethiopia by walking the streets of Jerusalem for three years in the garb of a slave (20:2). Jeremiah preached God's judgment on Judah at the hands of Babylon by wearing a yoke and breaking a flask (27:2-7; 19:1, 10-13). Ezekiel prophesied the reunion of Judah and Israel after the Exile by joining two pieces of wood, suitably inscribed, into one stick (37:15-22). Samuel tore his mantle to symbolize God's tearing the kingdom from Saul (1 Sam 15:27-28).

To such symbolic acts, the prophets added their spoken warnings of judgment and their proclamations of ultimate deliverance. Sometimes sights presented to their eyes became symbolic of the divine activity. Amos saw a plumb line against a wall and it symbolized the divine judgment (Amos 7:7-9). Much more significant are the uses made of agricultural and pastoral imagery. Israel is pictured in the symbolizing of the vine and of sheep. Israel is symbolized as a vine created by God to bear fruit for God. Israel's sin and rebellion is symbolized as yielding wild grapes, and Israel's judgment as the destruction of the vineyard (Isa 5:4; cf. Jer 2:21; 12:10). Again, in Ezek 34, Israel is portrayed as God's flock of sheep. Israel is so mismanaged by God's appointed shepherds, the nation's leaders, that it is scattered (cf. Jer 23:14; 50:6). Thus the theme of sin, rebellion, and judgment is dramatically symbolized.

Beyond the judgment, the prophets hoped for restoration of the people of God. They pictured a remnant that would be saved out of the judgment; a Davidic King, a MESSIAH or anointed one whom God would set on the throne; and a suffering servant, partly remnant and partly messiah, through whose suffering all nations would share in God's mercy (Isa 10:20; 9:6, 7; 11:1-5; Jer 23:5-6; 33:14-17; Isa 53:1-12). In the Book of Daniel we have another figure, the SON OF MAN who comes on the clouds of heaven, symbolizing the kingdom of the saints of the most high, and is thus a symbol for the remnant (Dan 7:13-14). At last Jesus came.

The Symbolic Presentation of Jesus. In Jesus the OT symbolism is gathered into a focal point. The symbolism of the word is gathered up into his historical personhood. In him the word has become enfleshed and assumed historical existence (John 1:14). In him the hope of a messiah finds its fulfillment. Jesus is the Christ, the anointed one of the living God and the suffering servant, in whose person the Messiah and the redeemed remnant become one, and through whose suffering everyone shall find redemption. Jesus is the Son of man, combining in his own person, as Messiah, the remnant which is reconstituted in him. It is Jesus' most frequently used self-designation. He seems to have been reticent about declaring himself overtly as Messiah. The term Son of man may, in some of its references, mean "humankind" (cf. Mark 2:28).

Much more significant theologically is the symbolic title for Jesus—SON OF GOD. At his baptism and transfiguration, Jesus is addressed by God as the beloved Son (Mark 1:11; 9:7). The title is used both in the temptation scene and while Jesus is on the cross (Matt 4:3ff.; 27:40). In the Gospel of John, the relation of Jesus to God as son is elaborated and the essential unity of father and son is affirmed (1:18; 10:30, 38). Paul affirms the unique sonship of Jesus (Gal 1:15f.; 4:4; Col 1:13). Jesus is the unique Son of God.

Associated with Christ's redeeming death, the most all-embracing symbol is the cross. The preaching of the cross is the heart of the gospel (1 Cor 1:18; Gal 6:14). Closely associated with this is the symbolic use of the lamb or the LAMB OF GOD. Here Jesus is symbolized as the paschal lamb (1 Cor 5:7; John 1:29). The Lamb is a principal title of Jesus in the Book of Revelation.

Symbolic Descriptions of Salvation. Three important symbols are used to describe the salvation wrought on the cross—JUSTIFICATION, RECONCILIATION, and REDEMPTION. Each has its appropriate aspect of human sin: guilt, alienation, and sinful bondage, respectively. Their backgrounds are, respectively, the law court, personal relationships, and the slave market. In each case, Christ accomplishes what human beings, independently, cannot. The sacrifice of Jesus Christ meets our judgment and covers our sin. By faith in him we can stand acquitted before the bar of God, justified not by our works, but by Jesus' gracious self-giving. We are graciously reconciled by God as we trust in Christ. Faith in Christ sets us free from the demonic bondage of sin. We are redeemed.

Symbolic Presentation of the Church and Its Worship. The community of the redeemed became the gathering of those whom God had called in Christ, the CHURCH, the New Israel, the new people of God. Symbolically it was described as the body of Christ, a community indwelt by his Spirit, unified by his love, and guided by him as its head.

There were two important symbolic acts in the worship of the NT church—BAPTISM and the LORD'S SUPPER. In baptism we have a symbolic presentation of the death and resurrection of Christ as that becomes effective in the life of the believer, who dies to sin and rises to newness of life in Christ. The symbolic burial in water has also overtones of lustration. In the Lord's Supper, the bread and wine symbolize the broken body and outpoured life of the crucified Christ. By faith, we open our lives to Christ's gracious risen presence.

See also COVENANT; CROSS; GOD, NAMES OF; LORD'S SUPPER; REVELATION, CONCEPT OF; SIGNS AND WONDERS; SON OF GOD; SON OF MAN; TEMPLE/TEMPLES; WORD; WORD OF GOD.

Bibliography. T. Boman, *Hebrew Thought Compared with Greek*; S. McFague, *Metaphorical Theology: Models of God in Religious Language*; P. Ricoeur, *The Symbolism of Evil*.

—ERIC C. RUST

Worship in the New Testament [MDB 970-71]

•**Worship in the New Testament.** "Worship" is derived from the Old English *weorthscipe* referring to a person of worth. People tend to worship that institution or person which has for them the greatest worth. In the Judeo-Christian tradition, GOD alone is worthy of worship for God is ascribed supreme worth.

Certain mystical traditions stress the sense of awe experienced in the presence of the Holy. Worship is linked to feeling a sense of transcendence and in its most intense form results in ecstasy for the worshiper. The ultimate goal of this form of worship is to be lost in union with the Ultimate One. Although there are mystical traditions in both Judaism and Christianity, the mainstream of the Judeo-Christian heritage has defined worship in terms of acts of ritual and SERVICE. The two most common linguistic expressions of worship in the Hebrew language suggest action. One word (הִשְׁתַּחֲוָה) means "to bow down" and describes an act of acknowledgment of the holiness of God. The most frequently used word for worship (עָבַד) is derived from the word for "servant" and is related to the verb which means "to labor." Biblical worship was a response to God's disclosure of himself through his mighty acts before and on behalf of his people. The call to worship for Israel encapsulated the essence of the nation's worship: "You shall love the Lord your God with all your heart, and with all your soul, and with all your might" (Deut 6:5). This command followed a review of God's saving acts, and a restatement of the basic commandments for relationships to God and community. The call was always to service. Worship was a ritual act which reminded the worshipers of what God had done for humans and what they were expected to do in return. Worship was a bridge between the acts of God in human experience and appropriate daily living by those for whom he had acted.

The worship of the patriarchs was marked by its pilgrim character. God spoke to various individuals, entered into COVENANT with them, rescued them, called them to repentance or renewed covenant with them, and they responded with worship. This worship usually included the building of an altar which became a memorial of the experience. There were no priests or prescribed rituals unless one chooses to interpret the head of the clan as functioning in such a role. Out of personal encounters emerged personal missions. The relationship between experience with God and service is inescapable. The devotion of the patriarchs and matriarchs was measured in terms of faithful service.

The Mosaic period produced a larger sense of community and introduced congregational worship. The community was formed in the EXODUS experience and the covenant which followed. The terms of the covenant, the expected response to God's deliverance, were spelled out in the TORAH which was at the center of worship and all life. Congregational worship was institutionalized with the construction of the TABERNACLE. The establishment of the priesthood created a body of interpreters of the Torah who assembled the people to hear and respond. The people were continually reminded of the presence of God among them. The mobility of the tabernacle symbolized the missionary character of the people and their worship. God was on the move with his people. The major development in this period was corporate as opposed to personal acts of worship.

The worship practices of Israel were shaped in part by Israel's interaction with Canaanite worship. The exposure to other forms of worship affected the rites but not the focus of worship as encounter between God and people. The building of the temple centralized worship and tended to diminish the pilgrim character of the experience. A pioneering spirit gave way to a settler mentality. The structure and trappings of the temple reflected the influence of Solomon's foreign wives. The distinguishing feature of Israelite worship continued to be its ethical faith. The end of worship was responsible living rooted in the righteousness of God. Long before the prophets' demands for reform, the emphasis in Hebrew worship was on righteous living as faith response. Ritual acts were only effective when the attitude of the people allowed the rites to be instruments of the Spirit.

The NT clearly records the birth of Christian worship from the womb of Jewish faith and expression. Christianity maintained much of what had been developed in the evolution of Israelite worship and its modification in the synagogues which arose during the EXILE. The major distinguishing feature of early Christian worship was celebration of the coming of the long-anticipated Messiah, Jesus of Nazareth. Christian worship is structured around promise and fulfillment. The OT promises which were fulfilled in Christ warrant Christian hope that the promises as yet unrealized will be fulfilled.

Christian observances such as BAPTISM and the Eucharist are symbols which replace CIRCUMCISION and the PASSOVER as reminders of deliverance and covenant, past, present, and future. Passover recalled Israel's salvation from slavery and the Eucharist is a meal of thanksgiving for salvation from sin. At the table of the Lord, the sacrifice of Christ on the cross is represented and the implied covenant of faith and personal responsibility is renewed.

Baptism symbolizes the new birth in Christ and initiates the convert into the community of faith. The act dramatically portrays the death and resurrection of Jesus and calls the baptized to live as those who have been reborn in the image of God and to reflect his righteousness in daily living.

The stress in NT worship continues to be on service. The Greek words most important to describing worship are similar to Hebrew counterparts. One word (λατρεία) is rendered "service" or "worship" and another (λειτουργία) is borrowed from secular life and refers to voluntary or obligatory service to the state or community. The connotations make it impossible to separate worship and service. Worship can be described as the hub around which the life of the believing community revolves. Evangelism, social action, education, crisis care, and other aspects of life together are spokes which arise out of the experience of God's revelation and continuing presence. Ritual is a dramatic portrayal of God's gifts that obligate his people to offer their gifts in return. Rom 12:1 echos the Israelite call to worship: "I appeal to you therefore brethren, by the mercies of God, to present your bodies as a living sacrifice, holy and acceptable to God, which is your spiritual worship." Christian worship is never completed in a sanctuary. It issues in the action of God and is completed in the action of the people of God.

The elements of worship take on different forms in various historical periods and diverse cultures but remain the same in essence. The primary elements of worship, apart from the rituals of sacrifice, changed little from OT to NT. Music is the language of the soul which often expresses the ineffable. Music combined with words in singing intensify feeling and support understanding. The reading and teaching of scripture are vital elements in putting meaning to revelation and explaining mission. Prayer dramatically portrays the revelation-response pattern of the divine-human encounter. It demonstrates the dependence of creature on creator. Offering of gifts and self is the ritual portrayal of the proper relationship between God and humanity. These elements have been ever-present in the history of Christian worship practice.

See also CIRCUMCISION; COVENANT; EXODUS; FASTING; FEASTS AND FESTIVALS; GOD; HOLINESS IN THE NT; HOLINESS IN THE OT; LORD'S SUPPER; MUSIC/MUSICAL INSTRUMENTS; PASSOVER; PRIESTS; REVELATION, CONCEPT OF; SERVICE; TEMPLE/TEMPLES; TABERNACLE; TENT OF MEETING.

Bibliography. H. Davies, *Christian Worship: Its History and Meaning*; G. Delling, *Worship in the New Testament*; R. P. Martin, *Worship in the Early Church*; H. H. Rowley, *Worship in Ancient Israel: Its Forms and Meaning*.

—RAYMOND BAILEY

General Epistles Dictionary Articles

Letter to the Hebrews [MDB 364-67]

• AN OUTLINE •

I. Introduction. The Son and Angels (1:1–2:18)
A. God's final revelation in his Son (1:1-4)
B. Christ higher than angels (1:5-14)
C. Admonition (2:1-4)
D. Subjection of the world to the Son—the way of suffering (2:5-9)
E. The pioneer of salvation made perfect through suffering (2:10-18)

II. Participation in the House of God and in the Rest along the Way (3:1–4:13)
A. Christ's faithfulness over God's house as Son compared with Moses' faithfulness as servant (3:1-6)
B. The rejection of Jesus more serious than the rejection of Moses (3:7-19)
C. The promise of rest remains but it may be forfeited (4:1-10)
D. Exhortation (4:1-13)

III. The Nature of the Son's High Priesthood (4:14–7:28)
A. Christ's high priesthood as encouragement to his people (4:14-16)
B. Christ's qualifications as high priest (5:1-10)
C. Readers' qualifications and challenge (5:11–6:12)
D. The steadfastness of God's promise (6:13-20)
E. Christ the perfect eternal high priest according to the order of Melchizedek (7:1-28)

IV. The Superiority of the Heavenly Reality over Its Earthly Copy (8:1–10:18)
A. The heavenly sanctuary and the new covenant (8:1-13)
B. The ministry of the levitical priests (9:1-10)
C. The character of Christ's sacrifice (9:11–10:18)

V. The Way of the Christian as the Way of Faith (10:19–12:29)
A. Privileges and duties of Christians (10:19-25)
B. The fate of the willful sinner (10:25-31)
C. Call for endurance (10:32-39)
D. The faith of past heroes and heroines (11:1-40)
E. Exhortation to faithful endurance as sons (12:1-29)

VI. Concluding Admonitions (13:1-21)
A. Ethical injunctions and examples (13:1-8)
B. Genuine Christian sacrifice (13:9-16)
C. Call for obedience and prayer (13:17-19)
D. Prayer and doxology (13:20-21)

VII. Postscript (13:22-25)
A. Personal notes (13:22-23)
B. Final greetings and benediction (13:24-25)

•**Hebrews, Letter to the.** We do not know who wrote Hebrews; we do not know to whom it was written; we do not know precisely why it was written; we do not even know how to classify the book as a writing. Hebrews is indeed the "riddle" of the NT. In order to gain some understanding of the writing, however, most commentators suggest a specific historical and religious situation which may be seen as the problem or the "question" to which Hebrews is the "answer." Exegesis, however, is often only loosely tied to the specific situation posited.

Hugh Montefiore, for example, argues that Hebrews was written by APOLLOS to the church at Corinth, especially to the Jewish Christians in that congregation. But his commentary "has been constructed in the hope that it may be of use to those for whom there is as yet no convincing solution to the difficult problems which this Epistle poses" (32).

Robert Jewett feels that effective exegesis of Hebrews demands that a particular hypothesis concerning the writer's situation be selected and used in interpretation. He suggests that Hebrews be read as a letter of Epaphras to the churches of the Lycus Valley designed to combat a unique Jewish-Gnostic heresy (evidenced in

COLOSSIANS). It would have been written at approximately the same time as Colossians to deal with the same sort of situation.

The suggestion of Helmut Koester that the writing be appreciated not in light of any specific situation but as a "fundamental theological treatise" seems to move away from the historical focus. Instead of moving outside the historical-critical argumentation, however, Koester simply generalizes the historical moment which is used for situating and interpreting the writing. Koester places Hebrews in the "general situation of the churches after Paul's time." Hebrews, then, is interpreted as "a witness for the efforts to develop the Pauline legacy" during the last decades of the first century (272).

This article is designed to survey the conventional historical-critical questions and to suggest a satisfying approach to the interpretation of Hebrews in light of the absence of compelling answers.

The Author. Hebrews is anonymous. In an early period, Hebrews was interpreted as a letter of Paul which was originally written in Hebrew or Aramaic and which was translated by Luke into Greek. Other early traditions name Clement of Rome, Apollos, or BARNABAS as the author. The vocabulary, style, and argumentation of Hebrews lead modern scholars to discount Pauline authorship and to envision the author as a Christian trained in rhetoric and Hellenistic learning. The writing itself is evidence that the writer is a Christian, a very well-educated Christian who uses a sophisticated style of Greek. His or her education and experience involved what we would call *literary* experience. This literary competency is used by the writer in viewing and explicating the OT, the person and work of Jesus Christ, and the place of Christians in the plan of God. The literary ability of the writer is used for religious purposes, but this does not negate the literary character of the writing. Modern critics have suggested as author the names of STEPHEN, PHILIP, PETER, SILAS, Aristion, Prisca, and JUDE.

The Recipients. Christians are being addressed. They are "holy brethren who share in a heavenly call" (3:1). They have been Christians for a period of time—long enough that they ought to be teachers (5:12). They have had a reputation for love and service directed toward other Christians in their need. They are facing difficult days, similar to their early times in Christian life and service. In those early days they suffered, "sometimes being publicly exposed to abuse and affliction, and sometimes being partners with those so treated" (10:33). At that time the Christians addressed in Hebrews "had compassion on the prisoners" and "joyfully accepted the plundering of your property" (Heb 10:34).

In this new period of suffering, the Christians have not yet resisted to the point of shedding their blood (12:4). The fact that the possibility of martyrdom is raised lets us know that the experience they are facing is not trivial, but we learn more about what is happening to the spirit and will of the readers than we learn of the actual cause of their suffering. The writer speaks of the danger of Christians drifting away from the message they have heard, failing to hold fast their confidence and pride, being hardened by the deceitfulness of sin. He warns of the danger of sluggishness. Some of the Christians have begun to neglect regular worship service. They are in need of endurance because they have drooping hands and weak knees (2:1; 3:6,13; 6:12; 10:25, 36; 12:12).

Readers have been sought among Jewish Christians because of the use of the OT and the arguments of the superiority of Jesus and the new COVENANT to Moses and the old covenant. The original readers were regarded for a long time as Jewish Christians living in Palestine, or more specifically in Jerusalem. Since the discovery of the DEAD SEA SCROLLS, some scholars have defended the thesis that readers were former members of the Qumran community—either priests who had been converted to Christianity or former members of the community who had come close to becoming Christians but who had not come all the way.

Some scholars have seen the readers as Jewish Christians outside Palestine—either Jewish Christians spread over the Roman world or Jewish Christians in a particular community (wealthy and cultured Jews at Ephesus, a small conservative enclave of Jewish Christians in Rome, or Jewish Christians in Alexandria or Cyprus who were being induced to espouse nationalistic Judaism).

The fact that the OT was the Bible for the Christian community everywhere—for Gentile Christians as well as Jewish Christians—makes it impossible to limit the readers to Jewish Christians in or outside Palestine. The readers, then, may also be seen as predominately Gentile Christians or simply Christians in general who are being warned concerning a general lassitude. These Christians have been located in such places as Corinth, Ephesus, the Lycus Valley, Antioch, Rome, or some other Italian community.

The one bit of information in the book itself which seems to be related to destination is the statement in 13:24 that "those from Italy greet you." It is possible that this is simply a greeting from Italy (perhaps Rome), but it is possible that the author is writing to Rome (or elsewhere in Italy) and sending greetings from Italians who are in his vicinity.

The Date. Since 1 CLEMENT refers to Hebrews, the writing had to be in existence before the end of the first century. The use made of the Temple in Hebrews (and silence concerning the destruction of the Temple in 70 CE) constitute no justification for dating the writing before 70 because abstract ideas and not the specific Herodian Temple is at issue.

What Sort of Writing Is Hebrews? How is Hebrews to be read? As a letter? Hebrews lacks the distinctive first-century salutation. Moreover, through chap. 12 the writing is too impersonal to be called a genuine letter (the epistolary ending may have been added by a later hand or by the author to give the writing the characteristics of a Pauline letter or to accompany the writing when it was sent to yet another community). In the last chapter of Hebrews, the writer describes the whole work as a "word of exhortation." The exhortation is made directly but it is also made indirectly in its presentation of Jesus Christ. What is the exhortation? We actually have to move along to the center of the writing to see the exhortation: "Let us leave the elementary doctrine of Christ and go on to maturity. . . . We desire each one of you to show the same earnestness in realizing the full assurance of hope until the end, so that you may not be sluggish, but imitators of those who through faith and patience inherit the promises" (6:1, 11-12). The elementary doctrine of Christ has to do both with an inferior concept of the person and work of Jesus Christ and with a superficial Christian faith and life. The maturity to which the writer is encouraging the readers is a Christological maturity and a maturity of Christian living.

The Form and Message of Hebrews. Hebrews is a sermon, but it is a particular type of sermon, one based on OT Scripture interpreted in a fashion reminiscent of the Alexandrian Judaism represented by PHILO. Hebrews and the other books of the NT looked at OT writings not in the context of the original situations or even in the context of the OT community as a whole. What was sought was not an original dated message to ancient communities. The OT writings were examined in the context of the church to discern the message to the contemporary community. The OT was examined in light of Jesus with the conviction that Jesus opens up the true meaning of the OT. Heb 5:8-10 is an excellent starting point for making sense of the message and form of the entire book. "Although he was a Son, he learned obedience through what he suffered; and being made perfect he became the source of eternal salvation to all who obey him, being designated by God a high priest according to the order of MELCHIZEDEK." The descending and ascending movement described here (although he was Son, he learned obedience through suffering; being made perfect through suffering he became the source of eternal salvation to all who obey him; he is designated HIGH PRIEST) follows the same motif of humiliation and suffering followed by exaltation and glory which pervades the primitive proclamation concerning Jesus. But the method of exegesis is different from that used in other NT writings which make essentially the same point concerning Jesus.

Particular methods are used in Hebrews to allow OT passages to speak to the present: the present is seen as the time of fulfillment of OT promises; specific OT persons, events, or things are seen as types which are related to their counterparts in the age of fulfillment; and OT passages are seen as allegories which refer to the period of fulfillment. In one respect, Hebrews is rather unique among NT books—the assumption and use of a Platonic worldview which sees the visible world of phenomena as an exteriorization, an imperfect imitation of the intelligible world. Material and sensible objects are not ultimate; more ultimate and "real" are the archetypes laid up in heaven. (The Platonic idealism of Hebrews is so pronounced that some scholars have attempted to defend the thesis that the author of Hebrews had a direct acquaintance with Philo and his attempt to reconcile Greek logic with OT teachings.)

The structure of Hebrews is related to its function as a word of exhortation and to its character as an exposition of OT passages. There is an interweaving of theological argument and earnest exhortation (2:14; 3:7–4:11; 4:14-16; 5:11–6:12; 10:19-29; 12:1-17; 13:1-17 all contain explicit exhortations). In the argument and exhortation, the Psalter is used extensively. The usual practice is to quote a section of the Psalter and then to use words and phrases from that quotation in the following exposition. At times the argument is elaborated with use of additional OT passages which deal with the same theme. The exegesis of Ps 95:7-11 in the exhortation of 3:7–4:13 contains references to the narrative of the wilderness wanderings; and the exegesis of Ps 110:4 in Heb 7:1-28 refers to the narrative of Melchizedek in Gen 14.

The form of Hebrews is also influenced by the use of the rhetorical device of *synkrisis* (comparison) and the use of the "more or less" type of *a fortiori* argument. In order to show the superiority of a person or object, that person or object may be compared with an outstanding specimen of the same kind. Hebrews shows the infinite worth of Jesus by comparing him with outstanding institutions and figures (angels, Moses, Melchizedek, etc.). The "more or less" argument is essentially the same as that used by the rabbis with the designation *qal-wa-homer* ("light and heavy").

The attempt to outline Hebrews in a definitive way has met with no general agreement. Proposals are based on the major exhortations (seen as standing at the end of the major sections (1:1–4:13; 4:14–10:31; 10:32–13:17); the Christological ideas of the writing; the distinction between the hortatory and Christological parts; or on the basis of the scheme of Greek hortatory address. Alexander C. Purdy explains that "no outline can do justice" to the interrelationship of the author's ideas, particularly because of the "subtle and skillful way in which he prepares his readers for the exposition of Jesus as high priest (in 2:17; 3:1), for the discussion of 'God's rest' (in 3:1, 18), and for the Melchizedek speculation (in 5:6, 10; 6:21)" (580).

The different historical situations and the different outlines suggested by commentators constitute not only evidence of the complexity of the book of Hebrews but also evidence that different readers—even critical readers—"concretize" or "actualize" Hebrews in light of their own psychological sets and historical and sociological situations. Hebrews invites readers to interact with the text to relate the text to their own needs in the very process of reading. The outline included here (above) is offered not to enable readers to bypass the active reading the author of Hebrews expects, but to suggest one way of organizing the result of reading and actualizing of the content.

See also ANGEL; APOSTASY; COVENANT; EPISTLE/LETTER; FAITH AND FAITHLESSNESS; HIGH PRIEST; MELCHIZEDEK; PERSECUTION IN THE NT; PREACHING; PRIESTS; SUFFERING IN THE NT; WORSHIP IN THE NT.

Bibliography. M. Barth, "The OT in Hebrews: An Essay in Biblical Hermeneutics," *Current Issues in NT Interpretation: Essays in Honor of Otto A. Piper*, ed. W. Klassen and G. F. Snyder; F. F. Bruce, *The Epistle to the Hebrews: The English Text, with Introduction, Exposition, and Notes*; G. W. Buchanan, *To the Hebrews: Translation, Comment, and Conclusions*; F. B. Craddock, "The Letter to the Hebrews," *NIB*; N. A. Dahl, "A New and Living Way: The Approach to God According to Hebrews 10:19-25," *Int* 5 (1951): 401-12; F. V. Filson, *"Yesterday": A Study of Hebrews in the Light of Chapter 13*; J. Hering, *The Epistle to the Hebrews*; F. L. Horton, Jr., *The Melchizedek Tradition: A Critical Examination of the Sources to the Fifth Century A.D. and in the Epistle to the Hebrews*; R. Jewett, *Letter to Pilgrims: A Commentary on the Epistle to the Hebrews*; W. G. Johnsson, "The Pilgrimage Motif in the Book of Hebrews," *JBL* 97 (1978): 239-51; E. Käsemann, *The Wandering*

People of God: An Investigation of the Letter to the Hebrews; H. Koester, *Introduction to the New Testament*, vol. 2, *History and Literature of Early Christianity*; F. Lo Bue, "The Historical Background of the Epistle to the Hebrews," *JBL* 75 (1956): 52-57; T. W. Manson, "The Problem of the Epistle to the Hebrews," *Studies in the Gospels and Epistles*, ed. M. Black; W. Manson, *The Epistle to the Hebrews: A Historical and Theological Consideration*; H. Montefiore, *A Commentary on the Epistle to the Hebrews*; A. C. Purdy, "Epistle to the Hebrews: Introduction and Exegesis," *IB*; S. G. Sowers, *The Hermeneutics of Philo and Hebrews. A Comparison of the Interpretation of the OT in Philo Judaeus and the Epistle to the Hebrews*; A. Vanhoye, *A Structured Translation of the Epistle to the Hebrews*; B. F. Westcott, *The Epistle to the Hebrews: The Greek Text with Notes and Essays*.

—EDGAR V. MCKNIGHT

Letter of James [MDB 427-28]

• AN OUTLINE •

I. Chapter 1
A. Address and greeting (1:1)
B. The Christian way of dealing with trials (1:2-4)
C. The relationship of wisdom, prayer, faith, doubt, and stability (1:5-8)
D. The transience of earthly wealth (1:9-11)
E. Distinctions among trial, temptation, and sin (1:12-15)
F. God, the source of all good (1:16-18)
G. Hearing, responding, and self-control (1:19-21)
H. On hearing and doing God's word (1:22-25)
I. One illustration (not a definition) of pure religion (1:26-27)

II. Chapter 2
A. Belief in Christ rejects partiality toward the rich (2:1-7)
B. Christian love for the "neighbor" rejects such partiality (2:8-9)
C. Love for neighbor illustrated as a kind of Christian "law" (2:10-13)
D. James's view on the relationship of faith and works (2:14-26)

III. Chapter 3
A. Teachings related to the use of the tongue (3:1-12)
B. An illustration of true wisdom (3:13-18)

IV. Chapter 4
A. On personal individual piety in contrast to a "worldly" life (4:1-10)
B. Relationship to others based on awareness of the law, the lawgiver, and judge (4:11-12)
C. Sin of presumption versus true humility (4:13-16)
D. The sin of omission (4:17)

V. Chapter 5
A. Judgment on rich people (5:1-6)
B. The virtue of patience (5:7-11)
C. Oaths forbidden (5:12)
D. Prayer and healing (5:13-18)
E. On reclaiming sinners (5:19-20)

•**James, Letter of.** The Letter of JAMES begins like other letters in the NT, but it is quite different from all other letters. Addressed to "the twelve tribes in the Dispersion," it is very general, whereas letters usually named individuals and came to focus on specific issues related to them or to their congregations.

What Kind of Literature? NT scholars usually refer to James as a diatribe or a paranesis. Paranetic literature is the more general ethical exhortation designed as moral instruction, and one is reminded a bit of the proverbs. Paranetic writing is not usually well outlined; it moves quickly from one issue to another and often returns to a subject which has already been covered.

James is cast in the form of a letter to the Christian community at large, similar to 1 Peter in many ways, but quite different from other epistles.

Authorship. The letter identifies the author as "James, a servant of God and of the Lord Jesus Christ." The name is actually "Jacob," but English translations use "James" and reserve "Jacob" for the OT patriarch.

Traditionally, the church identifies this James as the brother of Jesus who is prominent in the Jerusalem church (Acts 15:13-21; 21:18-25; Gal 1:19). James, the brother of Jesus, lived in Nazareth (Mark 6:3), and apparently, along with other siblings, Joseph, Judas, Simon, and sisters, did not understand or accept Jesus as Messiah during his lifetime. Evidently, James the brother of Jesus became a believer later. He did receive a resurrection appearance and appears as an apostle (1 Cor 15:7). This is the James who was obviously the leader in the Jerusalem church in Acts 15.

The other men named James in the NT are James the son of Zebedee, an apostle (Matt 4:21); James the son of Alphaeus, an apostle (Matt 10:3) and James the father of Judas (Luke 6:16). No serious case for the authorship of this letter has been made for any of these men named James. Tradition, although late and not well documented, focuses on James the brother of Jesus.

Arguments in favor of James the brother of Jesus are as follows. (1) His relationship to Jesus would have been a factor to encourage the canonization of the letter. (2) His prominence in the Jerusalem church is well known. (3) He was martyred in the seventh decade of the first century (notes in Josephus suggest a date of 60–62 CE; the second century Hegesippus dated James's death after the beginning of the Jewish revolt ca. 66–67 CE). (4) Only this James is well known enough to be seriously considered: almost nothing is known of James the son of Alphaeus, and James the son of Zebedee and brother of John evidently died about 42 CE (Acts 12:2). (5) The Judaistic flavor of the writing suggests a native Palestinian as author.

There are numerous arguments against the belief that James the brother of Jesus was the author. (1) There was strong resistance to the inclusion of the letter in the NT canon. Its acceptance was late. Such resistance is difficult to explain if it was written by this James. (2) There is no internal evidence to relate the author to Jesus' family. (3) The literary style, paranesis, and the superior type of Greek employed suggest that a peasant from Galilee could not have written it. Some commentators (e.g., Burton Scott Easton) consider it inconceivable that this James could have written it.

It appears, however, in light of the evidence, the best case is for James the brother of Jesus. Tradition favors him. There is no rival. A scribe's assistance could account for the Greek style, but why could not a Palestinian Galilean learn Greek? A date about 60–62 CE would fit the other evidence including knowledge of Paul's theology and letters. The Hebrew nature of the book is certainly understandable. In short, James's theology is almost exclusively the high moral teachings of first-century Judaism, basic OT thought.

There are distinctively Christian themes in the book, however, to justify its inclusion. James is a "servant of God and of the Lord Jesus Christ" (1:1). Reference is made to "the faith of our Lord Jesus Christ, the Lord of glory" (2:1). The early Christian hope of the coming of the Lord is mentioned twice (5:7,8). To be sure, James does not mention great Christian themes like atonement, death of Christ, resurrection, and so forth, but the nature of his letter may explain such omissions.

Doctrinal and Thematic Emphases. The writing is not a systematic composition. It switches subjects quickly without transition and often returns to a subject such as "the rich." It must be read for the truth taught in each brief statement.

The writing includes, incidentally, such great biblical themes as God the Creator and Father (2:19; 3:9); one universe (1:17); God is holy (1:13); God gives good gifts to us (1:17); God is the source of all good (1:5, 17); our ways are in God's hands (4:15); God is merciful (5:11); God hears prayers (1:5; 4:2; 5:13-18); and God forgives sins (5:15, 20); and the book sees salvation as JUSTIFICATION (2:21).

James deplored hypocrisy, sham, and pretense of any kind. His exhortations reflect an appreciation for the Hebrew prophets. He also believed that God and the Christian life were incompatible with the cultural world of his time. His repeated condemnations of the rich and powerful suggest a kinship with Amos and suggest a serious flaw in contemporary American Christian understanding.

See also FAITH AND FAITHLESSNESS; GENERAL LETTERS; JAMES; JUSTIFICATION; LAW IN THE NT; LOVE IN THE NT; WEALTH; WISDOM LITERATURE; WISDOM IN THE NT.

Bibliography. W. Barclay, *The Letters of James and Peter*; P. Davids, *The Epistle of James*; M. Dibelius, *James*; B. Easton, "The Epistle of James: Introduction and Exegesis," *IB*; L. T. Johnson, "The Letter of James," *NIB*; S. Laws, *A Commentary on the Epistle of James*; J. W. Roberts, *The Letter of James*; J. H. Ropes, *A Critical and Exegetical Commentary on the Epistle of St. James*; E. M. Sidebottom, *James, Jude, 2 Peter*; H. S. Songer, "James," *BBC*.

—MORRIS ASHCRAFT

Letters of Peter [MDB 677-79]

• AN OUTLINE OF FIRST PETER •

I. Opening and Greeting (1:1-2)
II. Blessing (1:3-12)
III. Exhortation to Holy Living (1:13–2:10)
IV. Social Code for Christian Households and Encouragement for Suffering Believers (2:11–4:11)
A. Preamble to the social code (2:11-12)
B. Social code for Christian households (2:13–3:7)
C. Conclusion to the social code (3:8-12)
D. Guidance for Christians who suffer for the faith (3:13–4:6)
E. Summary exhortation and doxology (4:7-11)
V. Encouragement in the Face of Suffering (4:12-19)
VI. Exhortation to Constancy under Suffering (5:1-11)
VII. Epistolary Conclusion (5:12-14)

• AN OUTLINE OF SECOND PETER •

I. Opening and Greeting (1:1-2)
II. Exhortation to Holy Living (1:3-11)
III. Reminder of the Inspired Tradition Guaranteed by Apostolic Testimony and the Sacred Hope Given by Inspired Prophets (1:12-21)
IV. Warning about and Execration of False Teachers (2:1-22)
V. Exhortation on the Parousia and the Apocalypse (3:1-13)
VI. Concluding Exhortation to Holiness and Steadfastness (3:14-18)

•Peter, Letters of. The Petrine Letters—1 and 2 Peter—are two of seven NT letters known as Catholic or General Letters (the others are James, 1, 2, 3 John, and Jude), so designated because they are addressed not to any single church or recipient but to the larger Christian community, and thus valuable for the universal (catholic) church. The letters are important as evidences of early Christian history and theology.

First Peter. First Peter was apparently known and used by the church in the East earlier than in the West. It was quoted by Polycarp in his *Letter to the Philippians* (ca. 135); accredited to PETER by Papias (first quarter of the second century) and Irenaeus (ca. 185); and used freely by Clement of Alexandria (ca. 200). In the West, it was omitted from the MURATORIAN CANON (the Christian scriptures accepted by the church at Rome ca. 180–190) and first appeared as accepted scripture in the writings of Tertullian (ca. 200–210). This is all the more striking, as much scholarship cites Rome as the place where the Epistle was written.

The author identifies himself as "Peter, apostle of Jesus Christ" (1:1) and a "fellow elder and witness of the sufferings of Christ" (5:1). Traditionally, this has been taken as a certification that the letter came from Jesus' chief disciple. Most modern scholars hold that the real author used "Peter" as a pseudonym. The style of the work is very literary, with traces of rhetorical expertise, deliberate rhythm and artistry, and a familiarity with the LXX—hence hardly from Peter (who was "illiterate" or "uneducated," according to Acts 4:13). Whether the linguistic elegance derives from Silvanus (SILAS), the scribe of the letter (5:12), is unresolvable. First Peter has Pauline traits: the use of "in Christ" (3:16; 5:10, 14), the view of Jesus' death as a ransom (l:18-19), and the use of a social code (2:13–3:7) similar to those in Colossians and Ephesians. This is in tension with the report in Gal 2 of the intense theological differences between Paul and Peter. First Peter lacks any evidence of firsthand knowledge of Jesus: no mention of Jesus' life, ministry, or teachings, no parables, no miracles, and not even any echoes of his striking proverbs. The phrase "witness of the sufferings of Christ" is so general it might be said by anyone for whom the passion of Jesus was his/her personally redeeming experience. Finally, the persecutions described in 1 Peter appear to be general and official, such as those inflicted on Christians under Domitian, well after Peter's death.

If Peter wrote this epistle, it should be dated about 64. Those who consider it to be from another author (or even from a Petrine school) date it late in the first century, about 90–95. Crucial to the question of dating the letter is the reference in 4:12-19 to their suffering as Christians. From the earliest days of the church Christians were subject to abuse and suffering for their faith; however, widespread and legally sanctioned persecution of Christians as Christians began only under Domitian in the 90s.

The letter mentions as its place of origin "Babylon" (5:13), a first-century symbol for Rome in apocalyptic literature (cf. Rev 14:8; 16:19). Early church tradition maintains that Peter went to Rome, served, and died there. The parallels between 1 Peter and *1 Clement* (the letter of the bishop of Rome to the Corinthians, ca. 96) show a possible Roman connection. And the greetings extended from "Mark" (5:13) also strengthen the proposal that 1 Peter came from Rome (Mark was with Paul in Rome: Col 4:10; Phlm 24).

The readers are addressed as "exiles of the Dispersion in Pontus, Galatia, Cappadocia, Asia, and Bithynia" (1:1), Christians dwelling in the more northern part of Asia Minor. Nevertheless, the exhortation to holiness and steadfastness under persecution, the reminder of the great hope laid up for God's people, and the encouragement to center one's life in Christ apply to Christians everywhere. The writer also addressed the readers as "exiles," chosen, destined, and sanctified, a description of who they were, not where they were. As God's people, this world for them was an alien place, because their home was with God. Consequently, they were encouraged to fortitude during their temporary sojourn or exile (see 1:17; 2:11).

The recipients were, in all likelihood, Gentiles. They were called on to avoid "the passions of [their] former ignorance" (1:14), reminded that they were "ransomed from [their] futile ways inherited from [their] fathers" (1:18) and called "out of darkness into his marvelous light. Once . . . no people but now . . . God's people" (2:9-10), and reminded that joining in with what Gentiles do was a thing of the past (4:3-6).

First Peter addresses two crises: temptation and persecution. The pagan society in which the readers lived posed a constant threat. Many religions, cultures, and cults were active and attractive. The Christian community survived by its close fellowship (Christ is here portrayed as shepherd and the church as a flock, 5:2-4). Moral perils at hand were to be avoided: passions of ignorance (1:14); futile ways (1:18); malice, guile, insincerity, envy, slander (2:1); passions of the flesh (2:11); evil (2:16); superficial and showy adornment (3:3); reviling (3:9); licentiousness, passions, drunkenness, reveling, carousing, lawless idolatry, wild profligacy (4:3-4); murder, theft, wrongdoing, mischief-making (4:15). The writer exhorts the exiles by pointing to Jesus as redeemer and spotless example, and by calling them to respond to Christ with resolute conviction (2:24).

While persecution appears to be a focus throughout the letter, in 1:1–4:11 persecution is only potential; but, from 4:12 on, it is real. While 1:6 says "you may have to suffer," and 3:14 "even if you do suffer," beginning with 4:12 the language shifts to "you share Christ's sufferings" (4:13), "let those who suffer . . . " (4:19). The danger they faced was intense. They were in peril of losing their well-being and their lives. That may be concluded fairly by the intense exhortation given and by the author's use of the example of Christ's suffering and death as their model.

By means of sermonic material (1:3–4:11) and admonitions (4:12–5:11), this Epistle aims to exhort the readers to be steadfast in God's grace (5:12), in the face of persecution, temptation, alienation, and social oppression. The readers are encouraged to be constant both for the sake of their witness for Christ and for the future hope for what they would receive (an imperishable, undefiled, unfading inheritance; the salvation of their souls; God's approval; and his blessing: things hoped for which are kept in heaven for those who suffer and persevere for Christ).

A striking feature of 1 Peter is its theology and ethics. Suffering is viewed as a testing, purifying experience, to be met with humility and love. A social code

(2:13–3:7, a feature which early Christians adopted from Stoic philosophers) instructs in correct living within given social roles. The writer starts from a point of radical eschatological hope when he offers his ethical guidelines: "the end of all things is at hand" (4:7). Irrespective of that starting point, it is quite problematic to modern readers that he calls for submission to all governmental powers and for slaves to be patient about being beaten (using Christ's passion as example), that he calls women "the weaker sex" and gives proscriptions against immoderate female attire, that his advice to husbands fosters patronizing, sexist roles, that he teaches a doctrine of Jesus' preaching in the world of the dead to people who died in Noah's day, and that his remarks about baptism are extremely sacramental. Apart from those factors, 1 Peter contains some of the richest expressions of Christian hope and piety in the NT. Its exhortation is consistent in putting Christ as the focus of Christian living, duty, and hope.

Second Peter. Probably the latest work in the NT to be written, 2 Peter was also the latest to be accepted as a part of the Christian Bible. It was not used by the apostolic fathers, not quoted by the church fathers until 250 (by Firmilian of Caesarea), not accepted by Eusebius, and questioned by Jerome, Erasmus, and Calvin. Its inclusion in the church canons cannot be dated with confidence before the late fourth century and in Syria before the sixth century. This is surprising to the general reader, since the author names himself "Simeon Peter" an "apostle" (1:1), claims to have been present at the transfiguration (1:17-19), and links this writing with 1 Peter (3:1). The church fathers were unconvinced of these claims to authority.

Many factors prevent most modern scholars from accepting 2 Peter's claim to be from Jesus' chief disciple. First, the work is a Jewish-Greek writing which makes an artificial effort at imitating Hellenistic authors. The style is a mixture of Hebraisms and secular Hellenistic traits. It uses a Hebrew-affected style of grammar and identifies the author with the strangely Hebraizing spelling "Simeon." There is also an apparent use of terms common to Hellenistic religions: "divine power" 1:3; "godliness" 1:3, 6, 7; "knowledge" 1:2, 3, 8; 2:20; "divine nature" 1:4; "self-control" 1:6; "eye-witnesses" 1:16; "corruption" 1:4; 2:12, 19; "brotherly affection" 1:7. Such a Hellenistic inclination is contrary to all we know of Peter from the Gospels and Acts.

Second, there is an almost unquestionable use of Jude as a source by the writer. Both writings address the PAROUSIA as a matter of teaching, and attack false teachers. Even more important is the high degree of similarity between the two in specific subject matter, choice of vocabulary, and even the order of ideas. Evident throughout the works, this is especially clear in 2 Pet 2:1-19 and Jude 4:16, where false teachers are described and OT allusions are drawn in exactly the same way by both writers. Since Jude was almost certainly written after Peter's death and 2 Peter after the Letter of Jude, 2 Peter could not have come from Simon Peter. Moreover, it is inconceivable that the chief disciple, the first to address Jesus as "Christ," the "rock" on which the church would be built, this member of the inner circle of disciples, would have to rely on Jude for his message.

Third, this is the only book in the NT that confronts heretical teaching against the parousia. Other writings confront heretical teachings about the parousia, but not teachings that the parousia would not occur. Such a heresy arose in the church during the second century when Gnostics with libertine antispiritualism opposed the doctrine of the parousia. The writing thus appears to come from a time much later than the lifetime of Peter.

Fourth, the work exhibits aspects of early Catholicism characteristic of the late first and early second centuries. The concept of apostleship held by the writer and the reference to "all [the] letters" of Paul (3:16) as if they were a collected body of works ranked as "scriptures" along with other "scriptures" indicate a time much later than the days of Peter. The "early Catholicism" in evidence here is one of the work's assets as a piece of history. Most scholars consider 2 Peter to be a pseudonymous letter, the latest written NT book, dating perhaps as late as 140–150.

Since authorship is uncertain, no certain place can be designated as its point of origination. In the address, no place-name advises us of its destination either. Such places as Palestine, Egypt, Rome, or Asia Minor have been proposed, but all proposals are guesses.

The purposes of the work are clearer and easier to decipher. The author intends to warn the readers about the heresy of false teachers who make light of Jesus' coming (1:16; 3:3ff.) and to protect them from the immoral ways of those libertines who are in their midst (3:17). The opponents he confronts are not two groups but one. False teaching and immoral living are interrelated.

The writer assails the false teachers who appear to have had a genuine conversion at some point (2:20-22), but who misuse Paul's letters (3:16) and teach error that probably derived from private or idiosyncratic interpretations (1:20). Such practice amounts to denying Christ (2:1, 20-22). The author's purpose is to stabilize the readers (3:17), so that they will not lose their "entrance into the eternal kingdom of our Lord and Savior Jesus Christ" (1:11). To achieve this, he attacks the ways and teachings of the heretics and also repeats his injunction for the readers to remember their heritage. They are founded on a trustworthy revelation that God promised and gave through inspired prophets, guaranteed through apostolic witness, certified by the work of the Holy Spirit, and will vindicate at the coming of the Lord. He launches an excited assault on the immorality of the heretics. Their assumed freedom is another slavery. Their ways will incur God's wrath. Their final state will be worse than if they had never come to Christ.

Second Peter is significant because of the view it gives us of emerging Catholicism in the second-century church. It is equally valuable as evidence for the lively contest the early church engaged in when deciding on what scriptures should be admitted to the canon, based primarily on the standard of apostolic authorship.

See also APOSTLE/APOSTLESHIP; CANON; EPISTLE/LETTER; JUDE, LETTER OF; MURATORIAN CANON; ETHICS IN THE NT; PAROUSIA/SECOND COMING; PERSECUTION IN THE NT; PETER; SUFFERING IN THE NT.

Bibliography. D. L. Bartlett, "The First Letter of Peter," *NIB*; E. Best, *1 Peter*, NCB; J. L. Blevins, "Introduction to 1 Peter," *RE* 79 (1982): 401-13; J. N. D. Kelly, *A Commentary on the Epistles of Peter and Jude*; W. G. Kümmel, *Introduction to the New Testament*; E. G. Selwyn, *The First Epistle of St. Peter*; D. F. Watson, "The Second Letter of Peter," *NIB*.

—RICHARD A. SPENCER

Gospel and Letters ofJohn [MDB 460-64]

• AN OUTLINE OF THE GOSPEL OF JOHN •

I. The Prologue (1:1-18)
II. Jesus before the World (1:19–12:50)
A. Introduction: the first disciples (1:19–2:11)
B. The revelation of eternal life: Cana to Cana (2:12–4:54)
C. Revelation and judgment at the festivals (5:1–10:42)
D. Withdrawal and return (11:1–12:50)
III. Jesus with His Own (13:1–20:31)
A. The farewell discourse (13:1–17:26)
B. The trial of Jesus (18:1–19:16a)
C. The death of Jesus (19:16b-42)
D. The resurrection of Jesus (20:1-29)
E. Conclusion (20:30-31)
IV. Epilogue (21:1-25)
A. The catch of fish (21:1-14)
B. The commissioning of Peter (21:15-23)
C. The postscript (21:24-25)

• AN OUTLINE OF FIRST JOHN •

I. The Prologue. The Word of Life (1:1-4)
II. Light among God's Children (1:5–2:27)
A. The incompatibility of light and sin (1:5–2:2)
B. Love as a test of knowledge (2:3-11)
C. Conflict with the world (2:12-17)
D. Conflict within the community (2:18-27)
III. Righteousness among God's Children (2:28–4:6)
A. The hope of the righteous (2:28–3:10)
B. The love of the righteous (3:11-24)
C. The two spirits (4:1-6)
IV. Love among God's Children (4:7–5:12)
A. The true nature of love (4:7-12)
B. The true nature of faith (5:1-12)
V. The Epilogue (5:31-21)

• AN OUTLINE OF SECOND JOHN •

I. Greeting. In Truth and Love (1-3)
II. Request. Love Those Who Walk in Truth (4-6)
III. Warning. Do Not Receive Those Who Spread Deception (7-11)
IV. Closing. The Fulfillment of Joy (12-13)

• AN OUTLINE OF THIRD JOHN •

I. Greetings to a Beloved Brother (1-4)
II. Praise for Gaius's Hospitality (5-8)
III. Criticism of Diotrephes' Defiance (9-10)
IV. Praise for Demetrius's Truthfulness (11-12)
V. Peace for "the Friends" (13-15)

•**John, Gospel and Letters of.** Called the "spiritual Gospel" by Clement of Alexandria, the Gospel of John has long been recognized as distinctive from the other three (the synoptic) Gospels. John preserves a tradition of Jesus' "signs," words, and crucifixion that seems to be independent of the synoptic Gospels. The Gospel of John has exerted a profound and pervasive influence on Christian theology, especially through its depiction of Jesus as the *logos* (Word) that became flesh.

Both John and the Synoptics give historical accounts of the ministry of Jesus from his baptism through the resurrection appearances, and both provide theological interpretation. Although the sequence in the Gospels varies, in both John and the Synoptics one finds the cleansing of the Temple, the feeding of the five thousand and the crossing of the sea, healing miracles, the anointing of Jesus by a woman, the entry into Jerusalem, and similarities in the accounts of the arrest, trials, crucifixion, and discovery of the empty tomb. The differences between John and the Synoptics are equally pronounced. In John the Kingdom of God, which is the major theme of Jesus' teachings in the Synoptics, appears only in John 3:3, 5, and 18:36. In its place, the kingship of Jesus becomes a primary theme of the trial and death of Jesus. In the Synoptics Jesus teaches in pithy sayings and parables; dialogues and long discourses dominate in the Gospel of John, where Jesus sounds more like the author of the Johannine Epistles than the Jesus of the synoptic Gospels. In the Synoptics Jesus spends all but the last week of his ministry in and around Galilee. John probably gives us a more accurate picture of the ministry of Jesus by recording several trips back and forth between Galilee (John 2; 4; 6), Samaria (John 4), and Judea (John 2–3; 5; 7–10; 11ff.). Whereas Jesus heals lepers and casts out demons in the Synoptics, neither lepers nor demons are mentioned in John; and the miracles that are reported are interpreted as signs that point to Jesus' identity as the Son of God. Clearly, John's account provides a different and extraordinarily valuable perspective on the significance of Jesus' life, his teachings, and his death and resurrection.

Authorship of the Gospel. From the latter part of the second century, church tradition has held that the Gospel, Letters, and Revelation were written by the apostle John, who lived to an advanced age in Ephesus. That tradition, however, is suspect on the grounds that the differences among the five writings make it highly unlikely that one person wrote all five, and the fact that the claim of apostolic authority helped the church rescue the Gospel of John from its use by the Gnostics. The author of the Book of Revelation claims the name "John" (1:1, 4, 9; 22:8), but he does not identify himself as an apostle.

Irenaeus, Bishop of Lyons in Gaul (ca. 130–200 CE), gives us the following account: "Afterwards, John the disciple of the Lord, who also had leaned upon His breast, did himself publish a gospel during his residence at Ephesus in Asia" (*AdvHaer* 3.1.1; cf. Eusebius *EccHist* 5.8.4). Is this John, "the disciple of the Lord," the apostle? In the course of weighing the evidence, Eusebius himself comments at one point: "This confirms the truth of the story of those who said that there were two of the same name in Asia, and that there are two tombs at Ephesus both still called John's" (*EccHist* 3.39.6). At least one of the Johns was probably the author of Revelation, but whether he was the apostle—and what his relationship to the Gospel was—is still debated.

The Gospel itself tells us that it is the testimony of the BELOVED DISCIPLE, but it does not identify the beloved disciple by name. At the end of the Gospel we read that he is the one who has borne witness and written these things; "we" know that his testimony is true; and "I" do not suppose the world could contain the books if everything were written down (21:24-25). From these verses we see the influence of the beloved disciple, a community that accepted his teaching, and an editor who speaks in the first person.

The Gospel scarcely mentions James and John, the sons of Zebedee (21:2), and we hear nothing of the three significant events in the synoptic Gospels at which only Peter, James, and John were present with Jesus: the raising of Jairus's daughter, the transfiguration, and the agony in Gethsemane. The beloved disciple appears only in John 13 and subsequent chapters, and he is known by the high priest in Jerusalem (18:15).

On the basis of the Gospel alone, one might conclude that the beloved disciple was Lazarus, who was from Bethany (so he could have been known by the high priest more easily than a Galilean fisherman), and who is introduced as "he whom you love" (11:3). Because he had been raised from the dead, the Johannine community could easily have thought that the Lord intended that he would not die again (21:23).

Life Setting of the Gospel. The Gospel of John probably originated in a community that had been forced out of the synagogue (9:22; 12:42; 16:2). At first a group of Christian Jews remained within the synagogue, but eventually differences over the observance of the law and the claim that Jesus was the Christ resulted in their being expelled from the synagogue. They rallied around the beloved disciple, who had been an eyewitness to the ministry of Jesus; and their identity as Christians was defined by their response to his teaching and preaching. In him they saw the Paraclete, the HOLY SPIRIT, at work in their midst.

The evangelist—either the beloved disciple himself or one of his followers—collected the traditions about Jesus, weaving together the signs material, the discourse material, and the passion narrative to form a first edition of the Gospel. The evangelist himself or another member of the Johannine community then enlarged the Gospel in a second or subsequent edition(s) by inserting material such as the prologue, John 15–17, and the references to the beloved disciple. At some point the sequence of chaps. 5 and 6 was reversed, and the cleansing of the Temple was moved to the beginning of the ministry of Jesus so that the raising of Lazarus could serve as the event that triggered Jesus' arrest. The Gospel once ended at the end of John 20, but an editor added John 21, resolving the question of the roles of Peter and the beloved disciple and giving the Gospel a second ending.

Date of the Gospel. In view of evidence for such an extended process of composition, we can speak only of a date at which the Gospel reached its final form. The Gospel rests on early tradition reaching back to Jesus, but it was composed over a period of decades. Most interpreters conclude that the Gospel was completed by 90–100 CE. The earliest fragment of a manuscript of the NT contains a few verses from John. Found in Egypt, it is dated between 125–150 CE.

Life Setting and Date of the Letters. The three letters were probably written by another member of the Johannine community shortly after or during the late stages of the composition of the Gospel. The three letters seem to come from a single hand, that of the Elder (2 John 1; 3 John 1), toward the end of the first century or in the opening years of the second century.

First John and 2 John reflect a division within the Johannine community and related churches. First John 2:19 refers to those who "went out from us." Later we read that "many false prophets have gone out into the world" (1 John 4:1). These false prophets may be recognized because they do not confess "Jesus Christ has come in the flesh" (4:2). The primary issue seems to have been the INCARNATION. The false prophets who had gone out from the community did not deny the divinity of the Christ; they denied that the Christ had come in flesh. The Gospel was written "that you may believe that Jesus is the Christ, the Son of God" (John 20:31), but now that confession is no longer sufficient.

The false prophets diminished the significance of Jesus' death and held a thoroughly realized eschatology which denied any future judgment of believers. Because they believed in Jesus as the Christ, they had been born from above. They had crossed from death into life (1 John 3:14), so they had already been raised to eternal life. The judgment is now, in how one responds to Jesus (John 3:19-21), so they were without sin (1 John 1:6, 8, 10; 2:1; 3:9). The Elder also complained that this group had failed to practice love for their fellow Christians (1 John 2:4-10). Perhaps they had refused to share their goods with needy believers (1 John 3:17).

In response, the Elder calls the community back to the affirmation of the incarnation, the command to love one another, the significance of the death of Jesus, and the reality of the resurrection and future judgment.

Literary Form and Primary Themes of the Gospel. The Gospel of John falls naturally into four basic sections. The first chapter constitutes a poetic and prose introduction to the Gospel. Chaps. 2–12 record Jesus' signs and public ministry. Chaps. 13–20 contain the footwashing; the farewell discourses; the prayer of consecration; the arrest, trials, and death of Jesus; the discovery of the empty tomb; and appearances to Mary Magdalene and the disciples.

The prologue introduces Jesus as the *logos*. This concept has deep roots in both Jewish and Greek thought. The opening words echo the first verse in Genesis. The wisdom tradition had identified WISDOM as the one through whom God had created the world (Prov 8:22), and all wisdom was believed to be contained in the law. Wisdom had been personified, so it was a short step to affirm that Jesus was the Wisdom of God that had become flesh. Greek readers would have understood that Jesus was the incarnation of the rational principle of the universe that the Stoics spoke of as the *logos*.

The prologue may have originally been a hymn to the *logos* into which prose sections have been added. John the Baptist is introduced as a witness to Jesus (John 1:6-8, 15), and Jesus' superiority even to Moses is defended (John 1:17). Jesus is the revealer who has revealed the Father. Those who accept him as the revealer have become the "children of God" (John 1:12).

Like the Synoptics, John begins with the baptism of Jesus. John the Baptist's only role is to bear witness to Jesus, and even the baptism of Jesus is reported in John's testimony. Followers of John could not argue, therefore, that John was first and that Jesus was his disciple, so John was the greater.

The changing of water to wine (2:1-11) introduces the ministry of Jesus as the beginning of the new life of the messianic age. Jesus is immediately brought into conflict with the Jewish authorities (2:12-25), so that all of the rest of the Gospel contains elements of a trial narrative.

Nicodemus, a teacher of the Jews, comes to Jesus at night, and Jesus instructs him about the necessity of birth from above (3:1-12). Here we meet a typical Johannine device. Jesus speaks in metaphorical, enigmatic sayings. His dialogue partners do not understand because they seize on the literal meaning of his words, and thereby the evangelist educates the reader to look for the metaphorical or symbolic significance of what Jesus does and what he says.

John 2–4 follows a progression parallel to the early chapters in Acts, as Jesus moves from the temple to dialogue with a Pharisee, to interaction with a fringe group in the Judean wilderness (John the Baptist), to Samaria, and finally to a royal official (who may have been a Gentile). The section begins and ends in Cana of Galilee and develops the theme of Jesus as the bringer of life from above.

The Samaritan woman learns—without any sign, though she has none of the advantages of Nicodemus—that Jesus is the giver of life and that this life is sustained by "living water," which must represent the Spirit of Jesus' revelation of the Father. The relationship between belief and life is then dramatically illustrated by the healing of the royal official's son (4:43-54).

Following the healing of the man at the Pool of Bethesda (5:1-18), the evangelist explains that "the Jews" sought to kill Jesus because he violated the Sabbath and blasphemously claimed that God was his Father. The rest of John 5 reads like a trial scene, as various witnesses are introduced in Jesus' defense.

The feeding of the multitude (John 6) becomes the basis for an extended discourse on Jesus as the bread of life. Jesus reenacts the Exodus experience, feeding the multitude in the wilderness and crossing the sea. But he himself is the bread from heaven, and one must feed on him to sustain the life he gives. This challenge was too much for most of Jesus' followers, however, so they abandon Jesus. Only the twelve are left—and one of them will betray Jesus.

John 7 and 8 present Jesus as the water of life and the light of the world against the background of the FEAST OF TABERNACLES, at which these two symbols were especially significant. These chapters show us an escalating hostility against Jesus. The revelation forces one either to accept Jesus or reject him, and so it sifts all humanity into two camps. The debate with the Jewish authorities reaches its most intense and hostile level in these chapters. Jesus debates with them his identity as the Son of God and their identity as the children of Abraham.

In John 9 Jesus, the light of the world, brings sight to a man born blind. The blind man is an "everyman" figure. We are all born blind and must be given sight. Sin consists not in being born blind but in refusing to see.

The next chapter develops the themes of Jesus as the good shepherd and his followers as those who hear his voice. At the feast of Hanukkah (DEDICATION), Jesus presents himself as the one in whom the glory of God may be seen. Consistently, therefore, Jesus fulfills and replaces the Jewish festivals. He is the reality to which they point.

As a result of the hostility against him, Jesus withdraws from Jerusalem (10:40-42), but he goes back to Judea—knowing that the authorities mean to kill him—in order to raise Lazarus, his friend, from the grave. Jesus, therefore, "lay[s] down his life for his friends" (see John 15:13-15; 3 John 15). The raising of Lazarus also emphasizes that those who believe in Jesus already have eternal life; it is a quality of life in relationship to God that begins now and continues forever.

Mary anoints Jesus' feet (12:1-8), ironically anointing Jesus as king and preparing for his burial. At the close of chap. 12 Jesus pronounces judgment on the world in a final soliloquy. Because "his own" did not receive him, Jesus turns to those who did believe in his name (1:11-12) in the chapters that follow.

John's account of Jesus' last evening with the disciples is peculiar in that it does not report the giving of the bread and the wine. At the last supper Jesus, knowing that his death was imminent, washed his disciples' feet. The footwashing illustrates the meaning of his death for them and provides a lesson on how they are to relate to one another (13:1-20).

In the farewell discourses Jesus teaches the disciples about the meaning of his death as his return to the Father, the coming of the Paraclete (Holy Spirit), and the persecution they will experience. The original discourse concludes at the end of chapter 14—"Rise, let us go hence" (14:31). The same themes are treated in the next two chapters. Then Jesus prays for himself, for the disciples, and for those who would believe as a result of their witness (17:1-26). He prays for the sanctity and unity of all who believe in his name.

In the garden there is no agony. Jesus is now supremely in control. The disciples do not abandon Jesus; he lays down his life for them. While Peter is busy denying Jesus, Jesus repeatedly stands by his witness to the truth. Jesus is tried before Annas and Caiaphas, though part of this trial is given earlier (11:47-53), and then he is taken to Pilate. The Roman trial is presented in seven scenes, with the Jews outside—because they will not defile themselves by entering a Gentile house—and Jesus inside. Pilate bounces back and forth between the two. Neither will give in, and in the end Pilate hands Jesus over to be crucified and wins from the Jews the confession that they have no king but Caesar. Actually, however, Pilate, not Jesus, has been on trial; and he stands condemned because he refuses to confess what he knows to be true, namely, that Jesus was "the king of the Jews."

The crucifixion is for John the exaltation or enthronement of Jesus as king. It is the first step in Jesus' return to the Father. Jesus' identity is heralded in Hebrew, Latin, and Greek: "The King of the Jews." The soldiers divided his garments; Jesus brings his mother and the beloved disciple into a new relationship with one another; he thirsts, and then when he is satisfied that his mission is complete, he lays down his life.

Jesus dies at the time the PASSOVER lambs were slaughtered; he was the true "lamb of God" (1:29, 36). No bones were broken, but his side was pierced (19:34-37). Joseph of Arimathea and Nicodemus then give him a kingly burial (19:38-42).

On the first day of the week Mary Magdalene finds the tomb open and tells the disciples. Peter and the beloved disciple race to the tomb, and the beloved disciple "saw and believed" (20:8).

Jesus then appears to Mary, to the disciples without Thomas, and a week later to the disciples with Thomas. The risen Lord commissions the disciples and breathes the Holy Spirit on them. Thomas's climactic confession, "My Lord and my God!" is followed by a final beatitude on all who will believe without seeing (20:28-29). A statement that the Gospel was written "that you may believe that Jesus is the Christ, the Son of God, and that believing you may have life in his name" (20:31) provides what may once have been the conclusion of the Gospel.

Chap. 21 reports an appearance of the risen Lord to a group of seven disciples while they were fishing. Following the Lord's instructions, the disciples enclose a great catch of fish. Symbolically, Peter draws the untorn net full of fish to the risen Lord, and together they eat a meal of bread and fish around a charcoal fire (cf. 18:18; 21:9). Peter is then challenged to tend the flock. Like the good shepherd, he will lay down his life for the sheep; but the beloved disciple will bear a true witness. An editor's note draws the Gospel to a close again (21:24-25).

Literary Form and Primary Themes of the Letters. First John was written by the Elder to the Johannine community about the threat posed by those who had departed from it. Because 1 John takes up relatively few themes and weaves them together in a spiral fashion, using transitional statements to link paragraphs together, it is difficult to outline. One common pattern highlights the three statements "God is light" (1:5), "He is just" (2:29), and "God is love" (4:8).

Three times in the first chapter we read "if we say" followed by a statement denying sin (1:6, 8, 10). Similarly, three times early in chap. 2 the Elder rejects the claims of those who say they know Jesus but do not follow his commands (2:4, 6, 9). Paradoxically, the Elder later claims that those who have been born from above cannot sin (3:6, 9). Both the Elder and his opponents share the ideal of perfectionism, but the Elder realizes that believers can and do sin. The opponents claim to be sinless already.

Repeatedly, the Elder exhorts the community to "believe in the name of his Son Jesus Christ and love one another, just as he commanded us" (3:23). Those who do not believe that Jesus has come in flesh (i.e., the incarnation; cf. 4:2) and have gone out from the community (2:19) show that they have violated both of these fundamental commands.

In response to the teachings of these false prophets, the Elder reaffirms the importance of the confession of sin, the death of Jesus, and the future coming of Jesus.

The second Letter seems to have been written to one of a network of churches linked to the Johannine community. In it the Elder warns "the elect lady" and her children of the danger of the false teachers who have gone out from the community. He instructs them not to receive anyone who does not "abide in the doctrine of Christ" (2 John 9-10).

The third Letter concerns difficult relations with another sister church. The challenge of this letter for modern readers is to understand the roles of the Elder, Gaius, Diotrephes, and Demetrius in the affairs that are referred to in passing. Diotrephes seems to have been a leader of the church who has ceased to receive the messengers sent by the Elder. His reasons for this action are open to speculation and debate. Gaius continues to receive messengers, such as Demetrius, who is commended to him.

See also BELOVED DISCIPLE; GNOSTICISM; GOSPELS, CRITICAL STUDY OF; HOLY SPIRIT; INCARNATION; JOHN THE APOSTLE; LOGOS/WORD; REVELATION, BOOK OF.

Bibliography. Surveys of Johannine Scholarship. W. F. Howard, *The Fourth Gospel in Recent Criticism and Interpretation*; R. Kysar, *The Fourth Evangelist and His Gospel: An Examination of Contemporary Scholarship*. Commentaries. C. K. Barrett, *The Gospel According to St. John*; G. R. Beasley-Murray, *John*; R. E. Brown, *The Gospel according to John*; R. Bultmann, *The Gospel of John*; C. H. Dodd, *The Interpretation of the Fourth Gospel*; E. Haenchen, *John*; B. Lindars, *The Gospel of John*; G. O'Day, "John," *NIB*; D. M. Smith, *John*; R. Schnackenburg, *The Gospel according to St. John*. Monographs and Articles. R. E. Brown, *The Community of the Beloved Disciple*; O. Cullmann, *The Johannine Circle*; R. A. Culpepper, *The Johannine School* and *Anatomy of the Fourth Gospel: A Study in Literary Design*; P. D. Duke, *Irony in the Fourth Gospel*; R. T. Fortna, *The Gospel of Signs: A Reconstruction of the Narrative Source Underlying the Fourth Gospel*; B. Lindars, *Behind the Fourth Gospel*; J. L. Martyn, *History and Theology in the Fourth Gospel*; J. Painter, *John: Witness and Theologian*; D. M. Smith, *Johannine Christianity: Essays on Its Setting, Sources, and Theology*; J. Staley, *The Print's First Kiss: A Rhetorical Investigation of the Implied Reader in the Fourth Gospel*. The Letters of John. C. C. Black, "The First, Second, and Third Letters of John," *NIB*; R. E. Brown, *The Epistles of John*; R. A. Culpepper, *1, 2, 3 John*; C. H. Dodd, *The Johannine Epistles*; I. H. Marshall, *The Epistles of John*; S. S. Smalley, *1, 2, 3 John*.

—R. ALAN CULPEPPER

Letter of Jude [MDB 479]

• AN OUTLINE •

I. Salutation (1-2)
II. Statement of Purpose (3-4)
III. Judgment against False Teachers (5-16)
IV. Warnings (17-19)
V. Exhortations (20-23)
VI. Doxology (24-25)

•**Jude, Letter of.** The short Letter of Jude is noted for its sharp rebuke of licentiousness, its predilection for triadic formulations, and its superb benediction.

Author. The writer identifies himself as JUDE the brother of JAMES and, by implication, the brother of Jesus (Matt 13:55; Mark 6:3). Many notable scholars hold that the letter is pseudonymous, that is, penned by an unknown author who gave his work greater credibility by attaching to it the name of one of Jesus' brothers. Christians can affirm either position with intellectual integrity and spiritual fidelity.

Date. Suggestions of date are found in v. 3, where the writer looks back to the apostolic age as past, and in v. 17, where the readers are reminded of words spoken to them by the apostles. Two issues influence the date assigned to the letter. The first question relates to authorship. If the Letter was written by Jude, then the date must be confined within the reasonable limits of his lifetime, i.e., before 65–80 CE. If the author was not Jude, then the writing may be placed any time within the lifespans of those who had heard the apostles, i.e., before 90–140 CE.

The second issue concerns the relationship of Jude to 2 Peter. Nearly all of the subject matter in Jude is common to 2 Peter and the organization of the material is similar. Three theories have been proposed to explain these parallels. The first holds that Jude borrowed from 2 Peter. Evidence for this contention rests on comparisons of Greek verb tenses. In 2 Peter warnings are voiced in future tenses. In Jude almost verbatim warnings are given in aorist (past) tenses (cf. 2 Pet 3:3 and Jude 18). Advocates of this view generally propose an early date for the Letter.

The second theory maintains that 2 Peter depends on Jude. Support for this opinion comes from literary and stylistic comparisons. Jude's letter is harsher in tone and appears to have been written with greater spontaneity than 2 Peter. Most significant is the impression that the author of 2 Peter intentionally excises Jude's references to apocryphal literature. Both Jude and 2 Peter allude to the pseudepigraphic *Assumption of Moses*, but 2 Peter removes the name of Moses (cf. Jude 9 and 2 Pet 2:11). In addition, while Jude directly cites the Book of *Enoch* (also in the pseudepigrapha; *1 Enoch* 1:9, cf. Jude 14-15), 2 Peter omits reference to Enoch entirely. Proponents of this theory usually assign a late date to the Letter.

A third theory suggesting a common source, either oral or written, has little support and few adherents.

Recipients and Purpose. The letter was written to the church at large. Its purpose was to warn Christians about libertines who were leading the church into error. Jude describes the heresy he is combating in very general terms. Some scholars have identified it as a form of Gnosticism or a proto-Gnostic Jewish dualism. The most that can be gleaned from internal evidence is that the heresy involved simple antinomianism and a practical infidelity.

See also ENOCH, FIRST; GNOSTICISM; JUDAS; JUDE; PETER, LETTERS OF.

Bibliography. A. E. Barnett, "The Epistle of Jude: Introduction," *IB*; D. Guthrie, *New Testament Introduction*; B. Reicke, *The Epistles of James, Peter, and John*; D. F. Watson, "The Letter of Jude," *NIB*.

—WILLIAM BRUCE PRESCOTT

Book of Revelation [MDB 759-61]

• AN OUTLINE •

Prologue (1:1-8)
I. Act One. The Seven Golden Lampstands (1:9–3:22)
sc1 The 1st golden lampstand—Ephesus (2:1-7)
sc2 The 2nd golden lampstand—Smyrna (2:8-11)
sc3 The 3rd golden lampstand—Pergamum (2:12-17)
sc4 The 4th golden lampstand—Thyatira (2:18-29)
sc5 The 5th golden lampstand—Sardis (3:1-6)
sc6 The 6th golden lampstand—Philadelphia (3:7-13)
sc7 The 7th golden lampstand—Laodicea (3:14-22)
II. Act Two. The Seven Golden Seals (4:1–8:4)
sc1 The 1st seal—the white horse (6:1-2)
sc2 The 2nd seal—the red horse (6:3-4)
sc3 The 3rd seal—the black horse (6:5-6)
sc4 The 4th seal—the pale green horse (6:7-8)
sc5 The 5th seal—the martyrs under the altar (6:9-11)
sc6 The 6th seal—the judgment of the world (6:12-17)
Interlude—the sealing of the 144,000 (7:1-17)
sc7 The 7th seal—the gold incense container (8:1-4)
III. Act Three. The Seven Trumpets (8:5–11:18)
sc1 The 1st trumpet—plague of hail, fire, blood (8:7)
sc2 The 2nd trumpet—plague on the sun (8:8-9)
sc3 The 3rd trumpet—plague on the fresh water (8:10-11)
sc4 The 4th trumpet—plague on the heavenly bodies (8:12)
Interlude—an eagle announces the three woes (8:13)
sc5 The 5th trumpet—plague of the locusts (9:1-2)
sc6 The 6th trumpet—plague of the 200 million horsemen (9:13-21)
Interlude—John eats a scroll; measuring of the temple; two witnesses appear (10:1–11:14)
sc7 The 7th trumpet—the worship of the twenty-four elders (11:15-18)
IV. Act Four. The Seven Tableaux (11:19–15:4)
sc1 The 1st tableau—woman, child, dragon (12:1-17)
sc2 The 2nd tableau—the beast from the sea (13:1-10)
sc3 The 3rd tableau—the beast from the land (13:11-18)
sc4 The 4th tableau—the lamb with the 144,000 (14:1-5)
Interlude—the announcements of the three angels (14:6-13)
sc5 The 5th tableau—the Son of man on a cloud (14:14-16)
sc6 The 6th tableau—the harvest of grapes (14:17-20)
sc7 The 7th tableau—the hymn of the lamb (15:1-4)
V. Act Five. The Seven Bowls of Wrath (15:5–16:21)
sc1 The 1st bowl—curse on the earth (16:2)
sc2 The 2nd bowl—curse on the sea (16:3)
sc3 The 3rd bowl—curse on the rivers (16:4-7)
sc4 The 4th bowl—curse on the sun (16:8-9)
sc5 The 5th bowl—curse on the beast's throne (16:10-11)
sc6 The 6th bowl—curse on the Euphrates (16:12-16)
sc7 The 7th bowl—curse on the air (16:17-21)
VI. Act Six. The Seven Judgments (17:1–20:3)
sc1 The 1st judgment—the woman and the scarlet beast (17:3b-18)
sc2 The 2nd judgment—the fall of Babylon (18:1-24)
sc3 The 3rd judgment—rejoicing in heaven and the marriage supper of the lamb (19:1-10)
sc4 The 4th judgment—the Word of God (19:11-16)
sc5 The 5th judgment—the angel on the sun (19:17-18)
sc6 The 6th judgment—battle of Armageddon (19:19-21)
sc7 The 7th judgment—Satan cast into abyss (20:1-3)

VII. Act Seven. The Seven Great Promises (20:4–22:5)
sc1 The 1st promise—the millennium (20:4b-10)
sc2 The 2nd promise—the judgment of evil (20:11-15)
sc3 The 3rd promise—the new heaven and earth (21:1-3)
sc4 The 4th promise—assurance for believers (21:4-8)
sc5 The 5th promise—the new Jerusalem (21:9-21)
sc6 The 6th promise—the city's illumination (21:21-27)
sc7 The 7th promise—the river of life (22:1-5)
Epilogue (22:6-21)

•**Revelation, Book of.** Scholars find it difficult to pinpoint the peculiar literary genre of the Book of Revelation. It is usually assumed that Revelation belongs to the literary genre of APOCALYPTIC LITERATURE. Many apocalyptic books were written by the Jews at the beginning of the Christian era. Apocalyptic seems to have emerged from the disappointments of the Jewish exiles in Babylon. The visions of the great prophets of a golden age for the Jews had not come about. The apocalyptic writers pushed those hopes and promises into a new age. Thus apocalyptic literature stressed a dualism consisting of this present evil age ruled by evil and the coming golden age ruled by Yahweh. There is no hope for the present evil age but a longing for its end with all kinds of catastrophic events. This genre also included such secondary elements as the pseudonymity of the author, visions, animal symbolism, numerology, and astral influences.

The word "apocalyptic," as used to define a genre of literature, comes from the Book of Revelation: the Gk. word *apocalypse*, "revelation," is the first word in the book. The adjective "apocalyptic" came to be applied to other works similar to the Book of Revelation. There are many dissimilarities between Revelation and the other apocalypses, however. Such essential themes as pseudonymity, secrecy, and historical periodization are not utilized by Revelation. Unlike other apocalypses, Revelation demonstrates a close affinity to the Hebrew prophetic literature and operates extensively from it. At the same time, Revelation has also been influenced by Greek tragic drama. The genre of Revelation thus seems to be a syncretistic one—setting forth a prophetic message in the form of Greek tragic drama.

The time sequence of Revelation shows the influence of both the Hebrew and Greek world. One cannot read Revelation straight through like other NT books. The visions come in cycles that often must be viewed side by side rather than in a straight-line progression. For example, the seven trumpets must be read along with the seven bowls of wrath. The closest analogy perhaps would be stereo speakers with the sounds of the seven trumpets coming out one speaker and the noise of the seven bowls from the other. One could also liken Revelation to a three-ring circus in which one must watch the action in all three rings at once.

The cyclical time sequence of the Greek world is wed to the straight-line progression of the Hebrew world. Revelation portrays a spiral effect—endless cycles of repetition but moving toward an end goal of history. The outer form of Greek tragic drama was used by the writer to make more dramatic the prophetic message of the book. In recent structuralist studies of Revelation, the affinity of the structure of Revelation to that of Greek tragic drama has been demonstrated. According to the compositional rules of the tragedy, the climax falls near the center of the action and the denouement comes near the end in an *a b c d c' b' a'* pattern. With that pattern there is a prophetic movement from promise to fulfillment within the structure of a cosmic, timeless drama.

Revelation as Drama. There are many similarities between Revelation and the extant Greek tragedies. A Greek theater was considered sacred ground for all who participated; actors, chorus, and patrons were considered ministers of religion. The technical Greek word for producing a play was "to teach" and the director was called "the teacher" while the plays were "the teaching." Actors were called priests and the throne of God stood on the lower stage. Thus, the readers of Revelation would have found much about Greek drama already a part of their religious heritage and a good background for understanding their new religion.

The role of the chorus in Greek tragic drama is very close to the role of the twenty-four elders in Revelation. At the beginning of a Greek drama, a chorus of twelve or twenty-four entered the stage and stood around the throne of Dionysius. The earliest tragedies had only choruses and no actors. The chorus could don masks and represent animals, birds, or beasts. At a later time (after 400 BCE) the dramas added one actor. The chorus however continued to be the medium for interpreting the drama. In Revelation the twenty-four elders sing and interpret the drama. They lead John around heaven and introduce many of the visions. Nine major hymns appear in Revelation in a balanced strophe-antistrophe pattern characteristic of the Greek dramas. The great composer Handel was so inspired by the hymns of Revelation that he made them a vital part of his work *The Messiah*.

At EPHESUS, a great amphitheater stood holding 24,000 seats. It had been built in the third century BCE and was the largest of the Greek theaters. The stage building, *skene*, was most unique in that it contained seven windows (*thuromata*) for scenery consisting of painted panels. All other Greek stages had three or five such openings. Thus for nearly 300 years before the writing of Revelation, the number seven had acquired great significance for the inhabitants of Ephesus. Everyone who has written on Revelation has remarked on its unique use of sevens—seven churches, seven trumpets, seven bowls, seven blessings, and so on. Revelation readily can be divided into seven acts with seven scenes.

The first blessing in Revelation is "Blessed is he who reads aloud the words of the prophecy" (1:3). The best way to begin a study of Revelation is to read it aloud with a recording of Handel's *Messiah* in the background. The factor that has made Revelation a lost book is that it has been left on the cold printed page. Revelation was meant to be seen and heard. A vision cannot be put into prose. The orality of Revelation is an essential element for interpretation. The enacted story possesses the power to transport the hearer into a different world. One enters into another universe and undergoes a new reality. The writer of Revelation had no hopes that his dramatic message would ever be enacted on the stage of Ephesus, but he used the dramatic medium of Greek drama and the stage of Ephesus to ensure the book would be heard and seen. A lector would read it aloud to a congregation made up mostly of slaves who could not read. As they heard it, they could envision it against the backdrop of the famous stage at Ephesus where they had witnessed so many Greek tragic dramas.

Apocalyptic Symbolism. The visions of Revelation came alive through the vivid use of colors, animals, and numerology. One cannot read Revelation as one would read a Gospel or a Pauline letter. The imagination must be used. Different systems of symbols may be found in Revelation.

The system of *numbers*: seven—divine number (seven horns, 4:6); six—imperfect, the enemy, Caesar (13:18); five—major penalties—the locusts torture people for five months (9:5); four—world (7:1); two—witnessing (11:3); one—unity (13:3); ten—complete (9:16); twelve—wholeness (21:14); one-third—incomplete (8:7).

The system of *colors*: pale green—death (6:8); emerald green—life (4:3); white—purity or conquering (1:14); red—war (6:4); black—famine (6:5); gold—worth or value (1:13); bronze—strength (1:15); scarlet—immorality (17:3).

The system of symbolism involving *animals* in the Book of Revelation is similar to the use of animals in political cartoons to depict current political figures. In Revelation, animals and monster beasts represent people or qualities: lamb with seven horns and eyes—Jesus Christ (4:6); frog—the most evil creature (16:13); monster beasts—Caesar, Satan, etc. (13:1); lion—wild animals (4:7); ox—domesticated animals (4:7); eagle—bearer of bad news (8:13).

In Revelation *places* take on symbolical meaning also: sea—the source of all evil in Revelation; desert—a place of strife and temptation; mountaintop—a place of revelation; Euphrates River—a dividing line or boundary point; Babylon—a code word for Rome or the enemy.

If the symbolic language in Revelation is taken literally, much of the message is lost. The book then becomes one of fear, gloom, and doom. In reality, the symbols are used by the writer to give a hidden message of hope to Christians being persecuted.

Authorship. The traditional view of John the disciple has many points in its favor. The church fathers tell us John was the only disciple to die a natural death at the age of 100 years. Eusebius reported that under Domitian, "the apostle John is banished to Patmos and sees his Apocalypse, as Irenaeus says" (*EccHist* 7.25). Dionysius, in the third century CE, however, pointed out that there were two church leaders in Ephesus by the name of John and concluded that Revelation was written by an Elder John, not the Disciple John. Perhaps one can conclude with certainty only that the book was written by a Jewish-Christian prophet named John.

Dating. The dating of Revelation is also much debated. Most modern scholars date the book during the reign of Domitian, 81–96 CE. The early church writers took that view. Eusebius, quoting Irenaeus, placed the writing in the fourteenth year of Domitian's reign. The persecution of Domitian's reign would fit well into the context of Revelation. Few details of that persecution exist in written form. Some scholars today believe this persecution was more of a perceived crisis than a real one. The Christians saw themselves as the outcasts, living in poverty over against the power of the ROMAN EMPIRE. Revelation serves as a catharsis to work through such feelings of rage and hostility.

Other scholars have suggested Nero's time (54–68 CE) or the period of Vespasian (69–79 CE). There is no real support for these positions in the early church fathers. Those who take the position base it on internal evidence such as the existence of the Herodian Temple in 11:1 and the church's flight to Pella mentioned in 12:1-6. Some have argued that the riddle of 17:10 (the seven emperors) fits Vespasian better than Domitian. However, the date of 95 CE during Domitian's reign continues to enjoy wide support.

Methods of Interpretation. There are many different ways of interpreting Revelation, from a futuristic document interpreting coming world events in detail to a mere history of the past. In the contemporary historical view, Revelation is interpreted primarily against the Roman Empire under Domitian in 95 CE. Revelation was written to bring hope to persecuted Christians of that period. The continuous-historical view sees Revelation as containing an overview history of the whole Christian church from the first century to the end of the age: the beast and the false prophet are the pope and the papacy. The futurist method views Revelation as dealing mainly with end-time events. Such interpreters look upon the last book of the Bible as largely a volume of unfulfilled prophecy. A very literal approach is taken to the book and very little symbolism is noted. One popular arm of this school is Dispensationalism founded by J. N. Darby of the Plymouth Brethren Church.

The dramatic-literary approach views Revelation as a literary whole with plot, characters, and themes. Greek tragic drama is viewed as the literary medium of the author. Emphasis is placed upon the visual elements of the book. This is the approach favored in this article.

In addition to various methods of interpretation, the student of Revelation also encounters a variety of views concerning the MILLENNIUM or the thousand-year reign of Christ (Rev 20:4-6). Although there are only three verses concerning the millennium in Revelation, many Bible students place exaggerated importance on the subject. The millennium becomes "the tail that wags the dog." Three basic schools are in vogue. The *premillennial* school teaches that Christ will come to earth before the thousand years and reign on earth. The *postmillennial* school asserts that Christ will reign in heaven during the thousand years and return to earth at the end of that period. The *amillennial* school views the millennium symbolically: Christ began his reign at his victory over Satan at the cross; he will reign for a complete period of time.

Canonicity. Revelation very early became authoritative in the church. Justin Martyr (150 CE) used the book and mentioned the author by name. It is mentioned in the MURATORIAN CANON. Papias (early second century) made use of it as authoritative and Melito of Sardis (160–190) wrote a commentary on it. Revelation also was included in the Latin Vulgate (391–404). The only place it encountered difficulty was in Syria.

See also APOCALYPTIC LITERATURE; DANIEL, BOOK OF; DUALISM; EPHESUS; ESCHATOLOGY IN THE NT; HYMN; JOHN THE APOSTLE; MILLENNIUM; NUMBERS/NUMEROLOGY; ROMAN EMPIRE; SYMBOL.

Bibliography. J. L. Blevins, *Revelation as Drama*; G. Caird, *The Revelation of St. John the Divine*; A. Collins, *Crisis and Catharsis*; C. Hemer, *The Letters to the Seven Churches*; J. P. Newport, *The Lion and the Lamb*; C. C. Rowland, "The Book of Revelation," *NIB*; R. M. Royalty, *The Streets of Heaven. The Ideology of Wealth in the Apocalypse of John.*

—JAMES L. BLEVINS

Hebrews

Marie E. Isaacs [MCB 1267-1281]

Introduction

The King James Version confidently designates this work as "The Epistle of Paul to the Hebrews." Modern scholarship, however, has shown this to be improbable on all counts. It is more a sermon than a letter, almost certainly not by the apostle Paul, and written to a Christian congregation rather than to the Jewish nation. About little else can we be certain, however. We know virtually nothing about the circumstances that led to Hebrews's composition, original destination, date, or authorship. What evidence we have is largely to be inferred from Hebrews itself—and that is far from unambiguous.

A Sermon

Only in its final greetings (13:22-25) does Hebrews resemble a first-century letter. Otherwise, from its opening prologue (1:1-4) to its closing warnings (12:29), it exhibits all the features of an expository sermon. (Some scholars think the sermon extends as far as 13:21.) Thus the work is highly rhetorical throughout, especially in those passages where the preacher interrupts his theological exposition and addresses the audience directly (see 2:1-4; 3:7-4:13; 5:11-6:20; 10:19-39; 12:1-29).

Although Ps 110 seems to be the homily's main text, it is by no means its only one. Thus the author of Hebrews uses a number of OT passages (mostly drawn from the Pentateuch and the Psalms) in his attempt to draw out the implications of Christ's death and ascension for the particular situation of the group to whom he is writing. Like all Christian preaching, Hebrews tries to grapple with contemporary experience on the one hand, and inherited religious tradition on the other, in order to make sense of them both.

The Situation Addressed

From the work itself we can infer a number of things about the congregation. It was a group whose knowledge of the Christian message had not come firsthand from the earthly JESUS but via the preaching and teaching of the earliest disciples (2:1-3). Although the preacher accuses them of spiritual immaturity (5:12-14), they were not recent converts. In fact theirs was an admirable record of fidelity even in the face of persecution and suffering, which they had encountered in the past (10:32-34; cf. 12:4). Now, however, that enthusiasm was on the wane.

Exactly what has caused this crisis of confidence we cannot say. Various suggestions have been made: the delayed PAROUSIA, the outbreak of the Jewish war against Rome in 66 CE, the Neronian persecution in 64 CE, the fall of the Jerusalem Temple in 70 CE, and so forth. What is clear is that they were a congregation in danger of drifting (2:2; 3:12; 4:11), tempted to go backward rather than forward. Many commentators have interpreted this to mean that they were tempted to revert to their original ancestral faith, JUDAISM. There is nothing in Hebrews that would suggest that the preacher is inveighing against Judaism, however. Rather, he finds examples of both fidelity (11:1-40) and infidelity (3:7-19) among the people of God in the past, and uses these by way of warning and encouragement to God's people in the present.

It is impossible to be sure as to the location of this particular group. JERUSALEM, ALEXANDRIA, CORINTH, SYRIA, and Asia Minor have all had their proponents. The current favorite is ROME, although this suggestion too is not without its difficulties. Both religiously and culturally its members seem to be Christian converts from the Greek-speaking Judaism of the dispersion. That of itself does not tell us where they were currently located, however.

As to Hebrews's date, it could have been written any time between the 60s and the 80s CE. It is first attested by Clement of Rome at the end of the first century. He cites parts of it, but not by name or title.

Central Theme

The main aim of this sermon is clearly pastoral. The author calls it *a word of exhortation* (13:22). The fundamental message to the group addressed could be summed up as:

> Don't give up! See in Jesus, seated at the right hand of God in heaven, the assurance that God's sovereignty will ultimately reign on earth. In the meantime, understand that the Christian's pilgrimage to final salvation inevitably involves suffering, just as surely as Jesus' own route to God was via the cross.

In conveying this message Hebrews expounds biblical texts that enable the author to interpret salvation as the process whereby access to God is achieved. To this end he focuses upon divinely appointed places of rendezvous between God and the people. In Jewish tradition these were, par excellence, the promised LAND of CANAAN (cf. 3:1–4:13; 11:1–12:3), and the cult place, where God was approached via sacrifice (cf. 4:14–10:8). In neither territory, Hebrews argues, has but a partial encounter with God occurred, since the barrier of sin, which hindered true access to God, remained. Hence, the only one who truly entered into the presence of God, that is, heaven, was Jesus. He was the *pioneer* who entered into the promised land (2:10; 12:2), the Melchizedekian high priest who has entered the superior Holy of

Holies (8:1–10:18), namely, heaven itself. And that by virtue of his death, which, by analogy, was the expiatory sacrifice that enabled the HIGH PRIEST to gain access to God. Other NT authors describe the work of Christ in sacrificial terms. Hebrews, however, is unique in comparing it to the sin offering of the Day of Atonement. Moreover, nowhere else in the NT do we find Jesus' death and entry into heaven depicted in priestly terms.

Author

From the second century, Christian tradition attributed Hebrews to Paul. Not until the fourth century was the Western church convinced, however. Even in the East there were those who were aware that there were problems, on stylistic grounds alone, of ascribing it to the APOSTLE. Hence, Clement of Alexandria suggested that Hebrews was originally written by Paul in Aramaic and then translated into Greek by Luke. Most NT characters have been suggested as the author of Hebrews, including BARNABAS, APOLLOS, and even a woman—Priscilla. Perhaps we should leave the last word on the identity of the author of Hebrews to Origen. "As to who actually wrote the epistle God alone knows the truth of the matter" (Eusebius, *EccHist* 6.12-14).

Nonetheless, from Hebrews itself we can deduce quite a lot about its author. There is nothing to suggest that the work was originally written in Aramaic or Hebrew. Its author (as well as presumably his audience) was, therefore Greek rather than semitic-speaking. Hence he uses the LXX version(s) of the OT. Indeed, in places (eg. 1:6,7) his argument would have made no sense had he been using the Hebrew of the MT. He also seems to be at home not only with the scriptures themselves, but also with accepted Jewish exegetical methods and traditions current in the first century.

Scholars are divided as to how far Hebrews has been influenced by current Hellenistic philosophy. Most agree that at the very least he draws upon the same wealth of literary vocabulary, and moved in the same circles of educated thought, as diaspora Jews such as PHILO of Alexandria, and the authors of the *Wisdom of Solomon* and the *Epistle of Aristeas*. Undoubtedly, he was trained in the rhetorical skills that loomed so large in the higher education of the Greco-Roman world of his day.

Equally evident is that the author stood firmly within first-century Christian tradition. Thus his homily—for all its unique features—is built upon two major tenets of Christian faith, which he assumes that his readers share: (1) that Jesus is now exalted in heaven; and (2) that his death was the means whereby that exaltation was achieved. He not only reaffirms these beliefs; he reinterprets and extends them to meet the needs of the situation of his audience. In so doing he has created a new and powerful theology of access to God, which has spoken to generations ever since.

For Further Study

In the *Mercer Dictionary of the Bible*: ATONEMENT, DAY OF; EPISTLE/LETTER; EXPIATION IN THE NT; HEBREWS, LETTER TO THE; HELLENISTIC WORLD; HIGH PRIEST; JUDAISM; MELCHIZEDEK; RESURRECTION IN THE NT.

In other sources: H. W. Attridge, *The Epistle to the Hebrews*, Herm; F. F. Bruce, *The Epistle to the Hebrews*, NICNT; F. B. Craddock, "The Letter to the Hebrews," *NIB*; J. Héring, *The Epistle to the Hebrews*; F. L. Horton, *The Melchizedek Tradition: A Critical Examination of the Sources to the Fifth Century AD and the Epistle to the Hebrews*; G. Hughes, *Hebrews and Hermeneutics: The Epistle to the Hebrews as an Example of Biblical Interpretation;* P. E. Hughes, *A Commentary on the Epistle to the Hebrews*; M. E. Isaacs, *Sacred Space: An Approach to the Theology of the Epistle to the Hebrews;* W. G. Johnsson, "The Pilgrimage Motif in the Book of Hebrews," *JBL* 97 (1971): 239-51; E. Käsemann, *The Wandering People of God*; H. Koester, "'Outside the Camp': Hebrews 13.9-14," *HTR* 33 (1962): 299-315; W. L. Lane, *Hebrews*, WBC; B. Lindars, *The Theology of the Letter to the Hebrews*; H. Montefiore, *The Epistle to the Hebrews*, BNTC; D. Peterson, *Hebrews and Perfection: An Examination of the Concept of Perfection in the Epistle to the Hebrews*; R. Williamson, "The Eucharist and the Epistle to the Hebrews," *NTS* 21 (1975): 300-12; R. McL. Wilson, *Hebrews*, NCC.

Commentary

An Outline

I. Prologue: The Exaltation of Jesus, the Son of God, 1:1-4
II. He Excels the Very Angels, 1:5–2:18
  A. Scriptural Proof of the Son's Incomparable Status, 1:5-14
  B. A Warning Aside: Heed the Christian Message, 2:1-4
  C. The Sovereignty and Solidarity of the Son of Man, 2:5-18
III. Fidelity and Infidelity, 3:1–4:13
  A. Jesus the Faithful Son Contrasted with Moses the Faithful Servant, 3:1-6
  B. A Warning Example: The Faithlessness of the Wilderness Generation, 3:7-19
  C. Beware Lest You Fail to Enter God's Promised Rest, 4:1-11
  D. A Coda : The Penetrative Power of God's Word, 4:12-13
IV. Jesus the High Priest, 4:14–10:18
  A. Merciful and Compassionate, 4:14–5:10
  B. An Exhortatory Aside: Grow Up! There Can Be No Going Back, 5:11–6:20
  C. According to the Order of Melchizedek, 7:1-28
  D. The Sacrificial Work of Christ, 8:1–10:18
V. An Exhortation to Persevere in the Faith, 10:19–12:29
  A. Perseverance: Some Encouragements and Warnings, 10:19:39
  B. The Faithful of the Past, 11:1-40
  C. The Faithful Endurance Required Now, 12:1-29
VI. Epistolary Exhortation and Conclusion, 13:1-25
  A. Christian Holiness and Its Obligations, 13:1-6
  B. The Implications of Jesus' Sacrifice, 13:7-19
  C. A Closing Benediction, 13:20-21
  D. A Farewell Note, 13:22-25

Prologue: The Exaltation of Jesus, the Son of God, 1:1-4

Hebrews opens with a prologue that extols the Son as God's supreme agent of REVELATION, creation, and salvation. These claims are put forward as commonly accepted Christian tradition. The tone, therefore, is confessional rather than argumentative.

1:1-2b. The Son, as God's definitive spokesman, supersedes all his predecessors. The genuine inspiration of the OT and its prophetic voice is not in dispute. Reference to the plurality and diversity of revelation in the past (*in many and various ways*), therefore, should not be understood pejoratively (*contra* NEB in fragmentary and piecemeal fashion). Nonetheless, it gives way to the single, definitive word articulated in Jesus.

Son is the name he has inherited (unlike Phil 2:11 where it is "Lord"). It signals his superior status to *prophets* (v. 1) and *angels* (v. 4) alike. This theme is developed in 1:5–2:18 concerning angels, and in 3:1-6 it is taken up with regard to MOSES (counted among Israel's prophets in Jewish tradition).

1:2c-3b. The Son as agent in creation. Here terms and functions, previously ascribed in Judaism to divine wisdom (Job 28:23-28; Prov 8; Sir 24:3-24; Wis 7:1–8:1), are applied to the Son. Thus he is God's agent in bringing *the worlds* (lit. "the ages") into being, and in the ongoing work of sustaining the universe. We find the selfsame functions ascribed by PHILO (the Alexandrian Jewish rabbi and older contemporary of the apostle Paul) to God's word (λόγος). In most respects Philo's *logos* is but wisdom (σοφία) in another guise.

Like wisdom in Jewish writings (cf. Wis 7:25f.), so the Son in Hebrews is described as God's *reflection*. Like *the word* in Philo (cf. On *Planting* 18) he is the *exact imprint*. The language of the divine wisdom/word is applied to the Son somewhat obliquely, however. Thus, unlike Paul in 1 Cor 1:24, 30, Hebrews does not directly describe Jesus as God's wisdom. Nor, unlike the prologue of John's Gospel, is he identified with the preexistent *logos* who became flesh.

The closest parallel in the NT to these verses is Col 1:15-20. It is possible that both Colossians and Hebrews are drawing upon an early Christian HYMN or confession. If so, Hebrews does not use it to stress the Son's preexistence so much as to assert his preeminence. Above all, the prologue is concerned to affirm the sovereignty of Christ in his postexistence.

1:3c-4. The Son as agent of salvation. Unique to Hebrews is the analogy that it draws between the death and ascension of Jesus and the actions of the Levitical high priest on the Day of Atonement (see Lev 16 and ATONEMENT, DAY OF). Thus the CROSS is likened to the sacrificial offering that was the essential prerequisite for entry into the shrine's inner sanctum, and heaven becomes that inner sanctum, the Holy of Holies in which Jesus is now situated.

This theme, developed at length in 4:14–10:18, is announced at the very outset: *When he had made purification for sins, he sat down at the right hand of the Majesty on high* (v. 3). The motif of session (sitting at the right hand of God) alludes to Ps 110:1, one of the most widely cited texts in the NT. It is used throughout this homily (1:13; 8:1; 10:12-13; 12:2) to affirm that Jesus is now in heaven, seated at God's right hand. A psalm that originally celebrated the enthronement of a Davidic king as God's son and viceroy is seen to find its fulfilment in the exalted Christ.

He Excels the Very Angels, 1:5–2:18

A discussion of Jesus' status vis-à-vis the angels arises out of the session theme of the prologue. From his heavenly location should not be inferred that Jesus is one of the angels, however. As Son he has a different status from the other occupants of heaven.

Scriptural Proof of the Son's Incomparable Status, 1:5-14

Seven OT texts are cited as confirmation. They are used to advance a carefully constructed argument:

1:5. Jesus is not an angel. He is Davidic Messiah, SON OF GOD. Ps 2:7 and 2 Sam 7:17 (texts that addressed the Davidic king as Son of God) are cited as twin testimonies to this.

1:6. Jesus receives homage. Jesus is the one who receives rather than pays homage, since he is God's *firstborn* (a term used of the Davidic king in LXX Ps 88 (MT 89):17).This is confirmed by Deut 32:43 (to be found only in the LXX).

1:7. Angels are changeable. Using the LXX Ps 103:4, Hebrews can claim that scripture shows that angels are so unstable that God can reduce them to the elemental forces of wind and fire, if he so chooses. (The MT Ps 104:4 says something quite different, i.e., that God can use winds and flames as his messengers.)

1:8-12. The Son, on the other hand, exercises eternal sovereignty. Ps 45:6-7 (LXX Ps 44:6-7), originally addressed as an encomium to the Davidic king, is here applied to Jesus. In both its Hebrew and Greek versions there are ambiguities in this psalm. Hence v. 6 (=Heb 1:8) can either be translated as, "Thy throne O God is forever," or "God is your throne forever," or "Your throne is a throne of God forever." Whether or not the original psalmist addressed Israel's king as "God" (cf. Exod 7:1; Ps 82:6), or Hebrews so designates Jesus, is far from certain. What is clear is that the emphasis here is upon the eternal sovereignty exercised by the Lord's anointed on God's behalf (1:9; cf. Isa 61:1). With the citation (vv. 10-12) of Ps 101:26-28 (MT 102:25-27), the permanence and stability of this rule is contrasted with the impermanence and instability of the created order.

1:13-14. Jesus is now enthroned in heaven. The section concludes with the text first cited in the prologue, Ps 110:1. Christ's heavenly session demonstrates his sovereignty over all things, angels included.

A Warning Aside: Heed the Christian Message, 2:1-4

This is the first of a number of instances where the author interrupts his exposition to address his audience directly. Here it is to issue a warning against the dangers of drifting away from the Christian faith.

The rhetorical question in v. 3 introduces an *a fortiori* argument. If the revelation mediated by angels is to be heeded, *how much more* so should the message of salvation, which was originally proclaimed by the Lord and validated by his original disciples? *The message declared through angels* (v. 2) probably reflects the tradition that had grown up in Judaism that angels were present when Moses was given the Law on Mount Sinai (cf. also Acts 7:28, 35; Gal 3:19). *Signs, wonders and various miracles,* together with the gifts of the *Holy Spirit,* act as corroborative testimony. Here the empowering work of the Spirit is to the fore (cf. also 6:4; 10:29). Elsewhere (3:7; 9:8; 10:15) the emphasis is on the HOLY SPIRIT as the source of scripture's inspiration.

The Sovereignty and Solidarity of the Son of Man, 2:5-18

2:5-9. The sovereignty of the son of man. Psalm 8:4-6 (MT vv. 5-7) is cited to show that God originally entrusted the exercise of sovereignty over the created order, not to angels, but to Man (=Adam; cf. Gen 1:26-30). The NRSV *human beings, mortals* (together with the plural verbs and pronouns) brings out well the corporate emphasis. This translation, however, obscures the singular *Man, Son of Man* of the original text. Whereas the psalmist was indeed using this language in a corporate rather than a titular sense, it was precisely the singular of the original that enabled Hebrews to see in the exaltation of one man, Jesus, the fulfilment of God's purposes for all humanity.

The MT of the psalm marvels that we should be made "a little lower than God" (*Elohim*). Following the LXX, however, Hebrews has *for a little while lower than the angels. Little while* is given a dual interpretation: (1) Applied to the earthly Jesus it refers to the interlude between his death and his heavenly exaltation. (2) Applied to the present it refers to the equally brief interlude between Jesus' heavenly enthronement and his exercise of sovereignty on earth. As yet the latter awaits its fulfilment until his return (see 9:28). In the meantime Jesus is the pioneer; the Son who leads *many sons* (NRSV *many children*) to their destiny of sovereignty (v. 1).

2:10-18. Jesus' solidarity with his followers. Three additional OT texts are used (vv. 12-13) to confirm this. As fellow members of the assembly (ἐκλλησία) of God he addresses them as his siblings (Ps 22:22), united with him in their praise of and trust in God (Isa 8:17), and counted as his (God's) children (Isa 8:18).

The chapter concludes with a statement of the genuine humanity of Christ. Unlike angels, he was subject to human limitations—including temptation (*testing*), suffering, and death. Therefore his help is directed, not towards angels in whose heavenly domain he now resides, but to human beings whose frailty he shared throughout the span of his earthly life. It is precisely Jesus' common humanity that qualifies him to act as *a merciful and faithful high priest* on our behalf.

Fidelity and Infidelity, 3:1–4:14

Picking up the word *faithful* from 2:17, the homily now moves to the topic of fidelity and infidelity. This section is predominantly an exhortation to remain steadfast and not to lose hope.

Jesus the Faithful Son Contrasted with Moses the Faithful Servant, 3:1-6

Both envoys (cf. v. 1, *apostle*) of God are comparable in their fidelity. Both were "faithful in my (i.e., God's) house." This is an allusion to Num 12:7 (LXX). Unlike the MT of this verse ("He is entrusted with all my house"), which points up Moses' status as Israel's supreme leader, the LXX stresses his constancy. He alone of all the wilderness generation continued to have faith in God's purposes for his people (=his *house*, household). On the other hand, Moses' status is lower than that of Jesus, and may be likened to that of a servant rather than the son of the house.

A Warning Example: The Faithlessness of the Wilderness Generation, 3:7-19

3:7-11. Israel's loss of faith in the past. In contrast to Moses' fidelity is the loss of faith on the part of those he sought to lead. Verses 7-11 cites Ps 94 (MT 95):7-11, which recalls Israel's resolve, in the face of the hardships of the wilderness, to turn her back on the promise of a homeland, and to return to a life of bondage in Egypt (cf. Num 14:1-35). The psalm also contains an allusion to an incident (Exod 17:1-7; Num 20:2-13) in which the people's complaint at their lack of water gave rise to the place names *Meribah* (=strife or contention) and *Massah* (=proof or test). The LXX translates rather than transliterates these Hebrew names. Hence they become: *as in the rebellion*, and: *as on the day of testing* (v. 8). The psalmist saw Israel's demand for water as putting God to the test—itself a demonstration of her loss of faith. By altering the punctuation and adding *therefore* (v. 10) Hebrews makes *forty years* refer, not to the duration of God's anger, but to the length of time Israel had been privileged to experience God's works (v. 17 reverts to the more usual reading). The effect of this is to heighten the enormity of the people's ingratitude.

3:12-4:11. A commentary on Psalm 95. Here the preacher applies the psalm to the present situation of his Christian audience. He draws an analogy between the experience of the wilderness generation and that of the group he is now addressing. Like their predecessors, they too are living through testing times. Unlike them, however, they should stand firm and not lose hope in the promises of God's future. They should take warning from the fate that befell the faithless of the past, whose punishment was that they were forbidden to enter the promised land of Canaan.

Like the psalmist, the author of Hebrews confines himself at this point to the threat of disinheritance. *They will not enter into my rest.* He does not mention that, in the case of CALEB, JOSHUA, and those Israelites under twenty years of age, God relented, in response to Moses' pleading (see Num 14:29ff.). To have done so would have detracted from the main purpose of this particular sermon. The preacher wants to use the words of the psalm as an exemplary warning to his own generation of the dangerous consequences of abandoning their faith.

Beware Lest You Fail to Enter God's Promised Rest, 4:1-11

By *enter* and *rest* Hebrews is not simply referring to Israel's possession of the land of CANAAN. He is well aware that that was achieved under Joshua (cf. 4:8). In

Jewish tradition however, the land had come to represent more than a place of rest from Israel's wanderings (cf. Deut 3:20; Josh 1:3), or from the assaults of her enemies (cf. Deut 25:19; Josh 11:23). The land, more specifically Jerusalem (cf. Ps 132:14) and its Temple (cf. Deut 12:18), came to be thought of as God's abode or resting place. Thus *rest*, understood as the presence of God (cf. Exod 3:14; LXX Deut 33:14), could be a metaphor for salvation. Clearly that is how it is understood by the author of Hebrews.

Linking the psalm's noun *rest* with the verb "to rest" found in (LXX) Gen 2:2 enables Hebrews to move from the idea of salvation as the possession of the LAND to its depiction as the attainment of heaven itself. Salvation is thus to be in the presence of God in heaven, there to share that "rest" that he himself enjoyed on the seventh day, having created the universe. *Sabbath rest* (σαββατισμός) is the word coined by Hebrews (4:9) to characterize salvation as heavenly rather than earthly in its locus. Understood thus, the promised "rest" was not obtained when JOSHUA (v. 8) entered Canaan. (Chapter 11 reverts to this theme. The land sought in faith by Israel's patriarchs was not the earthly Canaan but a heavenly inheritance.)

What is more, neither the promise nor threat of this particular word of God was intended for the wilderness generation alone. Hence the psalmist (assumed by Hebrews to be DAVID) could and did address both to the *today* of his own time. Had the promise been fulfilled in Joshua's day there would have been no need for the psalmist of a later generation to have repeated it. For Hebrews this demonstrates that the promise is still outstanding (vv. 7-10). Thus he uses the psalm to challenge his contemporary audience to seize the *today* of God's word, lest they fail to become heirs of salvation. Like the wilderness generation, they stand on the brink of entry. They are *in the process of entering* God's rest. The NRSV *enter* (v. 3) obscures the continuous force of the Greek at this point. The recurrent warnings in this section (3:12-14; 4:1,11) remind the readers that, even for them, salvation *remains* (3:9) to be attained in the future.

A Coda: The Penetrative Power of God's Word, 4:12-13.

The homiletic exposition of Ps 95 concludes with a coda in praise of the word (λόγος) of God. Clearly this is not a reference to Jesus, but to God, speaking through the scriptures that have just been cited. The Bible is seen as no dead letter of the past, but *living and active*; of continuing and contemporary relevance.

The image of divine judgment as a sword is a traditional one (cf. Isa 34:5-6). Wis 18:14-16 depicts the word as a warrior, wielding the divine sword of judgment against Israel's enemies at the EXODUS (cf. Eph 6:17; Rev 1:16; 2:12; 19:15). *Spirit* and *soul, joints* and *marrow,* and *thought* and *intentions* are used as three pairs of synonyms to emphasize the penetrative power of God's word and its ability to bring judgment even to the seemingly impenetrable.

Jesus the High Priest, 4:14–10:18

In this central section the principal soteriological model employed is that of the high priest, and the role he played in the Day of Atonement ceremonies. In this analogy, the death and ascension of Jesus represent both the offering and the offerer, the expiatory sacrifice that was the essential prerequisite for entry into the Holy of Holies and the high priest who was thus enabled to enter into the presence of God on the people's behalf.

Not only are comparisons made but contrasts are also drawn. Thus Jesus is superior both to the Day of Atonement's sacrificial victim, and its high priest. Furthermore, the cult place that Christ has entered far excels even the Holy of Holies, since it is nothing less than heaven itself. When in 8:7-13 and 9:15-22 Hebrews moves from the image of Jesus as expiatory sacrifice to one whereby he is seen as a COVENANT offering, we find a similar stress on his supremacy over what has gone before. His was a superior sacrifice that inaugurated a new and better covenant.

Merciful and Compassionate, 4:14–5:10

Hebrews 4:14-16 acts as a transition from the theme of access to God in terms of entry into the promised land (3:1–4:13), to its depiction in terms of the Jewish cult that dominates 4:14–10:18. Christ's priesthood, hinted at 1:3 and first stated at 2:17, *a merciful and faithful high priest*, is now pursued.

By way of encouragement to hold fast to their faith, the readers are once more reminded that Jesus is now in the presence of God in heaven. Earlier images of heaven as a royal court where Christ is enthroned now give way to its depiction as the inner sanctum of Israel's cult place. Thus it contains a *throne of grace* (4:16), i.e., the *mercy seat* located in the tabernacle's Holy of Holies (cf. 9:5). This is a reference to the lid or covering of the ark, upon which the victim's blood was sprinkled by the high priest on the Day of Atonement. Since the effect of this action was expiatory, the ARK could be spoken of as the place where mercy was dispensed. In the light of Jesus' expiatory work, Christians should be confident (NRSV *approach . . . with boldness*; cf. 3:6; 10:19) that they may approach God.

The source of Jesus' compassion as HIGH PRIEST lies in his genuine humanity—*one who in every respect has been tested as we are* (4:15). This picks up the theme of testing from 3:8 where it referred to the wilderness generation's desire to put God to the test. Thereby their own faith was tested and found wanting. By contrast, Jesus' response to testing was quite different. He was *without sin*.

Excursus: Priesthood in Postexilic Israel.

With the demise of the Davidic monarchy in postexilic Judaism, it was the institution of priesthood that came to the fore. Hence the covenant made by God with LEVI came to be seen as analogous to the one he made with Moses (cf. Jer 33:14-26—a passage regarded by many scholars as a postexilic interpolation). Like the Davidic covenant (2 Sam 7:12-16), the Levitical one was portrayed as permanent (Num 25:11-13; Sir 45:6-21)—*forever.*

The dominance of the priestly model of leadership in the postexilic period is evident from the second century BCE, with the installation of the Hasmonean high priesthood. In 140 BCE, Simon Maccabeus claimed the dual role of high priest and ethnarch both for himself and in perpetuity for his heirs (cf. 1 Mac 14:41). JOSEPHUS tells us (*Ant* 13.301) that by the time of John Hyrcanus (130–104 BCE) the Hasmoneans had adopted the title "king" as well as high priest.

The QUMRAN community seems to have come into being originally as a protest, not against Hasmonean claims to (non-Davidic) kingship, but to their right to the high priesthood. According to the Covenanters, although of the tribe of Levi, they were not descended from the Zadokite line (cf. *1QpHab* 12:7-8; 10:10; *CD* 12:2). They therefore regarded Hasmonean incumbency of the office to be invalid. The restoration of the true Zadokite line became part of their eschatological vision of the cult in the future. Thus, unlike Hebrews, the Qumran Covenanters looked forward to the purification of Judaism's Levitical high priesthood, rather than to its replacement by something wholly other—a Melchizidekian order.

5:1-4. The Aaronic priesthood. The major qualifications for the Aaronic priesthood are: (1) Common humanity. The priest must be part of what he represents. Hence he is *chosen from among mortals* (v. 1). (2) He should display a tolerant understanding towards those who err (v. 2), since he himself has human weaknesses (cf. 4:15) that require that he offer sacrifice, not only for the people, but for himself (v. 3). Here Hebrews has in mind the Day of Atonement ritual, where the two separate offerings were clearly distinguished (cf. Lev 9:7; 16:6-17). Later (7:27; 9:7) he is to assert the superiority of Christ's priesthood over that of the Levitical order, not least in his sinlessness (cf. 4:15), which precluded the need for two sacrifices and two entries into the Holy of Holies. (3) Priesthood requires a call and appointment that has God rather than oneself as its instigator (v. 4). "Appointed" (RSV) is preferable (as in 7:28 and 8:3) to the NRSV *put in charge of* (v. 1). 5:5-10 applies these qualifications to Jesus in inverse order:

5:5-6.10. His is a divine appointment. He has not only been called by God as his Son (Ps 2:7; cf. Heb 1:5); he has also been designated *a priest forever according to the order of Melchizedek* (Ps 110:4). In their original setting both Pss 2 and 110 were addressed to a Davidic king. Although Israel's preexilic kings could and did exercise what were later to become the exclusive functions of the priesthood (cf. 2 Sam 6:13-18; 24:17; 1 Kgs 3:15), since they were of the tribe of JUDAH rather than Levi, they were not priests. Hence the Psalmist addressed the Davidic king as of *the order of Melchizedek*, rather than Levi. Hebrews can therefore appropriately designate Jesus, the Davidic Messiah, as priest. In what sense he is *after the order of Melchizedek* will be developed in chap. 7.

Although Ps 110:1 is widely used in the NT, it is striking that Hebrews is the only Christian writer before JUSTIN MARTYR in the second century to use verse 4. Even those Qumran writings that feature MELCHIZEDEK (*11QMelch*; *1QapGen*) make no use of it.

5:7-10. Jesus shares human weakness. He is thus part of the humanity he represents. Unlike the Levitical high priest, however, in the case of Jesus it is not sin that is the common bond between representative and people; it is suffering and mortality (cf. 2:14-15). *Having been made perfect* (v. 9) is not a reference to moral perfectibility, and should not be understood as parallel with, *He learned obedience through what he suffered* (v. 8). That would be to suggest that Jesus' death was designed to correct his prior disobedience, whereas Hebrews stands firmly within the tradition that regarded him as sinless (cf. 2 Cor 5:21; 1 Pet 2:22; 1 John 3:5). His suffering is certainly portrayed as educative—but not in a punitive sense. Rather, it developed (cf. Luke 2:52) and expressed his filial obedience to God.

The language of *perfection* (τελείωσις) and its cognates (τελεῖουν and τελειωτής) in Hebrews, whether applied to Jesus or his followers, never loses the sense of achieving an end or goal (τελός). In terms of the Jewish cult that end was access to God, symbolized by the entry of the high priest into the Holy of Holies. *Perfection* (cf. 7:11) for the Christian author of Hebrews is the attainment of that goal in terms of entry into heaven. It is, moreover, a process (*being made perfect*) that includes not only the end, but the means to that end. In the case of Jesus, his passion was the path to his perfecting (cf. 2:10; 5:9; 7:28). His disciples also, if they follow Jesus the *perfecter* (12:2), may achieve access to the presence of God, that is, heaven (cf. 10:4; 12:23), although, unlike Christ, for them that lies in the future.

Verse 7 is unlikely to refer to Jesus' prayer in Gethsemane (cf. Matt 26:36-46 || Mark 14:32-42 || Luke 22:40-46), since there his petition, "Remove this cup from me," was not granted. Here, however, *his prayer was heard.* Far from being a fearful entreaty, this prayer exudes the confidence that is the hallmark of the truly *reverent*. It displays that frank expression of emotion (*loud cries and tears*) that, according to Jewish tradition, characterized the prayer of the righteous. Thus Philo can say of Moses' prayer: "But the man of worth has such courage of speech that he is bold not only to speak and cry aloud, but actually to make an outcry of reproach, wrung from him by real conviction, and expressing true emotion" (*Who Is the Heir of Divine Things* 19). As vv. 6 and 10 make clear, this is the confidant prayer of Jesus, the Melchizedekian high priest, which accompanied the offering of the sacrifice of his own life.

An Exhortatory Aside: Grow Up! There Can Be No Going Back, 5:11-6:20.

Before further developing the theme of Jesus' Melchizedekian high priesthood, Hebrews urges his readers to become more mature (v. 1 *maturity* is preferable to NRSV *perfection*).

5:11–6:3. In spiritual matters they are mere babes. They have yet to progress beyond the ABCs of the faith. These are listed in vv. 1-2. *Repentance from dead works* = behavior that will ensue in spiritual death. There is nothing here to suggest the contrast that we find in Paul between faith and works. *Contra* NRSV, *instruction on baptisms* (6:2) is unlikely to refer to Christian baptism since: (1) The NT word for baptism is neuter, whereas here it is masculine, and (2) it is in the plural. If it were baptism we would expect the singular. It is better understood, therefore, as referring to purificatory rites of ablution in general.

Similarly, we should not confine *laying on of hands* to any one specific Christian rite of initiation. In biblical tradition it occurs in a whole variety of different contexts as the mode whereby power was transferred and blessings bestowed (Lohse 1974). *Resurrection of the dead* refers to the general resurrection that lies in the future (see 11:19) rather than to the resurrection of Christ that has already taken place. Only once in Hebrews (13:10) do we find a reference to Jesus' resurrection.

All these beliefs and practices can be found in JUDAISM. Nonetheless, for the author of Hebrews, convinced as he was that Judaism's scriptures are *about Christ* (6:1), they may be described also as Christian *basic teaching*. This is therefore no call to reject the inspiration of the past in order to embrace Christianity, but a call to see in Jesus the true fulfilment of God's previous revelation.

6:4-12. Hope versus despair. Here the hopelessness that comes from giving up one's Christian discipleship is contrasted with the hope that is held out to those who remain steadfast. It is impossible for renegades to be readmitted to the community of faith once they have left (6:4-6; cf. 10:26-31), not because they have committed postbaptismal sin. Nor because there is a special category of "mortal" sins for which there can be no forgiveness. Like Num 15:30-31, Hebrews believes that there can be no expiatory sacrifice for one who *acts high-handedly*, that is, for one who refuses to accept the very jurisdiction of God. To *fall away* in this context means to deliberately place oneself outside the new covenant community. To abandon Christian discipleship is to ally oneself with that very rejection that originally brought about Christ's crucifixion. As the rest of this homily goes on to assert, that sacrifice was unique and cannot be repeated.

All this is merely by way of warning. So far the recipients have remained loyal (v. 9). So they are not only warned; they are encouraged (vv. 10-12) to look forward in hope rather than go back via a path that can only lead to a dead end.

6:13-20. God has confirmed his promise by an oath. Christian hope is grounded in the twofold character of God's word: (1) the *promise* that is the believer's inheritance, and (2) the *oath* that guarantees the promise (v. 17). Hebrews cites the example of ABRAHAM. God's promise that he would father a great nation (Gen 12:1-4) was emphatically renewed (by God swearing an oath) after the patriarch had demonstrated his willingness to sacrifice his son (Gen 22:16-18). Both promise and oath are to be trusted (v. 18, *two unchangeable things*), but the word accompanied by the oath is the superior, definitive, last word of God.

This argument paves the way for chap. 7. It enables the author to claim that Melchizedekian high priesthood is superior to the Aaronic order since it was confirmed by an oath. Although v. 16 acknowledges the problem, unlike some Jewish authors (cf. Philo, *Allegorical Commentaries* 3.207), Hebrews does not discuss how it is possible for God to swear by himself.

According to the Order of Melchizedek, 7:1-28

In order to pursue the analogy of Christ's death and ascension in priestly terms, it is essential for the author to establish the non-Levitical order of his priesthood. Jesus could not at one and the same time be Davidic Messiah of the tribe of Judah (vv. 13-15) and Aaronic high priest of the tribe of Levi.

7:1-3. The order of Melchizedek. In the two references to MELCHIZEDEK in the OT (Gen 14:17-20; Ps 110:4) Hebrews finds a type of priesthood that is non-Levitical. In vv. 1-2 he focuses on two things mentioned in Gen 14: (1) Melchizedek's blessing of Abraham, and (2) his receiving tithes from the patriarch. In these actions is to be found evidence of Melchizedek's superiority (vv. 4-8).

Melchizedek was probably originally a Canaanite priest-king. Little more can be said of this figure from the mists of Israel's prehistory. Perhaps precisely because of this he came to exercise the creative imagination of both Jewish and Christian writers.

Verse 2 reflects first-century Jewish exegetical belief that the *zedek* of the priest-king's name was derived from the Hebrew *sedeq* (righteous-ness) and therefore meant *king of righteousness*. In fact it may have had its origins in Zedek, the name of a Canaanite deity, and meant "Zedek's king." By the time of Hebrews, Melchizedek had become associated in Jewish thought with the city of *Salem* (=Jerusalem), whose name was supposedly derived from the Hebrew *shalom*, *peace*.

The Qumran Covenanters were also interested in Melchizedek (cf. *1QapGen* 14; *11QMelch*). Their interest in him was not as a priestly figure but as a heavenly being, whom they thought would come in the final jubilee year to exercise judgment on God's behalf.

From scripture's silence as to Melchizedek's origins and final destiny v. 3 infers that he was *without father, without mother, without genealogy, having neither beginning of days nor end of life*. He therefore typifies a kind of priesthood that is neither inherited nor bequeathed. Jesus' resurrection, *the power of an indestructible life* (v. 16), demonstrates that he *remains a priest forever* (v. 3 = Ps 110:4), and therefore has no successor (cf. 7:24). From this the reader might be led to think that Melchizedek was the model for Christ. Yet, as v. 3 shows, for Hebrews it is Melchizedek who resembles the SON OF GOD rather than *vice versa*.

7:4-10. Melchizedek is superior to both Abraham and Levi. Abraham acknowledged this in receiving his blessing and giving him tithes. And Levi, although as yet unborn, did likewise, since he may be regarded as seminally present (= *in the loins of*) in his great grandfather.

7:11-19. Failure of Levitical order. The Levitical order failed to effect access to God, which was its whole purpose. Therefore it has been superseded by a new priesthood. Hebrews (vv. 12, 18) is aware that to abrogate the Aaronic office is effectively to overthrow the Mosaic Law that legislated for its provision. Apart from a brief mention at 10:1, however, the issue of the Law is not pursued further. The discussion is confined to priesthood.

7:20-28. The superiority of Jesus' high priesthood. Psalm 110:4, initially introduced at v. 17 to stress the eternity (*forever*) of Christ's priestly order, is now used to assert that Melchizedekian priesthood is God's final word—*The Lord has sworn and will not change his mind.* Just as 6:13-20 argued that in the case of Abraham God's promise was even better when confirmed by an oath, so here the asseveration that prefaced the address to a Davidic king in Ps 110 is seen to confirm that it is Melchizedekian rather than Levitical priesthood that is God's definitive word. This priesthood is *the guarantee of a better covenant* (cf. 8:7-13; 9:15-27).

7:23-25. Christ's priestly ministry is singular and permanent. It is therefore better than that of AARON, since it requires no line of succession (cf. 7:3). The ministry of the ascended Christ is that of *intercession* (cf. Rom 8:34) rather than sacrifice. The latter was but the means whereby Jesus entered heaven.

7:26-28. He was a high priest who was sinless. Unlike the Aaronic high priest, who needed to offer two sacrifices and therefore make two entries into the Holy of Holies on the Day of Atonement, Jesus had no need of personal expiation. He entered the presence of God but once. He *has been made perfect* (v. 28) does not imply his own need of moral perfectibility. Rather, the language of "perfection" in Hebrews refers to the process whereby he achieved the goal of entry into heaven (see note on 5:9).

The Sacrificial Work of Christ, 8:1–10:18

At this point the cultic imagery is expanded to make way, not only for Christ as priest, but Christ as sacrificial victim, whose death was the essential prerequisite for his access to God. This is worked out in terms of Jesus as (1) the new covenant sacrifice (8:7-13; 9:15-22), and (2) the superior Day of Atonement offering.

The whole purpose of expiatory sacrifices in the Jewish cultic system was to remove the barrier of sin which separated the profane from the holy. They were the divinely appointed means whereby the worshiper could approach God. Above all this was exemplified in the Day of Atonement ceremonies. Using this model, Hebrews compares the death of Christ to that offering, and his ascension to heaven with the entry of the high priest into the Holy of Holies. Thus the goal of all sacrifice has been achieved, making the cult itself redundant.

8:1-6. Jesus is now in the presence of God. With yet another allusion to Ps 110:1, *seated at the right hand*, the preacher brings us back once more to this *the main point* (v. 1) of his sermon. He cites (v. 5) Exod 25:40 (LXX), *"See that you make everything according to the pattern that was shown you on the mountain,"* to claim that the plans of the tabernacle shown to Moses by God were but a shadowy copy (NRSV, v. 5, *a sketch and shadow*) rather than the real thing. That superior reality, which now replaces the earthly shrine, is heaven itself—*the sanctuary and the true tent* which Christ has entered.

Hebrews 8:6 at once concludes this section on Jesus as *minister* in the superior shrine, and introduces the new theme of him as *the mediator of a better covenant.*

8:7-13. The promise of a new covenant. Here the Mosaic covenant on Mount Sinai (see Exod 19) is contrasted with that promised by JEREMIAH (31:31-34). COVENANT, especially as developed in Deuteronomistic circles in the years leading up to the EXILE, became the term that encapsulated Israel's faith that she had been chosen as God's people. The bond between God and Israel was not thought of as a contract between two equal partners. Nonetheless, it was bilateral in nature. God's commitment to his people carried with it a solemn obligation to serve him alone and to be obedient to his commandments. It was because of Israel's lamentable failure to fulfil her side of the obligation that Jeremiah looked forward to a new covenant.

8:8-12. The prophecy of Jeremiah. This is cited from the LXX (=Jer 38:31-34). Hebrews goes further than Jeremiah, however. He suggests that failure to keep the covenant was not merely weakness on the people's part; it was inherent in the Mosaic covenant itself, as the very mention of *a second* one demonstrates. *For if the first had been faultless, there would have been no need to look for a second one* (v. 7).

What lies at the heart of Jeremiah's promise of a new covenant is the same notion of adoption that lay behind the Mosaic covenant. To this, however, the prophet has added some striking new features: (1) *I will put my laws in their minds and write them on their hearts* (v. 10). It is this interiorization of the will of God that leads to radical obedience. (2) With the universal knowledge of the Law's demands will come the redundancy of its teachers and interpreters. *For they shall all know me from the least of them to the greatest* (v. 11).

8:13. The new covenant. This new covenant has been inaugurated by the death of Christ. It heralds a new order (a theme that runs throughout 7:1–10:18) that makes what went before *obsolete, growing old* and *soon to disappear*. For Hebrews, the new covenant is thus part of the new age that, like the promised land, has yet to be attained. It is the promise held out to the believer of God's future, to be experienced in the present as hope.

9:1-10. The inadequacy of the earthly cult. The author returns to the theme that dominates this central section—the Day of Atonement.

9:1-5. The layout and contents of the shrine. Clearly, the simple twofold division of the wilderness TABERNACLE (Exod 25-26) rather than the more complex structure of the Jerusalem Temple (see TEMPLE/TEMPLES) is in mind. In the former was an outer tent (*the first one*), *the Holy Place* (v. 2), beyond which was an inner sanctum, *the Holy of Holies* (v. 3).

In the accounts in Exodus (25:1–31:11; 36:2–39:43; 40:1-15; 40:16-38) the only furnishing in the Holy of Holies was the ARK. The final fate of the ark remains unknown. It was probably removed and/or destroyed by the Babylonians when they sacked the Temple (cf. Jer 3:14-17). JOSEPHUS (*BJ* 5.219) tells us that in the Temple of his day the inner sanctum was completely empty. In Hebrews's account the ark is made to contain within it certain sacred objects: the *tablets of the covenant* (cf. Deut 10:2; 1 Kgs 8:9; 2 Chr 5:10); the urn containing the *manna* (cf. Exod 16:33-34); and *Aaron's rod* (cf. Num 17:16-24). Furthermore, unlike Exod 30:1-10; 38:25-28, Hebrews (v. 4) locates the *altar of incense* inside rather than outside the Holy of Holies.

9:6-10. The regulations for worship on the Day of Atonement. These are briefly alluded to. Two points are emphasized: (1) The Holy of Holies was the exclusive domain of the high priest, who was permitted to enter on but one day of the year. (2) Expiatory sacrifice was the *sine qua non* without which even he was not permitted access. He in fact made two sacrifices and two entries into the inner sanctum. First he offered a bull to expiate for the sins of himself and his household (cf. Lev 16:6,11). Then he sacrificed a goat to purify both the people and the cult place (cf. Lev 16:16). *Sins committed unintentionally* (v. 7), reminds us that Israel's sacrificial system (including its "sin" and "guilt" offerings) was largely intended to expiate unwitting rather than "high-handed" sins (see Num 15:30-31).

The sins of the people were laid upon the head of a second goat (the "scapegoat") by the high priest. Since nothing that is sinful can be offered to God, this animal was not sacrificed, but driven out live into the wilderness (cf. Lev 16:20-22). Nowhere in the NT is Jesus depicted as the scapegoat. The emphasis rather (v. 14) is upon Jesus as the spotless victim.

The Mosaic ritual itself (= *the first tent*, v. 8) was a parable in action (= *symbol*, v. 9) of the fact that it provided no definitive, lasting access to God. Even during the period of its dispensation (=*standing*, v. 8), it could only deal with external rather than internal purification. It could not cleanse the *conscience* (v. 9). That had to await the sacrifice of Christ (= *the time . . . to set things right*, v. 10).

9:11-14. The superiority of Christ as priest and victim. This lies in the fact that Jesus has entered the presence of God, not through the sacrifice of an animal, but through the superior offering of himself. Verse 13 alludes to another of Israel's expiatory rites—the ceremony of the red heifer (Num 19:2-20) in which the animal was burned with cedar wood, along with hyssop and scarlet "stuff" (cf. Heb 9:19). The resultant ashes were then mixed with water and sprinkled upon the people (see HEIFER, RED).

It is the contrast between the exterior and the interior that is drawn at this point in the homily. Judaism's expiatory rites could only cleanse what is outside (= the *flesh*, v. 13), whereas Jesus' sacrifice dealt with the interior sense of guilt (= *conscience*), that inner accuser that condemns a way of life that leads to death. (*Dead works*, v. 14, should not be understood in the Pauline sense of "works of the law" over against faith.)

By capitalizing *Spirit* the NRSV gives a trinitarian interpretation to v. 14. It is better understood, however, as a reference to Jesus' own spirit or person, which is *eternal* by virtue of his resurrection (cf. 7:16).

9:15-22. The new covenant and its sacrifice. This resumes the theme of 8:7-13. Now the death of Christ is likened, not to the Day of Atonement offering, but to the sacrifice that accompanied the ratification of the Mosaic covenant (Exod 24:1-8). Apart from Luke 20:20 and 1 Cor 11:25, Hebrews is the only NT work to depict Jesus as the *new* covenant victim. (Mark 14:24 || Matt 26:28 mentions covenant but not new covenant.) Unlike them, however, Hebrews does not place this within the context of the last supper. In fact, Hebrews displays no interest in the Eucharist whatsoever.

9:15. The death of Jesus ratifies a new covenant. *Redeems* (cf. 9:12) conjures up a picture of God's manumission of his people from slavery in Egypt. The bondage envisaged here, however, is that of sin.

9:16-17. A testator must first die before a will can take effect. This argument depends upon the double meaning of διαθήκη, the LXX's translation of the Hebrew word for *covenant (berith).* In secular Greek it means "will" (cf. Gal 3:15-17).

9:18-22. A death was also necessary to ratify the Mosaic covenant. Whereas in Exodus the covenant offering was concerned with consecration, here it is interpreted as expiatory. This is probably because the Day of Atonement, rather than the inauguration of the covenant, dominates Hebrews's thinking. The one becomes interpreted in terms of the other. Thus, unlike the biblical account, not only the people, but the book (v. 19) together with the contents of the tabernacle (v. 21) are sprinkled with the blood of the covenant victim. Hebrews 9:19 also contains elements drawn, not from the covenant, but from the ceremony of the red heifer (see note on 9:13).

9:23-28. Christ's death as the means whereby he entered heaven. Once more we are back with the dominant motif of the Day of Atonement. Hebrews 9:23-24 is another *a fortiori* argument. If the contents of the material shrine needed cleansing, *how much more* the *heavenly things themselves.* The latter is probably a metaphor for that which is interior, namely, the CONSCIENCE. Thus this section looks back to 9:11-14 and forward to 10:1-10, which focus upon the internal as opposed to the external.

9:25-28. Levitical sacrifices and the death of Christ. The repetitive character of Levitical sacrifices is contrasted with the *once for all* (vv. 26, 27, 28) of the death of Christ. A *reductio ad absurdum* argument is employed to show that if this were not the case Jesus would have had to die repeatedly. As we all know, however, humans die but once! Jesus' return will not be to atone for sin, but to bring final salvation. Throughout Hebrews salvation is held out as a future hope—not a present possession.

10:1-18. The sacrifice to end all sacrifices. This passage functions as both a recapitulation of the argument of 8:1–10:18 and as its climax. Thus it reiterates:

(1) 10:1-3. Christ's sacrifice needs no annual renewal. Sacrifices of the cult, on the other hand, had to be repeated. This proves that they, together with the Mosaic Law that legislated for them, were not God's final revelation (*true form*) but only a precursor (*shadow*). Far from absolving guilt (*consciousness of sin;* cf. 9:14), they merely acted as its constant reminder.

(2) 10:4-10. Unlike animal sacrifice, that of Jesus was a voluntary self-offering. Ps 40:6-8 is cited (vv. 5-7) in its LXX form (=Ps 39:7-9). *A body you have prepared for me* (v. 5) is the LXX translation of the obscure Hebrew phrase, "Ears you have dug for me," which the NRSV of Ps 40 freely renders, "You have given me an open ear." This is used to echo the Psalmist's insistence upon the supremacy of obedience over sacrificial offerings *per se* (v. 9). Above all, Jesus' death is seen as superior to that of animals, since they had no option. Putting the psalm on the lips of Jesus (v. 5; cf. 2:12-13) is not to claim his preexistence, but to identify his death with the superior self-offering spoken of by the psalm.

(3) 10:11-18. Since it was effective, it does away with all further need of sacrifice. Having offered the definitive sacrifice, Jesus is now enthroned in heaven (Ps 110:1). His enemies have as yet to be subjugated on earth (cf. 2:8; 9:28). Nonetheless, he has gained access to God (= *perfected*) not only for himself but ultimately for his followers (= the *sanctified*). His death has thus fulfilled the two promises that lay at the heart of Jeremiah's new covenant: (a) a genuine change in humanity that affects the interior and not simply the exterior; and (b) the removal of sin. With this achieved, there is no further need of a sacrificial system at all.

An Exhortation to Persevere in the Faith, 10:19–12:29

The sermon proper is concluded by a series of encouragements and warnings aimed at a readership who may be tempted to abandon their discipleship in the face of present hardships. Once more the theme of pilgrimage (cf. 3:1–4:14) is taken up.

Perseverance: Some Encouragements and Warnings, 10:19-39

10:19-25. Trust in the faithfulness of God. An appeal to the fidelity of the Christian is grounded in a belief in the fidelity of God: *He who has promised is faithful* (v. 23). Heb 10:19-20 is best understood as an allegorization of the *curtain* that divided the Holy of Holies from the rest of the shrine. It now represents the death (= *flesh*) through which Jesus passed in order to gain access to God.

10:26-31. Go forward rather than back. The warning of 6:4-6 is renewed. *Anyone who has violated the law of Moses dies without mercy* (v. 28) alludes to Deut 17:8. Here what is condemned is not every breach of the Law, but idolatrous APOSTASY. What makes that unforgivable is that it constitutes a refusal to accept God's jurisdiction. That is as true of the new covenant as it was of the old. To go back on Christian discipleship is to spurn the Son of God, to treat the cross as if it were merely a profane death, rather than a sacred sacrifice that inaugurated a new covenant, and thus to outrage the spirit of God that mediated that grace (v. 29).

10:32-39. Be encouraged by your own past good record. *Enlightened* (v. 32) became a metaphor for BAPTISM from the second century onwards. Here, however, it is used as an image of spiritual conversion in general. The references to public ridicule (= *exposed to abuse*), *persecution*, and the *plundering of . . . possessions* (vv. 32-34) are too vague and general to enable us to pinpoint either the date or destination of this epistle. Habakkuk 2:3-4 (LXX) is cited (vv. 37-38) to affirm, by way of encouragement: (1) that Jesus will shortly return (*in a very little while*); and (2) that his readers will not be among those who renege on their commitment.

The Faithful of the Past, 11:1-40

The theme of faith is now picked up from the Habakkuk quotation cited at the end of chap. 10. *By faith* is the repetitive refrain by which a list of various heroes and martyrs of Israel's past are introduced as exemplars of faith. Nowhere in the biblical accounts themselves are their exploits attributed to faith.

Such listings of the achievements of people and events of the past in order to bolster up the resolve of the faithful of the present seem to have been traditional. Thus Wis 10 appeals (although not by name) to ADAM, ABEL, NOAH, JACOB, JOSEPH, MOSES, and the EXODUS generation as examples of those who triumphed over adversity with the aid of God's wisdom. An even closer formal parallel is PHILO (*On Rewards and Punishments* 11-14), in his definition and exposition of hope. He, however, confines himself to types in general of those who have exemplified hope. Hebrews, on the other hand, cites particular individuals and events that have demonstrated faith, i.e., a belief and trust in God's as-yet-unseen future, which was to find its fulfilment in Jesus.

11:1-3. What is faith? Commentators disagree as to the meaning of two crucial words in v. 1. The NRSV choice of *assurance* for ὑπόστασις and *conviction* for ἔλεγχος find no parallel in first-century Greek usage. It is therefore preferable to translate v. 1: "Now faith is the *title deed* of things hoped for, *the evidence* of things not seen."

Faith is not purely subjective. It is trust in the reality of God's consummation of his purposes in the future. Our ancestors "received confirmation" (v. 2, lit. "testimony," *contra* NRSV, *approval*) of God's promises. In their case, that final salvation was as invisible as was the material, visible world, before God brought it into existence through his divine command (v. 3).

11:4-7. Abel, Enoch, and Noah. Genesis 4:3-10 does not explain how or why Abel's was the superior sacrifice. Here (v. 4) it is ascribed to his faith. Hebrews 11:5 follows the LXX of Gen 5:21-24 and understands the enigmatic, "and he was not because God took him" of the MT, as implying that Enoch was translated to heaven (cf. *1 Enoch* 12.3; 15.1; *2 Enoch* 27.8; 71.14; *Jub* 4.23; Philo, *On the Changing of Names* 38; Josephus, *Ant* 1.2.4). Noah (cf. Gen 6:13-22) believed in God's warning of the impending flood (v. 7, *events as yet unseen*).

11:8-12. Abraham and Sarah. The story of Abraham's migration in response to God's call (Gen 12:1-8) enables Hebrews to link faith with obedience (v. 8). Like that of his successors ISAAC and JACOB, Abraham's sojourn in Canaan was but temporary (v. 9; cf. Gen 17:8; 23:4), since God's promise was not of an earthly but of a heavenly reality (v. 10). (The theme of the heavenly city will be resumed at 12:12.) Unlike those traditions that looked forward to the descent of the heavenly Jerusalem to earth (e.g., *4 Ezra* 13:36; Rev 21:2, 10), for Hebrews the land/city that is the true destination of pilgrimage is wholly transcendent.

11:13-16. The goal of faith. The true goal of faith is a heavenly rather than an earthly homeland. This recapitulates the main point of the chapter. None of these heroes of the past lived to see God's promises fulfilled. They lived in the faith that a *better country, a heavenly one* was to be theirs in the future.

11:17-22. Isaac, Jacob, and Joseph. Abraham was willing to offer his *only son* Isaac since he had faith in God's power to raise the dead (v. 19). A belief in a future resurrection of the dead was widespread in the first century. It is not, however, attributed to Abraham in the biblical account.

The NRSV translation *figuratively speaking* (v. 19) is to be rejected. Rather, as in 9:9, it means a *symbol* of future salvation: "Isaac's rescue from virtual death on the sacrificial pyre is symbolic of the deliverance that all the faithful can expect" (Attridge 1989, 336). Isaac's blessing of his sons (Gen 27:27-29, 39-40) is also seen to have a future reference (v. 20).

By adopting the LXX of Gen 47:31, "bowing in worship over the top of his staff" (v. 21), Jacob's blessing of his sons (Gen 48:8-22) is seen as an act of homage to God. (The MT, "Israel bowed himself on the end of his bed," means rather that he was prostrated by old age.)

11:23-27. Moses. Even Judaism's supreme agent of revelation (cf. Exod.33:11; Num 12:1-8) was motivated by a vision of the future. It was this, rather than fear (v. 27), that led him to leave Egypt. (His murder of an Egyptian overseer [Exod 12:11-12] is not mentioned.)

Abuse suffered for the Christ (v. 26) could either have Jesus the Messiah, or Moses the Lord's *anointed* (cf. LXX Ps 88:51-52 [MT 89:50-51]) as its referent. Probably both are intended. Thus, Moses, in obedience to and solidarity with the reproach that will be endured by the future Christ, accepted his fate as an exile. This glimpse of the future motivated his endurance.

11:28-31. The Passover, the Exodus, the fall of Jericho, and Rahab. These (cf. Exod 12:21-30; 14:21-31; Josh 6:12-21; 2:1-21; 6:22-5) all similarly reflect a faith in the future.

11:32-8. Other heroes and martyrs. Beginning with various military and political leaders of the postsettlement period (vv. 32-34), the list now includes not simply the victors, but the persecuted, many of whom lost their lives (vv. 35-38). *Women received their dead by resurrection* (v. 35), probably refers to the miracles performed by ELIJAH (1 Kgs 17:17-24) and ELISHA (2 Kgs 4:18-37). The picture of torture and death in vv. 36-38 has probably been colored by the stories of the Maccabean martyrs (see 2 Macc 6:18-31; 7; 4 Macc 6–12).

11:29-40. A summary. Their faith was to find its fulfillment in Christ. They awaited a *better* resurrection. This was what inspired them to endure—even in adversity.

The Faithful Endurance Required Now, 12:1-29

12:1-3. Look to the example of Jesus, the pioneer and perfecter of faith. The array of *witnesses* paraded in chap. 11 find their climax in Jesus. He has not only blazed the trail (= *pioneer*); he has reached its goal (= *perfecter*)—heaven. In their preparation for and participation in the contest (cf. *race*) of faith, Christians should take courage from his example.

12:4-13. View suffering as God's fatherly discipline. The readers, unlike Jesus, have not yet had to face a martyr's death. Their present *trials* (v. 7) should be seen as a sign of their true membership of the household of God. Far from being evidence of God's displeasure, they are signs of his fatherly care (cf. Wis 11:9-10). The educative value of suffering (cf. Prov 13:24; 22:15; Wis 3:3-5; Rom 5:3-4; 1 Cor 11:32) is confirmed by way of a citation (vv. 5-6) from Prov 3:11-12 (LXX). Painful though their present plight might be (v. 11; cf. the athletic imagery of vv. 1-2), its aim is educative rather than punitive.

12:14-17. Take warning from the example of Esau. Hebrews 12:14-15 appeals for harmony (= *peace*) within the Christian community. *See . . . that no root of bitterness springs up and causes trouble* (v. 16) alludes to Deut 29:17 (LXX)—a passage which, in its original context, warned against APOSTASY from the covenant community. Similarly, the author of Hebrews is concerned that his readers should not abandon their Christian commitment. Otherwise they could become like Esau (cf. Gen 25:27-34; 27:30-40), who sold his birthright cheap. The biblical account has no reference to Esau's belated and futile repentance. In introducing it (v. 17), Hebrews echoes the previous warning (6:4-6; 10:26-31) that repentance for the apostate is impossible.

12:18-24. The heavenly Zion contrasted with Mount Sinai. Although not explicitly named, vv. 18-21 clearly alludes both to the site (Mt. Sinai) and the events that surrounded the ratification of the Mosaic covenant and the giving of the Law. In his summary the author of Hebrews combines features drawn from Exod 19:12-19; 20:18-21 with those of Deut 4:11-12; 5:23-27 in order to stress the distance imposed upon the people by the very awesomeness of that theophanic revelation. Mount Sinai's site was so sacred that not so much as an animal was permitted to set foot upon it. Unlike the Exodus account, Hebrews will not even exempt Moses from the taboo. He, too, was terrified.

Verses 22-24 contrasts this with Mount Zion. This is not to be identified with the Jebusite stronghold captured by David (cf. 2 Sam 5:6-9), which became the capital city, Jerusalem. For Hebrews, heaven, not earth, is God's abode. This *heavenly Jerusalem*, unlike Mount Zion, may be *touched* (cf. v. 18).

Even so, that salvation has yet to be achieved by the believer. As yet only Christ has attained it. "You have approached" is a better translation than the NRSV *you have come* (v. 22). Meanwhile, the author has a proleptic vision (v. 23) of that future heavenly Jerusalem, peopled by the faithful of all ages, who, having been perfected through the work of Christ, will finally make up the completed assembly of the people of God. Chief among their number is Jesus. The blood of his new covenant sacrifice speaks of forgiveness and reconciliation, unlike that of Abel (cf. Gen 4:10-11) which cried out for vengeance.

12:25-29. A final solemn warning. The awesome responsibility of having access to God is to be taken seriously. The theme of the infidelity of the wilderness generation (cf. 3:7–4:13) is once more touched upon (v. 25). Part of an oracle, originally a promise to the postexilic remnant of the restoration of the Jerusalem Temple, is cited: "*Yet once more I will shake not only the earth but also the heaven*" (v. 26 = Hag 2:6). Here it is used, however, as an assurance of the replacement of all that is earthly and transient (= *what is shaken*, v. 27) by the heavenly and permanent (i.e., what *cannot be shaken* , vv. 27, 28). Verses 28-29 conclude with a call to worship. The offering now acceptable to God is that of gratitude and reverence on the part of the worshiper.

Epistolary Exhortation and Conclusion, 13:1-25

An abrupt change in tone and style signals the beginning of the author's epistolary conclusion. Here he appends a number of injunctions concerning the implications of his sermon for Christian living.

Christian Holiness and Its Obligations, 13:1-6

The ethical hallmarks that should characterize the new covenant community are briefly listed: (1) *Mutual love* between its members. (2) Hospitality. Probably this refers also to fellow Christians; visitors, who are *strangers* to the particular community. Heb 13:2 alludes to Abraham and Sarah's unrecognised guests (Gen 18:2-15). (3) Empathy towards those who have been imprisoned or otherwise maltreated (NRSV *tortured* is too specific) for their faith. (4) Marital fidelity and sexual chastity. (5) An absence of material greed. This is reinforced in v. 5 by the citation of a combination of Deut 31:6,8 and Josh 31:8, and in v. 6 by LXX Ps 117 (MT 118):6. These texts exhort reliance upon God.

The Implications of Jesus' Sacrifice, 13:7-19

Between an injunction to remember leaders—past (v. 7) and present (vv. 17-19)—is now placed a parenthetical summary of the epistle's main argument. Its condensed style makes this passage initially difficult to follow. Once "unpacked', however, it becomes clear. What is being said is: (1) The gracious act of God (= *grace*) in the death and exaltation of Jesus is superior to the Mosaic cult (=*regulations about food*, v. 9). (2) Christians have an expiatory sacrifice (= *an altar*) which, like those offered on the Day of Atonement, was not eaten (v. 10). Just as the carcases of these animals were *burned outside the camp* (v. 10; cf. Lev 16:27), so Jesus was disposed of *outside the city gate* (v. 12; cf. Mark 15:20 = Matt 27:31).

(3) Therefore, look beyond the fate of Jerusalem and its sanctuary, which is but transitory. Follow instead the way of Jesus. *Abuse* (cf. 11:26) will be the necessary lot of those who journey with him to the heavenly city (vv. 13-14). (4) Now, the only sacrifice required of the Christian is the praise of God in worship and the performance of good works in life (vv. 15-16).

A Closing Benediction, 13:20-21

This takes the form of a prayer for the recipients, and a doxology in praise of Christ.

13:20. Led up from the dead. "Led up from the dead" is a better translation than the NRSV *brought back*: Hebrews presents Christ's victory over death as exaltation rather than resurrection. In keeping with Jewish traditions of the Messiah as the shepherd of God's flock (cf. *PsSol* 17:40), Jesus is the *great shepherd of the sheep* (cf. John 10:11,14; 1 Pet 2:25; 5:4).

A Farewell Note, 13:22-25

Here more practical matters are dealt with. The author describes what he has written as a *word of exhortation* (v. 22)—the usual designation of a sermon (cf. Acts 13:15). The mention of *Timothy* (v. 23) led later interpreters to link Hebrews with PAUL (cf., e.g., Rom 16:21; 2 Cor 1:1; 1 Thes 1:1), and to conclude that the apostle was its author. It is unclear whether Timothy *has been set free* (v. 23) means from prison, or from some task that has, until recently, detained him. Equally ambiguous is *those from Italy* (v. 24). This could mean that Italy was the place from which Hebrews was written. It could, however, designate Italians who were sending their greetings home, in which case Italy would be its destination. Given these ambiguities (and that some scholars do not attribute vv. 21-25 to the original author), it is impossible to determine from these verses either the epistle's origin or destination.

Works Cited

Attridge, H. W. 1989. *The Epistle to the Hebrews*, Herm.
Lohse, Eduard. 1974. "The Laying on of Hands." TDNT 9:431-34.

James

R. Alan Culpepper [MCB 1283-1294]

Introduction

James is an eminently practical letter, manifesting a passionate concern for the role of faith in the concrete circumstances of life. Rather than deal with SANCTIFICATION, James challenges believers to control their tongues. Rather than debate the meaning of JUSTIFICATION, James calls on Christians to treat the POOR and the rich with equal respect. James, therefore, shuns abstract arguments and pointedly calls for PURITY and faithfulness in all areas of life.

Literary Character

Although James begins with an epistolary greeting, it lacks other characteristics of the letter form. Instead, one finds a series of exhortations with affinities to Jewish wisdom materials and Greco-Roman philosophical, ethical instruction: lack of topical continuity, eclecticism, repetition of motifs, and admonitions that do not apply to a single audience or situation.

Some fifty to sixty imperatives have been counted in James's 108 verses. Lists of traditional virtues and vices are featured (3:16-17). Occasionally, various maxims are gathered around one topic, as in Jas 5:13-18, where prayer is discussed from several perspectives. In Jas 2 one finds the only sustained argument in the letter, on the dangers of partiality and the relationship between FAITH and works. More often, however, the reader of James finds a series of different maxims or exhortations, often organized by a mnemonic device called *catchword linkage*. Sayings are strung together in such a way that a significant term in one saying also appears in the following saying. For example, note the succession of linking terms in Jas 1:2-6: *trials* (v. 2)–*testing* (v. 3); *endurance* (v. 3)–*endurance* (v. 4); *lacking* (v. 4)–*lacking* (v. 5); *ask* (v. 5)–*ask* (v. 6). The exhortations in James are carefully selected; it is not just a random collection of sayings. At the same time, the paraenetic character and catchword linkage employed in James make it difficult to reduce the letter to an orderly topical outline.

Social Setting

James is concerned about oppression of the poor by the rich and reciprocal hostility from the poor. The Christians meet in assemblies (2:2) led by *elders* (5:14), and one might be expected to aspire to the role of teacher (3:1). Some justify their lack of faithfulness by boasting Pauline slogans (2:14-26), and echoes of words of JESUS recur frequently. Envy and malicious talk are constant threats to the fabric of community life (4:2, 11). Laborers work for unfair wages (5:4). Life itself poses trials for the believers, who are encouraged to endure hardship patiently, anoint the sick with oil, and replace oaths with prayer.

James 1:1 contains the address and greeting: *To the twelve tribes in the Dispersion: Greetings*. Three interpretations of this address have been advanced: (1) all Jews living outside of Palestine; (2) Christendom conceived as the fulfillment of Israel; and (3) Jewish Christians living outside of Palestine who still looked to Jerusalem for leadership. The first has largely been abandoned because the epistle is clearly from a Christian leader to other Christians. The figurative interpretation is held in one form or another by all who claim that the epistle is pseudonymous and hold to a late date. The third position is compatible with the view that the epistle derives directly or indirectly from James, the brother of Jesus and leader of the Jerusalem church.

Authorship and Date

Among the factors that must be accounted for are the following: JAMES does not claim to be an APOSTLE, only *a servant of God and of the Lord Jesus Christ* (1:1). There is no claim to a familial relationship with Jesus. In fact, there are only two references to Jesus in the entire letter (1:1; 2:1). Although James seems to know both the tradition of the sayings of Jesus and some of the tenets of Paulinism, it does not quote any other NT book and is not quoted elsewhere in the NT. At most, one may argue that Jude 1 echoes Jas 1:1. James is also written in excellent Greek and reflects both Hellenistic and Jewish Christian features.

The traditional view is that James was written by James the Just, the brother of Jesus, prior to his death in 62 CE Alternatively, some scholars maintain that James is a pseudonymous work, written in the name of James late in the first century. It has also been suggested that the letter was originally a Jewish document that was subsequently reworked by a Christian, but this position has failed to gather much support.

A mediating position seems to be gaining favor. It holds that James contains material from the teachings of James in Jerusalem that was later compiled or edited by someone else. It was then sent to Jewish Christians who had been dispersed from Jerusalem during the turbulent events of the 50s and 60s. On this reading, James gives us a glimpse of the early Palestinian church just before it was dispersed by the war of 66–74 CE (see Davids 1982).

For nearly two centuries the early church was remarkably silent about James. The first clear reference to the letter appears in Origen (third cent.), who referred to it as scripture and attributed it to James the Just. In his "Preface to the New Testament" in 1552, Luther concluded, "Therefore St. James' epistle is really an epistle of straw, compared to these others, for it has nothing of the nature of the gospel about it." His reasons for discrediting James were that it opposed Paul in "ascribing justification to works" (*Luther's Works*, 35:396) and because of its apparent lack of organization.

Nevertheless, evidence for the origin of the material in James in the early days of the church (before the composition of the Gospels or the collection of Paul's letters) seems strong. The absence of anything peculiar to James the Just is also significant. The epistle preserves the traditional, ethical concerns of early Jewish Christianity, but drops its emphasis on the Law, circumcision, and dietary restrictions. At the same time, it embraces and endorses the authority of James and combats a misinterpretation of Paul. The letter, therefore, appears to be the work of one who gathered up the teachings of the early church in Jerusalem, attached the name of the late head of the church (since it contained his teachings), and sent it to Jewish Christians who had been dispersed as a result of the anarchy in Judea in the 60s.

For Further Study

In the *Mercer Dictionary of the Bible*: FAITH AND FAITHLESSNESS; JAMES, LETTER OF; GENERAL LETTERS; JAMES.

In other sources: P. H. Davids, *The Epistle of James: A Commentary on the Greek Text*, NIGTC; M. Dibelius, *James*, Herm; D. E. Hiebert, *The Epistle of James: Tests of a Living Faith*; L. T. Johnson, "The Letter of James," *NIB*; S. Laws, *A Commentary on the Epistle of James*, HNTC; R. P. Martin, *James*, WBC; D. P. Scaer, *James, the Apostle of Faith: A Primary Christological Epistle for the Persecuted Church*; H. S. Songer, "James," *BBC*.

Commentary

An Outline

I. Introductory Address and Greeting, 1:1
II. The Obedience of Faith, 1:2-27
  A. Testing Produces Joy, 1:2-4
  B. Prayer Produces Wisdom, 1:5-8
  C. Wealth Is Transient, 1:9-11
  D. Sin Results in Death, 1:12-16
  E. God Gives Perfect Gifts, 1:17-21
  F. The Obedient Persevere, 1:22-25
  G. The Obedient Care for the Oppressed, 1:26-27
III. The Obedience of Faith in Worship and Works, 2:1-26
  A. The Heresy of Partiality, 2:1-13
  B. The Relationship of Faith and Works, 2:14-26
IV. The Obedience of Faith in Words and Wisdom, 3:1-18
  A. The Power of Words, 3:1-12
  B. The Wisdom from Above, 3:13-18
V. The Obedience of Faith in Community, 4:1–5:6
  A. Faith as a Response to Dissension, 4:1-12
  B. Faith as a Response to Presumption, 4:13-17
  C. A Warning to the Rich, 5:1-6
VI. The Obedience of Faith in Patience, Oaths, and Prayer, 5:7-18
  A. A Call for Patience, 5:7-11
  B. Rejection of Oaths, 5:12
  C. The Power of Prayer, 5:13-18
VII. Concluding Exhortation: Restoring the Wayward, 5:19-20

Introductory Address and Greeting, 1:1

James, the brother of Jesus and leader of the early church, greets the Jewish Christians dispersed from Jerusalem.

The Obedience of Faith, 1:2-27

The first chapter is composed of a series of ethical instructions. A definition of pure religion concludes the chapter.

Testing Produces Joy, 1:2-4

Appropriately, the first word is one of encouragement for those who face trials. The term *trials* (*peirasmos*) can mean either (1) temptation to do evil, or (2) trial or stress. Here it means the latter. The main thrust of these verses is that trials are an opportunity for joy and growth. Stubbornly refusing to give in to anxiety, despair, or grief is both the test and the testimony of authentic faith. These verses echo the saying of Jesus in Matt 5:11-12 (= Luke 6:22-23) and call not just for brave endurance but for joy in the midst of trial.

Prayer Produces Wisdom, 1:5-8

Two new concepts are introduced in these sayings: WISDOM (cf. 3:13-18) and double-mindedness (4:8). Wisdom is the ability to transcend our circumstances and see life from God's perspective.

Care must be taken to let James be James. Do not read James's words with Paul's meanings. By *faith* James does not mean a saving belief but loyalty and commitment under trial, faithful living. By *wisdom* James means God's gift of discernment and empowerment, something akin to Paul's understanding of the role of the Spirit, or being "in Christ." Unlike the rabbis, James does not depend on the study of TORAH for wisdom but on prayer. If wisdom is a gift from God, it is natural to insist that the Christian ask for it (Luke 11:13 = Matt 7:7-8). By *double-mindedness* James does not mean doubt but divided loyalty or conflict of interest.

Verses 7 and 8 have been handled variously by the translators: as distinct but related statements (KJV), as subject and predicate (RSV), or as appositional (NEB, JB, NIV, GNB, NRSV).

The doubter is a "two-souled person" who is unwilling to trust God completely, contrary to the SHEMA that calls for the faithful to love God with all their heart, soul, and might (Deut 6:4-5). The double-minded vacillate; they are uncommitted, refuse to take sides, and do one thing wishing they were doing another. When James encourages us to ask without doubting, he is not talking about drumming up a particular kind of feeling when we pray but about living out a steadfast trust in God.

Wealth Is Transient, 1:9-11.

These verses introduce James's concern for poverty and WEALTH. This theme too is deeply rooted in the teachings of Jesus, especially in Luke. The humble person is a Christian, but does James think of the rich person as a Christian or not? In contrast to the NEB, JB, and GNB, it is doubtful that James considered the rich man to be a brother also.

James contrasts the humble, lowly person with the arrogant, godless person. *Rich* and *poor* are not exclusively economic terms but carry contrasting connotations of pious humility and wicked arrogance. Here the social location of James's readers must be kept in mind.

Boasting usually carries a negative connotation in the NT, but it can also mean rejoicing and glorifying God. The reversal of fortunes is a common biblical theme (e.g., Luke 12:13-21; 16:19-31). The humble should rejoice because God has chosen them and will exalt them. Both the present grace of God and its future fulfillment call for exultation. James challenges us to see life from the vantage point of the fulfillment of God's redemptive work.

The lowly will be exalted and the wealth of the rich will pass away. The only thing that is worthy of our glory and praise is the completion of God's work. Wealth is meaningless in the face of death (Isa 40:6-7; Ps 103:15). James returns to the dangers of wealth in 2:5-7, 4:13-16, and 5:1-6.

Sin Results in Death, 1:12-16

This unit deals with both trials and temptations. Verse 12 returns to the theme of enduring trials (cf. 1:2-4). It offers two good reasons for enduring trials: (1) one who endures is blessed, and (2) that one will receive *the crown of life*, eternal life.

The term for standing the test is one that was also used in connection with the testing of coins to determine whether they were genuine. The goal for the Christian is keep faith genuine in the midst of life's tests. The reward is salvation.

Verse 13 is the first instance of diatribe style: entering dialogue with an imaginary opponent. Does God test persons of faith or tempt us to sin? Commentators are divided on the issue of whether the term *peirasmos* has the same meaning in v. 13 as it has had previously (i.e., "trial") or whether it now means "temptation." If the meaning is temptation, then v. 13 is the beginning of a new section that is joined to v. 12 by catchword linkage. Trials are to be endured, but temptations are to be resisted. Still, the two cannot be completely separated; some temptations may call for endurance also.

James warns us that we cannot blame our sin on God. God is not tempted, and God tempts no one. Neither does James introduce the notion of the demonic here (cf. 3:15; 4:7). Instead, he requires us to face our own culpability. James emphasizes the human side of sin. Whatever the origin of the temptation, we are the ones who choose to sin.

The EVIL we do begins with the desire we enjoy. The imagery is drawn from hunting and fishing. The fish is lured, and the prey is enticed to a trap (2 Pet 2:14, 18). The image is also used of the harlot enticing to FORNICATION. Hiebert (1979, 105) comments: "Temptation has its source not in the outer lure but in the inner lust."

Evil is seldom born full-grown. James therefore unveils the process of its growth. Sin always has the insidious power to grow into something we never intended. At its birth SIN is hardly recognizable, but when it has grown up it is death. Many people would like to sin and then be done with it; but sin, once born, always grows up. The problem with sin, therefore, is not that we may get caught but that sin itself kills.

God Gives Perfect Gifts, 1:17-21

These verses speak of God's good gifts and our need to receive them with gladness. Verse 17 sets forth the principle of God's goodness and changelessness. If God is good and cannot change, then God cannot entice people to evil. There is no variation in God's goodness either. It does not wax or wane. As the creator of the stars, God is the "father of lights." The technical terms in v. 17b, which have been translated variously, can all refer to astronomical phenomena. God neither changes nor is changed.

Verse 18 supplies an illustration of God's goodness. The issue is whether it refers to God's giving life in creation or in redemption. The reference to our being *a kind of first fruits of his creatures* tilts the matter in favor of God's activity in redemption. God's work, therefore, stands in opposition to sin. Sin brings death; God brings forth new life. The new life begins in God's resolute will. The instrument of regeneration is the gospel message, but Christians are responsible for demonstrating the reality of the new life by the way they live. Our changeless, steadfast, creative God gives only good gifts, the chief of which is salvation; but this is just the beginning of God's work.

The cluster of three related, short sayings on receiving the word (vv. 19-21) is typical of Jewish wisdom (e.g., Prov 13:3; 15:1; 29:20; Eccl 7:9; Sir 5:11; 6:33). The reference to being *quick to listen* indicates a ready, responsive attitude. It is probably tied to hearing the preached word. *Slow to speak* counsels against hasty, ill-considered reactions. *Slow to anger* guards against a flash of temper, but it does not mean that anger has no place in Christian life.

Verse 21 begins with the common image of taking off clothes, which was often used to speak of repentance and BAPTISM (Rom 13:12; Eph 4:22; Col 3:8; 1 Pet 2:1). The word *all* reminds us that God is never satisfied with partial purity. Then, receive God's word with meekness—which means not weakness but humility. *The implanted word* is not inborn or "engrafted" (KJV). It is the seed planted in us through the word of God or the preaching of the gospel (compare Jesus' seed PARABLES). Salvation is still future, but *the implanted word* has the power to bring it about. Like sin, the word grows in a dynamic process. Rather than death, however, it results in salvation.

The Obedient Persevere, 1:22-25

These sayings continue James's refrain that the only faith that makes any difference is the faith that is obedient to God's direction. In the previous section he said that we should be quick to receive the word. Now he tells us what he means by that: be quick not only to listen but to obey. Hearing and doing was a common theme both in Jewish wisdom and in the teachings of Jesus (Deut 6:4-5; Matt 7:24-27; Rom 2:13). Having stated the principle in v. 22, James illustrates the point in vv. 23-24, and then draws a positive conclusion (v. 25). The illustration of the mirror was common in ancient ethical teachings (cf. 1 Cor 13:12). Mirrors were made of polished copper or bronze and were neither common nor very clear. The person who hears the word and does not seize the opportunity to respond with obedience is like the person who gets a chance to see what he or she looks like and then forgets.

By *the perfect law, the law of liberty* (v. 25), James probably means the higher standard of righteousness in the teachings of Jesus. Literally, James enjoins the reader to be not a "forgetful hearer but a workful doer." The beatitude then pronounces blessing on the doer *in their doing*.

The Obedient Care for the Oppressed, 1:26-27

These verses aptly sum up most of the message of the letter. The Christian is instructed to control the tongue, care for others, and resist temptation. Here is the positive side of hearing the word.

James echoes the prophets' critique of religion that is vain and futile. Some persons may do all the right, religious things, but if they *do not bridle their tongues,* their religion is futile. These persons are not hypocrites who pretend in order to deceive others; they themselves are deceived. They think they are religious but show no inner character that is consistent with the religion they profess.

Verse 27 offers a penetrating definition of pure religion that stands in contrast to the vain religion James has just described. The language is drawn from the practice of ritual cleanness. *Pure and undefiled* here means that which is free from moral pollution and corruption in the presence of God—the Father of those who are hurt by an abusive tongue, the Father of the widows and orphans also. *Orphans and widows* were traditional examples of the powerless and neglected (Isa 1:10-17; Deut 14:29; 24:17-22; Jer 5:28).

James spotlights both the personal and the social elements of true piety in v. 27: care for the helpless and moral purity, or as one commentator put it, "charity" and "chastity."

The Obedience of Faith in Worship and Works, 2:1-26

Chapter 2 offers the most sustained argument in the letter. Essentially it has two parts, one dealing with showing partiality and one demanding works of faithfulness.

The Heresy of Partiality, 2:1-13

Most commentators treat v. 1 as a prohibition, but it may also be an opening question (NRSV). The author gives an illustration of partiality in the context of a meeting of the church either for worship or to hear a legal case. The term for partiality or favoritism literally means "face receiving."

Two men enter the assembly. We are not told whether they are Christians or visitors. The rich person is distinguished by his rings and fine clothing. By contrast the POOR person (a *ptōchos*—one almost has to spit to say the word!) has dirty or shabby clothes and no rings. Both enter. How does the church respond? They do not see the persons. Instead, they take note of the clothing. The man in fine clothing is shown to a prominent seat. The poor man is told to stand out of the way or sit at someone's feet.

Verse 4 issues the first of the condemnations by means of a question that expects an affirmative answer. Yes, they have made judges of themselves, and they have *become judges with evil thoughts* (cf. Lev 19:15; Luke 18:6). Distinguishing between persons robs Christian community of its distinctive character.

Verses 5-7 expose the awful consequences of such partiality. God has chosen *the poor of the world* (cf. Deut 4:37; 7:7; 14:2; 1 Cor 1:26). God has refused to favor the wealth of the rich and has thereby nullified social distinctions. The role reversal is dramatic. In God's eyes it is not a person's *face* but one's *faith* that matters. The oppressed are favored and exalted. They will be *rich in faith*, heirs of the inheritance coveted by others. Verse 5 contains the only reference to the *kingdom* in James; it is promised to those who love God (1:12).

Two penetrating questions follow. James charges that the church shows favor to the rich, but it is the rich who oppress them. The next charge is the most devastating: the rich also blaspheme the excellent name that was invoked over you—which is probably an allusion to the name of Christ invoked in the context of BAPTISM. By siding with the rich, the church has taken the side of oppressors and blasphemers. Care must be taken today, of course, to distinguish the first-century connotations of rich and poor. These verses should not be treated as a general condemnation of wealth or as a blessing of poverty. The issue here is partiality, not possessions.

The argument of vv. 8-13 is that the law commands love of neighbor. Therefore, anyone who shows partiality has violated the law, and anyone who has violated any part of the law has violated the whole law. Love of neighbor (Lev 19:18) was viewed as the essence of the law. *Royal law* (v. 8) may mean the supreme law, God's law, or the OT law as interpreted by Jesus. Partiality, therefore, is a serious offense, not something to be tolerated or excused. Love, on the other hand, is partial to the needy and the neglected.

One cannot despise or dishonor another person by showing partiality and still please God. The principle of the unity of the law was taught by the rabbis. Since every commandment expresses the lawgiver's will, the violation of any commandment is an offense against the lawgiver. To drive home the point, James appeals to two central laws of the Decalogue, ADULTERY (IN THE OT) and MURDER. One who violates any commandment is a transgressor of the whole law.

Verse 12 draws the practical conclusion: speak and act as persons who are about to be judged by the law of FREEDOM (cf. 1:25). As elsewhere in James, an eschatological urgency is brought to bear on the ethical dimensions of life. The closing verse of this section reflects the paradox of judgment under the gospel. No MERCY will be shown to one who shows no mercy (Matt 5:7; Luke 16:19-31). Mercy does not triumph at the expense of JUSTICE, but the cross is the greatest testimony to the triumph of mercy.

The Relationship of Faith and Works, 2:14-26

James is apparently confronting a situation in which people in the church were professing faith in Christ but felt no need for moral purity or ethical living. Faith alone was regarded as essential, while works were unnecessary. James is not addressing the question of how one "gets saved." He is concerned about Christians who have grown complacent about living faithfully.

The argument takes the form of a question: *What good is it . . . if you say you have faith but do not have works?* (v. 14). In this hypothetical instance the person's faith is confirmed only by the claims he or she makes for it. This kind of argument by constructing an imaginary dialogue was characteristic of a diatribe between CYNICS and STOICS, but may have been common in synagogue sermons as well. The second question, *Can faith save you?* (v. 14) expects a negative answer. The question is deliberately provocative. One hardly wants to admit that a person of faith will not be saved. The implications are disturbing. The question, therefore, forces reflection on the nature of faith. Underlying James's attack may be his concern over misinterpretation of Paul's insistence that we are saved by faith alone.

Verses 15-16 give an illustration, and v. 17 draws the obvious conclusion. The illustration has parallels with Matt 25:35-45 and 1 John 3:17. A Christian meets a brother or sister who is in need of food and clothing, but all the Christian does is extend sympathy and best wishes. But prayer and sympathy are of little value when one refuses to share the basic necessities of life with those in need. The question, "What good is it?" echoes v. 14. The obvious conclusion is that faith without works is dead. James is not arguing for the superiority of works over faith but for the inseparability of faith and works. An authentic faith will make a difference in how a person lives.

Verse 18 is difficult, and no solution to its difficulties is entirely satisfactory. An imaginary speaker interjects a comment, but is the speaker James's ally or his opponent, and how far does the comment extend? Is the comment only *"You have faith and I have works,"* or does it extend through v. 19? The problem is that the comment seems to express James's point, not that of an opponent. Although no satisfactory solution is evident, the gist of the objection is that faith and works may be separated, and it is this separation that James disallows. Works demonstrate the existence of a vibrant faith.

Even orthodox belief is no substitute for a living faith. Verse 19 seems to be part of James's response to the interlocutor, pointing to the intellectual content of faith: *you believe that*. The affirmation that *God is one* was the central affirmation of Jewish worship (Deut 6:4). Knowledge, even confession, without commitment is of no value. *Even the demons believe!*

The rhetorical question in v. 20 sets up an appeal to biblical characters: ABRAHAM and RAHAB. The question plays on the contrast between *works* (*ergōn*) and *barren* (*argē*). Abraham demonstrated faith by offering ISAAC. Verse 23 cites Gen 15:6, just as Paul does in Rom 4:3. The next statement, *You see that a person is justified by works and not by faith alone* (v. 24), seems to be a rebuttal to Rom 3:28: "For we hold that a person is justified by faith apart from works prescribed by the law." The difficulty is largely resolved when one pays close attention to the different problems JAMES and PAUL were addressing, and the difference in the meaning of the terms in each context. Paul was arguing that one is justified by reliance on God's grace rather than by works of the law. James was addressing complacent Christians, arguing that intellectual belief in God is of no value unless it gives rise to deeds that demonstrate one's faith.

Even recognizing these differences, it still appears that James is responding to Christians who are misinterpreting Paul and quoting Pauline slogans. James uses language that echoes Paul's teaching (the formula, *by faith alone* (v. 24), occurs elsewhere only in Paul's letters); appeals to Abraham as Paul does in Rom 4; quotes Gen 15:6 as Paul does in Rom 4:3; and his affirmation reverses the points of Paul's affirmation in Rom 3:28. James was probably not responding directly to Paul, however, but to distortions of his teachings.

Rahab was a popular heroine in contemporary literature (Matt 1:5; Heb 11:31). She was considered to be a model of the ideal proselyte. Verse 26 concludes the chapter with an analogy: *faith without works* is as dead as a *body without . . . spirit* (cf. v. 17).

The Obedience of Faith in Words and Wisdom, 3:1-18

James 3 treats two subjects of vital importance to Christian living: controlling the tongue (vv. 1-12) and recognizing true wisdom (vv. 13-18).

The Power of Words, 3:1-12

The tongue can easily serve as a barometer of character and spiritual maturity (Matt 12:34-37), so control of one's speech is not optional for Christians. The chapter begins with a specific warning that *not many . . . should become teachers*. The reason given is that teachers will be judged more strictly than others.

As sensitive as James is to the many subtle forms of sin that can insinuate themselves into the life of a Christian, it still holds out the ideal of perfection. By steadfastness "you may be perfect" (1:4, NRSV *mature*), and faith is perfected by works (2:22). An echo can again be found in the sermon on the mount: "You, therefore, must be perfect, as your heavenly Father is perfect" (Matt 5:48). James does not require perfection but uses it to underscore the difficulty of complete mastery over one's speech.

Two metaphors drive home the point that a small member can control the whole body: *bridle* and *rudder*. Although the metaphors lend themselves to the positive sense that one small member could actually harness and control the whole body, James emphasizes the difficulty of harnessing the tongue rather than its power to subdue a wild or undisciplined body. The paragraph reaches a pointed conclusion in v. 5a. The tongue's influence does not correspond to its size. James paints graphic, disturbing pictures of the tongue's potential for perversity and leaves it up to each individual to decide what to do about the problem of unrestrained speech.

The third metaphor introduces the tongue's potential for destruction: a spark can destroy a whole forest. Verse 6 is so difficult to translate that commentators have often suggested the text is corrupt. The NRSV, however, renders it intelligible by simply reversing the sequence of the second and third clauses and translating the verb as passive (*is placed*). The tongue can stain, defile, or render a person unclean before God.

The phrase *the cycle of nature* is peculiar. It reflects the view that life is an eternal, cyclical procession. The phrase had entered into common usage, however, and James uses it without adopting the philosophy it once conveyed. The tongue not only exposes the whole realm of evil within us; like a spark it sets on fire the whole arena of human life. Consequently, the tongue can ignite far greater EVIL than we may ever intend. The source of the tongue's iniquity is finally revealed: hell itself.

The progressive growth of evil can be charted through this tangled verse. GEHENNA, place of torment and home of demons, the inexhaustible source of iniquity, lights the fiery tongue. The tongue introduces the whole world of evil into our bodies and puts to flame the whole order of life. Paul would have introduced a list of vices; James paints a graphic picture of the most destructive fire imaginable.

Verses 7 and 8 advance James's series of hyperboles on the evils of the tongue by comparing its untamed and poisonous nature to that of wild beasts. The second point of comparison follows quickly: the tongue is *full of deadly poison*. Few things evoke fear more quickly than the sight of a scorpion or a poisonous snake. The hissing tongue is full poison (Ps 140:3; Rom 3:13). Who can still claim, "but words will never hurt me"?

Having condemned the wild, poisonous nature of the tongue, James finally gives specific examples. The tongue is fickle. James did not know the idiom "forked tongue," but it expresses the tongue's inconsistency. The tongue is used both to curse and to bless, and that *ought not to be so*. This admonition may refer to casual cursing, but James may be referring to the church's worship, and specifically to preachers who both praise God and invoke curses on others in God's name. One cannot bless God and curse those made in his image. Such speech is evidence of the double-mindedness James condemns (1:8; 4:8).

Two further metaphors follow, illustrating the incompatibility of blessing and cursing. Springs were vital to life in Palestine. Yet, in the same area one found both fresh and bitter water—but never from the same opening. Each spring was known for the water it produced. Similarly, a fig tree cannot produce olives, nor can a grapevine produce figs (cf. Matt 7:16). Verse 12 ends abruptly. The shorter text reads: *No more can salt water yield fresh*. The longer text draws the statement in line with the previous metaphors: "Thus no spring can yield both salt water and fresh water." The longer text, however, says no more than v. 11, while the shorter text maintains that one product cannot become another.

The Wisdom from Above, 3:13-18

Verses 13-17 form a unit that contrasts the evidences of wisdom from above with earthly wisdom. Verse 18 provides a transition to the sayings on conflict that follow in 4:1-12.

The unit begins with a question that invites self-examination. An imperative follows. If one has both wisdom and discernment, then let that person demonstrate spiritual maturity not in devastating arguments but in the good works that come from *gentleness born of wisdom* (v. 13). If faith results in works (2:14-26), so too true wisdom is manifested in one's conduct and manner of life. True wisdom produces humility not arrogance.

Verse 14 conveys the implication that the church is plagued by bitter jealousy and ambition. These may be especially evident in its teachers and would-be leaders. James echoes words of Jesus again at this point: these sins come from the heart (cf. Matt 15:19). The admonitions that follow may stand in coordinate relationship to one another ("do not boast about it or deny the truth," NIV) or causal relationship ("do not be arrogant and so lie against the truth," NASB).

Verse 15 explains why boasting is excluded. Ambition and arrogance are the fruit of a kind of wisdom, but not the true wisdom that comes down *from above*. True wisdom is one of God's good and perfect gifts (1:17). Nevertheless, the wisdom of the arrogant and ambitious who create dissension in the church is indeed inspired: it is inspired by the devil. The three adjectives form a crescendo of sinful alienation from God. Such wisdom is *earthly, unspiritual, and devilish* (v. 15).

Verse 16 pushes the argument one step further: if counterfeit wisdom is exposed by jealousy and selfish ambition, these in turn give rise to disorder and every kind of evil. True wisdom bears seven identifying marks (v. 17):

1. *Pure*. Like the works of God, the life of his people should be morally perfect and undefiled.

2. Ready for peace (*peaceable*). The wisdom from above is therefore diametrically opposed to the divisiveness of the earthly, sensual, and demonic inspiration of the arrogant and ambitious.

3. *Gentle* or "considerate" (NEB, NIV). In a position of strength, the wise person is considerate of those who might otherwise be dominated or manipulated.

4. Compliant (*willing to yield*). In a position of weakness, the wise one is reasonable, yielding, and obedient.

5. *Full of mercy and good fruit*. True wisdom results in the true religion (acts of mercy, 1:27) and true faith (acts of charity, 2:15-17).

6. *Without a trace of partiality* or "unwavering" (NASB). The sense is either that true wisdom does not "make a distinction" or that it is not fickle and inconsistent—like the tongue that both blesses and curses (vv. 9-12).

7. Sincere. Having nothing to hide, wisdom is *without . . . hypocrisy*, genuine. It can be taken at face value.

The aphorism in v. 18 closes this section on the contrasting effects of the two wisdoms. Its interpretation hinges on two issues: (1) is *the harvest of righteousness* (a) an appositional genitive (in which case the fruit is righteousness) or (b) a subjective genitive (in which case righteousness produces its own fruit); and (2) is the fruit *sown in peace* (a) *by* or (b) *for* those who make peace? The similarity to the blessing of the peacemakers (Matt 5:9) is unmistakable. Peace and righteousness are mutually dependent; each requires the other. The mark of true wisdom is, therefore, its capacity to produce peace and righteousness. Peacemaking and jealousy are antithetical; one creates unity, the other division.

The Obedience of Faith in Community, 4:1–5:6

As with most of James, the section that follows is composed of loosely related instructions for ethical living. Various divisions of the chapters have been proposed. Here Jas 4:1–5:6 is viewed as a series of exhortations on living faithfully in community. Three of the chief dangers to the communities of faith are dissension (4:1-12), presumption (5:1-6), and inappropriate use of wealth (5:1-6).

Faith as a Response to Dissension, 4:1-12

This section is an extension of the previous one in that it exposes the consequences of earthly wisdom: the quarrels that destroy (vv. 1-3), the world that corrupts (vv. 4-6), the humility that restores (vv. 7-10), and the judgment on those who judge (vv. 11-12).

The first verse raises two questions. The first diagnoses the situation; the second challenges the readers to accept James's diagnosis of the cause of quarreling and infighting. The wars and fightings are generally understood as metaphorical references to quarrels and factions within the community. The second question suggests that the quarrels are caused by "pleasures" that war in your members. The thought that our pleasures are the cause of fighting among members of the Christian community places pride, ambition, and vanity in their true context.

The charge *you . . . murder* seems so harsh as a charge concerning the church that Erasmus (1519 ed. of Greek NT) proposed that the text was corrupt and that "you envy" (*phthoneite*) should be read instead of "you murder" (*phoneuete*). This conjecture was accepted by Calvin and the KJV, but is now generally rejected. There is no manuscript support for the conjecture. On the other hand, murder is often connected metaphorically with sins of the tongue.

The tragedy is that by fighting we do not obtain what we desire. On the other hand, we have only to ask God for what we need. God is the giver of every good and perfect gift (1:17). Again, we ask but we do not receive because we do not ask rightly. James does not say that we are asking for sinful things, but we are asking sinfully. We are not praying for forgiveness or righteousness, but to further our own interests. We may ask for good things for the wrong reasons. This does not mean, of course, that all unanswered prayer is due to praying wrongly.

Using a term that evokes echoes of Hosea's condemnation of Israel, James charges that such Christians are adulterers and adulteresses (v. 4). *World* is used here in the hostile sense found in the Johannine literature (1 John 2:15-17). God and the world are set in opposition to one another, so that friendship with one means hostility toward the other (Matt 6:24; Luke 16:13). The desire for pleasure divides and distorts our entire existence. This forced choice means that neutrality toward God is impossible.

Verse 5 announces a quotation from scripture, but the remainder of v. 5 cannot be found anywhere in the OT. Psalms 41:2 and 83:3 come as close as any reference, but James may paraphrase material such as Gen 6:3 or Exod 20:5. The first part of v. 6 promises that God does not readily give us up. Instead, he gives more grace. God helps wavering Christians!

There are ten imperatives in vv. 7-10. Together they provide an expanded definition of repentance.

1. *Submit . . . to God.* The imperatives that follow explain this first, basic demand. It is a military term meaning to put oneself under the command of a superior.

2. *Resist the devil.* The second command is the counterpart to the first. The first requires the second. Again, James uses a military metaphor: to stand against.

3. *Draw near to God.* This is a cultic term for worshiping God.

4. *Cleanse your hands.* This is the language of ceremonial cleansing (Exod 30:19-21; 2 Cor 7:1).

5. *Purify your hearts.* Again, ceremonial language. To cleanse one's heart means to cleanse one's entire inner being (cf. Ps 24:4).

6. *Lament* (lit. "be wretched"). True repentance is accompanied by remorse.

7. *Mourn.*

8. *Weep* (Luke 6:25; Mark 14:72).

9. *Let your laughter be turned to mourning and your joy to dejection.*

10. *Humble yourselves.* Any other road to exaltation is the result of sinfulness.

True repentance, however, does not lack for results. Three promises follow the ten imperatives: (1) the devil *will flee from you*; (2) *God will draw near to you*; and (3) God *will exalt you.*

Verses 11-12 form a conclusion to Jas 3:1–4:12 in that they return to the sins of speech and dissension within the community. Verse 11 begins with the only imperative in these two verses. The command is not to disparage or belittle one another. The present tense implies that such disparagement is currently taking place. The issue is not whether what is being said is true or not. James leaves no room for those who would justify their damaging words by saying, "Well, I am just telling the truth." The rest of vv. 11-12 gives a theological justification for this command: (1) The one who disparages or judges a brother disparages or judges the law: "inasmuch as ye have done it unto the least of these my brethren ye have done it unto God's law" (cf. Matt 25:40).

The command not to slander appears both in the OT (Lev 19:16) and in the NT (Rom 1:30; 2 Cor 12:20). (2) Breaking the law highhandedly implies that we are not bound by the law. (3) If we place ourselves above the law, as judges, we have usurped God's prerogative. We have taken God's place as the lawgiver. Are we able to give a better law or a more righteous judgment? God is the only one who is able to save and to destroy. Breaking the law by disparaging others is therefore a disparagement of God. It is blasphemy. The conclusion of v. 12 puts us in our place again: *So who, then, are you to judge your neighbor?*

Faith as a Response to Presumption, 4:13-17

This section turns again to the rich and the results of love of the world. James has in mind here the merchants in particular, the small businessmen who worked ambitiously and industriously, traveling to whatever place held the prospect of profit. James does not condemn their business dealings as dishonest. What he condemns is the presumptuous disregard of God's sovereignty as they make their plans. The businessmen are merely an illustration of the attitude that ignores God in our daily affairs. Their plans assume that they are in full control of their lives. First, they do not know the future. Second, their lives are mortal and transitory.

James is not saying that it is wrong to make plans, only that we ought to live our lives under God's sovereignty.

The saying "If the Lord wills" (RSV) is common in hellenistic writings. It may express either genuine or superficial piety. James, therefore, may intend a bit of irony. If the pagans at least say, "If God wills," then should not Christians recognize their finiteness and place the planning of their lives under God's sovereignty? By placing our lives under God's will we also have a sure defense against dread, despair, and fear of the future. In contrast, those who worship God on Sunday and live in complete disregard of God's sovereignty the rest of the week show an attitude of sinful arrogance.

Verse 17 is a maxim or proverb, such as James quotes in 2:13 or 3:18. If we know what is good and do not do it, we sin. The word order emphasizes that such compromise is nothing less than sin. Sin is not related just to certain absolutes, therefore, but also to the level of our spiritual maturity and discernment.

A Warning to the Rich, 5:1-6

With this paragraph James shifts both his target and his tone. He offers a sharp, prophetic warning to the rich landowners who oppress the poor. These are apparently not members of the community because he never calls them brothers (as in 5:7-11). He does not call them to repent; he laments the judgment on them. His primary concern, however, is to dissuade Christians from falling into envy towards the power and privilege of the wealthy.

The call to weep and howl (RSV) depicts a scene of utter despair and misery. The present participle vividly describes the scene as already occurring. In vv. 2-3 James describes the effects of the judgment upon the wealth of the rich. Perfect tense verbs are used, as though the judgment had already been accomplished.

1. Their wealth is ruined, decayed, *rotted.* We may have a list of three types of wealth: foodstuffs, garments, and metals.

2. Their garments are *moth-eaten.*

3. Their *gold and silver have rusted.* These metals, of course, cannot rust. So James is either thinking of the coins of the time that had so much alloy that they did rust, or else he is describing the corruption of riches by a power greater than rust.

Moreover, the rich will be condemned by their wealth. The rust will bear witness against them that they did not use their wealth responsibly. The rust that eats at the metals in an awful turn of events will eat at their flesh. The final irony of this verse is that they have been storing up treasure *in the last days*. While they should have been preparing for the Lord's coming by righteous living, they have hoarded their goods and oppressed the poor. The goods they hoarded now condemn them (Matt 6:19-21; Luke 12:15-21; 16:19-31).

Verse 4 describes the charges against landowners. The charges, though, are brought by the wages they have wrongfully held back from those who labored in their fields. Jewish law required that laborers be paid at the end of each day, since some depended on the day's wage for food. The harvest, of course, was a time of great income for the landowner, but he defrauds the poor who work his fields. These cries rise to the Lord, the Lord of Hosts! (cf. Isa. 5:7-9). The wealth of the rich has been gained at the expense of the poor.

The rich have lived a life of ease and pleasure, supported by the suffering and oppression of others. They have fattened their hearts (cholesterol!) like fatted calves that continue eating even on the day of their slaughter. Now the day of the Lord has come, and they themselves are the fatted calves. Yet they live in complete disregard for the imminence of the Judgment.

Verse 6 states the third and most serious offense. These landowners have condemned and killed the righteous. They have killed the righteous sufferer, perhaps by means of judicial proceedings. Some see it as an allusion to the crucifixion of Jesus or the martyrdom of James the Just. Neither is really called for, however. "The righteous" is probably a collective term (NIV).

The Obedience of Faith in Patience, Oaths, and Prayer, 5:7-18

The remaining verses of the letter can be divided into four sections: a call for patience (vv. 7-11), rejection of profanity (v. 12), the power of prayer (vv. 13-18), and restoring the wayward (5:19-20). The main themes of the letter are found in this closing section: rich—poor, the need to control speech, concern for harmony within the community, and the need for endurance.

A Call for Patience, 5:7-11

The word for patience means literally to have a long temper, or we might say "a long fuse." James turns from condemnation of the rich in 5:1-6 to concern for the community. Although the poor may be abused by the rich, James calls on Christians to be patient. Some have understood *the coming of the Lord* as a reference to God's coming in judgment, as in the OT prophets, but most interpreters are convinced it is a reference to the PAROUSIA of the risen Lord.

James draws an illustration from the life of the small farmer. The farmer awaits the "precious fruit from the earth" (RSV). His livelihood depends on the harvest. He plants his carefully saved seed, hopes, waits, and stretches his resources and rations—everything depends on the harvest. *The early and late rains* are characteristic of the climate of the east end of the Mediterranean. The early rains came in October and November, the late rains in April and May. Without the early rains the crops would not survive; without the late rains the harvest would be small.

Verse 8 draws the conclusion: "So you be patient also." The best response to impatience is new resolve. The basis for such resolve is offered by the promise that the coming of the Lord is "at hand" (RSV).

Discouragement and impatience can easily lead to grumbling, and grumbling to disunity. James therefore warns the Christians not to "moan" about one another. Even if some complaining about the rich might be tolerated (vv. 1-6), the Christians should not turn their impatience against one another. Both hope and judgment are expressed by the rest of v. 9. Don't complain about one another lest you be judged also. The judge is standing at the doors even now (Mark 13:29; Rev 3:20). He is coming to judge both the rich and the poor. Wait on his judgment and do not incur condemnation at the last minute by sowing dissension within the community of believers.

Christians are not in a unique situation just because they have suffered. The prophets suffered too. The Christians will do well to take the prophets as an example of suffering and patience. They too spoke in the name of the Lord. Verse 11 turns to a specific example of patience: Job. Actually JOB does not seem all that patient in the OT book, so James may be referring to contemporary tradition regarding Job. This is the only reference to Job in the NT, and James speaks of Job's endurance or steadfastness rather than his patience. The main point is that Job remained faithful in spite of his suffering. The issue is whether we will endure and not lose faith.

The Lord is full of compassion and mercies. The one who is patient and endures trial faithfully will see the good that the Lord is doing.

Rejection of Oaths, 5:12

This verse appears with little context. It may be that James has in mind again the dangers of the tongue and the ways it disrupts community. Harold Songer (1972, 136) finds the sequence of admonitions meaningful: "Suffering Christians (vv. 7-11) must guard their speech and not grumble (v. 9) or swear (v. 12) . . . but pray (vv. 13-18) and confess their sins (v. 16)."

This verse is closely paralleled by Matt 5:33-37 (cf. Matt 23:16-22). James's concern is not oaths sworn in court but the practice of using oaths in everyday discourse. This practice had developed to the point that some oaths were binding, while other, similar formulas were not. One could give the appearance of swearing a sacred oath, therefore, but actually use a defective form with no intention of being bound by it. Jesus and James both condemn such hypocrisy. If this is the central concern, then James is saying that Christians should always speak in such a way that no one would ever doubt our word. Oaths would then no longer be needed.

The Power of Prayer, 5:13-18

Following the warning against swearing in the previous verse, James turns to the positive admonition to be diligent in prayer. The section opens with three questions: Is anyone *among you suffering*? Is *any cheerful*? Is *any among you sick*? The answers give his response: Let him *pray*. Let him *sing praise*. Let him call for the *elders of the church*. Prayer is not just an aid in time of distress; it is the appropriate response to every circumstance in life.

The first question seems not to have illness in view but rather distress, misfortune, or calamity. In the NT the term for singing is used of singing praises to God in public worship (1 Cor 14:15; Eph 5:19). Don't forget God in the good times.

Is any sick? The term can denote any illness or weakness, here apparently a serious illness. *The elders of the church* were probably the senior, respected men of the community. Prayer is primary. The anointing with OIL is mentioned in a participle. There is no instruction to consecrate the oil. It is the common term for olive oil, which was at times used medicinally (Mark 6:13; Luke 10:34). Here it is an external sign of the inward power of prayer. James is apparently describing a common practice of the church rather than prescribing a new procedure. James does not prescribe this procedure for every illness, nor does he assure that we will always be cured or spared from death. Obviously that is not the case. Instead, James is describing a procedure by which one in need is upheld by the church and God's mercy and healing power is invoked.

The last part of v. 15 forms a transition to James's closing emphasis—rooting sin out of our lives. Sin and sickness were closely connected in popular thought. James does not contend that sickness is always the result of sin, but he allows that it may be. Prayer can deal with both sickness and sin. In times of need we are to pray for God's care and deliverance.

James exhorts Christians to confess their sins to one another. He does not say the sick person is to confess his or her sins to the elders. He seems to have in mind open, public confessions of specific sins in the context of worship and prayer for one another. Apart from confession we cannot experience forgiveness. Excesses are to be avoided, of course. In some instances specific, public confession would not lead to restoration or harmony.

The latter part of v. 16 states the theme of the whole section. The entreaty or petition *of the righteous [person] is powerful and effective.* The prayer of ordinary persons has great power when God makes it effective. James is not just talking about the prayer of saints. He illustrates the power of prayer by appealing to the example of ELIJAH. The period of three and a half years is based on a rabbinic estimate of the time of the drought based on 1 Kgs 18:1. Elijah is the fourth OT character James has used, following Abraham (2:21-24); Rahab (2:25); Job (5:11). James takes pains to say that Elijah was human and subject to the same suffering the rest of us endure. Legend emphasized the effectiveness of Elijah's prayer. James argued that it wasn't Elijah; it was the power of prayer at work.

Concluding Exhortation: Restoring the Wayward, 5:19-20

A Christian's responsibility for sinners does not stop with prayer. James closes the letter by calling on us to take responsibility for erring Christians. To wander *from the truth* means to turn aside from God's will and live in moral corruption. James is not talking about converting an unbeliever but restoring an erring brother or sister. He does not specify how this restoration takes place. Death is the final result of sin. If we minimize the gravity of the erring one's position, we also minimize the significance of restoration.

One who restores another also covers a multitude of sins. The term to *cover* comes from the OT and means to secure their forgiveness (Ps 32:1; 85:2). Some commentators take this to mean that the agent of restoration has secured forgiveness for his or her own sins, but the idea that meritorious works bring forgiveness cuts against the NT emphasis that sin is forgiven by grace.

This last admonition, to be active in turning others from sin, captures the purpose of the letter. So, with no closing greetings, it ends abruptly, leaving us to consider its claim upon our lives.

Works Cited

Davids, P. H. 1982. *The Epistle of James: A Commentary on the Greek Text.* NIGTC.

Hiebert, D. Edmond. 1979. *The Epistle of James: Tests of a Living Faith.*

Luther's Works. Ed. Theodore G. Tapert. 1955–1958.

Songer, Harold S. 1972. "James." *BBC*.

First Peter

J. Ramsey Michaels [MCB 1295-1304]

Introduction

First Peter is one of two NT letters bearing the name of the apostle PETER. Nothing in the letter itself identifies it explicitly as the "first" of the two. In the NT it is given the title "First Peter" or "the First Epistle of Peter" because of 2 Pet 3:1, where that work refers to itself as "this second letter," and perhaps also because in "Second Peter" the apostle is represented as expecting his own death very soon (2 Pet 1:14). First Peter presents itself not as the beginning of an ongoing correspondence, but as a once-for-all directive from the apostle to a large number of Christian congregations spread over five Roman provinces of Asia Minor (1:1).

Authorship and Genre

The authorship of 1 Peter is disputed because its elegant Greek style is believed to be inconsistent with the tradition that Simon Peter was an uneducated Galilean (Acts 4:13). Defenders of Petrine authorship, such as E. G. Selwyn and Peter Davids, have resorted to the theory that Peter's coworker *Silvanus* (5:12) was responsible for putting some of Peter's ideas into good Greek style. This in effect makes Silvanus the real author of the letter. More likely, Silvanus (or Silas) was simply the messenger who delivered the letter to its Asian destination, just as he helped deliver the decree of the JERUSALEM COUNCIL to ANTIOCH according to Acts 15:22-32.

A better theory is that 1 Peter was a semiofficial communication from the church at ROME. Like *1 Clement* at the end of the first century CE, 1 Peter claims to be written from a congregation in *Babylon* (5:13), which by the latter half of the century had become a designation for the city of Rome (cf. Rev 17:4-5, 18). If Peter was the Roman congregation's resident apostle at the time, it is not surprising that a circular letter from Rome to Christians scattered throughout the Asian provinces might have been written under his supervision and authority. If so, the letter's style can be attributed to an anonymous learned scribe without resorting to theories about Silvanus.

The appropriateness of a circular letter from *Babylon* (5:13) to the Diaspora, or *Dispersion* (1:1) is unmistakable, for Babylon was the city that had first scattered the Jews from their homeland in 587/6 BCE. Peter is drawing an analogy between the Jewish community scattered throughout the world and the worldwide Christian community of his day (5:9). The church at Rome is telling its sister churches in the provinces that they all share a common lot as *aliens and exiles* in the ROMAN EMPIRE (1:1; 2:11), and that they must know how to respond to slander, hostile questioning, and even persecution, whether from the populace or the imperial authorities.

Another major objection to the traditional view that Peter wrote 1 Peter is the assumption, itself based on tradition, that the apostle Peter died in the persecution under Nero in 64 CE, a decade before Jews and Christians began referring to Rome as "Babylon." The traditions about Peter's death are relatively late, and the later they are the more detailed and specific they become (as, e.g., in *ActPet* 30-41). John 21:18-19 may or may not suggest that Peter was martyred, but in any case gives no information as to when or under what circumstances. The same is true of the reference to his death in 2 Pet 1:14. What is usually considered the earliest explicit reference to Peter's martyrdom merely states that Peter "suffered not one or two, but many trials, and having thus given testimony went to the glorious place which was his due" (*1 Clem* 5.4).

Although there is no consensus on the authorship of 1 Peter, the letter is well known and well attested in the ancient church (POLYCARP, PAPIAS, IRENAEUS, Tertullian, Clement, and Origen; see Michaels 1988, xxxi– xxxiv). The burden of proof still rests with those who want to assign it to someone other than Peter.

Integrity

Many questions have been raised in the past about the integrity of 1 Peter. The apparent sharp break between 4:11 and 4:12 has suggested to some that a letter consisting of 1:1–4:11 dealt with persecution as a rather remote possibility, and that 4:12–5:11 was added as a postscript when the persecution suddenly broke out. Alternatively, some have argued that 1:3–4:11 was not a letter at all but a baptismal sermon, or even a baptismal liturgy, later framed into a letter by the addition of 1:1-2 and 4:12–5:14.

In keeping with more recent literary approaches to the NT, the tendency in the past two or three decades has been rather to interpret 1 Peter as a literary unit, and in most instances as an actual letter. Although there has been continued recognition of rhetorical forms in 1 Peter such as "household duty codes" (2:18– 3:7), and even of possible hymnic or creedal fragments (e.g., 1:18-21; 2:21-25; 3:18-22), these are now generally discussed under the heading of Peter's "sources" (along with the OT and the sayings of Jesus), not as generic features which somehow call into question the work's integrity or its identity as a real letter.

For Further Study

In the *Mercer Dictionary of the Bible*: ESCHATOLOGY IN THE NT; ETHICS IN THE NEW TESTAMENT; GENERAL LETTERS; PERSECUTION IN THE NT; PETER; PETER, LETTERS OF; ROME; SUFFERING IN THE NT.

In other sources: D. L. Bartlett, "The First Letter of Peter," *NIB*; W. J. Dalton, *Christ's Proclamation to the Spirits: A Study of 1 Pet 3:18–4:6*; P. H. Davids, *The First Epistle of Peter*, NICNT; J. N. D. Kelly, *A Commentary on the Epistles of Peter and of Jude*, HNTC; J. R. Michaels, *1 Peter*, WBC, and *Word Biblical Themes: 1 Peter*; E. G. Selwyn, *The First Epistle of St. Peter*; C. H. Talbert, ed., *Perspectives on First Peter*, NABPR/SSS 9.

Commentary

An Outline

I. Greetings, 1:1-2
II. The Identity of the People of God, 1:3–2:10
  A. The Great Salvation, 1:3-12
  B. The New Way of Life, 1:13-25
  C. The Chosen Community, 2:1-10
III. The Responsibilities of the People of God, 2:11–4:11
  A. Respect for Everyone, 2:11-17
  B. Slaves and Masters, 2:18-25
  C. Wives and Husbands, 3:1-7
  D. Seeking Peace, 3:8-12
  E. The Hope of Vindication, 3:13–4:6
  F. Christian Community, 4:7-11
IV. The Responsibilities of Elders, 4:12–5:11
  A. The Fiery Ordeal, 4:12-19
  B. Elders and Their Congregations, 5:1-11
V. Conclusion, 5:12-14

Greetings, 1:1-2

Peter, like PAUL, identifies himself as *apostle of Jesus Christ*, but writes to a far larger audience than Paul. While Paul wrote only to individual congregations, or (in one instance) "the churches of Galatia" (Gal 1:2), Peter's audience encompasses five Roman provinces roughly equivalent to present-day Turkey. He addresses his readers as Christian believers chosen by the God of Israel and thereby alienated from the religion and culture of the ROMAN EMPIRE. Like the Jews, they are a Diaspora (cf. Jas 1:1), a chosen people scattered throughout the empire. Peter attributes their conversion to God's foreknowledge and the purifying work of the HOLY SPIRIT. Like the Jews in Moses' time who promised to obey God as the blood of sacrificial animals was sprinkled over them (Exod 24:3-8), these Christians have obediently accepted the blood of Jesus Christ poured out for them. Peter wishes them abundant *grace and peace*.

The Identity of the People of God, 1:3–2:10

The Great Salvation, 1:3-12

A long introductory "blessing" embraces the present experience and future hope of Christians, setting both against the background of biblical (and extrabiblical) prophecies out of the Jewish past. The whole section is loosely held together by relative pronouns (e.g., vv. 6, 8, 10, 12), as Peter moves back and forth between praise of God and the instruction of his readers.

1:3-9. Salvation as revelation and joy. Peter praises God for the power evident in raising Jesus Christ from the dead, and for the mercy evident in giving Christians (himself included) a new birth as children of God with a sure promise of eternal salvation (v. 3). Shifting from *us* to *you*, he assures his readers that God will keep them safe through whatever persecutions they may now be facing (vv. 5-6). His knowledge of their actual circumstances in the Roman provinces seems general and rather limited, yet he is confident that whatever is happening to them now is God's way of testing their faithfulness, as gold is tested and purified *by fire* (v. 7; cf. Ps 66:10 and Wis 3:5-6). He is confident that their faith will turn out stronger than ever, bringing them *praise and glory and honor* at the time "when Jesus Christ appears" (v. 7b).

Peter's mention of the "appearing," or "revealing," of Jesus in v. 7b reinforces and personalizes his reference to *salvation ready to be revealed in the last time* (v. 5b; cf. 1:13; 4:13; 5:4). "Salvation" *is* JESUS, now invisible, but soon to become visible in power and splendor. To be saved is to see him when he appears, and know the joy of his presence (vv. 6, 8). Until then, one must love him and trust in him sight unseen (v. 8). *Indescribable and glorious joy* (v. 8; cf. 4:13b) is still future, reserved in HEAVEN for all who love Jesus even though he is now hidden from human view (cf. 1 Cor 2:9; 2 Tim 4:8).

1:10-12. Salvation's witnesses. Salvation to Peter is the "end," or goal, of Christian faith (v. 9), not its beginning, but he reminds his readers that this future salvation and the sufferings that made it possible were prophesied long ago (v. 10). By mentioning both *prophets* (v. 10) and *angels* (v. 12b), Peter places his audience at the end of time, and at the center of the universe. The ancient Jewish prophets were already Christians in that the *spirit of Christ* (v. 11) was speaking through them about the *sufferings* intended for Christ (i.e., his death on the cross), and the "glorious events" to follow: his resurrection from the dead, his journey to heaven (cf. 3:19, 22), and his final "appearing" again on earth. Not even the prophets understood when or how this would all take place. They tried to find out, but God told them it was not for them or for their time. Instead, Peter claims, it is for our benefit today (cf. Matt 13:17 = Luke 10:24). The Holy Spirit sent from heaven has made the good news known through missionaries in Asia Minor, and even God's angels long to look down from heaven on the wonders of human salvation (v. 12b).

The New Way of Life, 1:13-25

1:13-21. Hope and holiness. *Therefore* in v. 13 introduces a call to action on the basis of the salvation just described. Yet Peter cannot stop celebrating the salvation itself. The section begins, like the preceding one, with *hope* (v. 13; cf. 1:3), and ends on the same note (v. 21). Peter keeps weaving into his call to action reminders of what God has done and will do for Christian believers (compare such phrases as *the grace that Jesus Christ will bring you when he is revealed*, v. 13; the holy one *who called you*, v. 15; and all of vv. 18-21). Consequently, the call to action is general, not specific. The imperatives of hope (v. 13) and godly fear (v.

17) have more to do with attitudes of mind than with behavior, and are directed not toward other people but toward God. Only the command to *be holy* (vv. 15-16) focuses on day-by-day Christian living. To be holy as God is holy (cf. Lev 19:2, which Peter cites) was traditionally understood as a religious or cultic goal, but Peter identifies holiness here as something expressed in *conduct* (v. 15). "Holy conduct" for Peter is something that runs counter to the values of Roman society (i.e., *the futile ways inherited from your ancestors* [v. 18]), but only in later sections of his letter (e.g., in 2:11–3:12), will he define it more concretely.

In vv. 18-21 Peter resumes his celebration of God's saving work through Jesus Christ. He describes Christian salvation here as "redemption" (*ransom*) or release from slavery by the payment of a price. The price is not *silver or gold* (cf. Isa 52:3), but something far more precious—the blood of Christ understood as a ransom (cf. Mark 10:45; Titus 2:14). Drawing on the Exodus story (e.g., Exod 12:1-7), Peter compares the blood of Christ to *that of a lamb without defect or blemish* (v. 19; cf. Exod 12:5), and places Christ's death in the context of God's eternal plan, from *before the foundation of the world* to *the end of the ages* (v. 20). By the shedding of Christ's blood (cf. v. 2) and his *resurrection . . . from the dead* (cf. v. 3), the readers of this letter have become for the first time "believers in God" (v. 21)—the God of Israel—and sharers in Israel's redemption. The implication is clear that these Christian readers are gentiles by birth and not Jews.

1:22-25. Undying love. Peter now brings his argument to a focus in a single ethical command: *love one another deeply from the heart* (v. 22b). The love command proper is framed by references to purification through OBEDIENCE (v. 22a; cf. vv. 2, 18-19), and spiritual rebirth (v. 23; cf. v. 3). The key word is *deeply* or "constantly" (cf. 4:8). Love among Christians should be as strong and as lasting as their faith *tested in the fire* (cf. v. 7). Theirs is an undying love because they have been reborn by the planting of *imperishable seed*—that is, by the preaching of the Christian gospel understood as *the living and enduring word of God* (vv. 23-25). Peter drives home his point with a citation of Isa 40:6b, 8: all humanity fades away like the grass and the flowers, but *the word of the Lord endures forever.* To Peter the word of the eternal God, the message spoken by Jesus the Lord (cf. Mark 13:31), and the good news about Jesus announced by his followers (cf. v. 12) all amount to the same thing—an eternal Word summoning those who hear it to eternal and genuine love for each other.

The Chosen Community, 2:1-10

2:1-3. Growing toward salvation. For the time being, Peter continues on the theme of hearing the word of God, without exploring further the love command. With the image of rebirth still in mind, he compares his readers to *newborn infants* (v. 2), urging them to do what comes naturally to babies—that is, to long for the *pure, spiritual milk* consisting of *the Lord* (v. 3) and the Lord's message. This means rejecting all other spiritual food as impure: all the *malice* and *guile*, all the *insincerity, envy, and all slander* evident to Peter in Roman society (v. 1). *Milk* here is not elementary Christian instruction intended to give way later to "solid food" (as, e.g., in 1 Cor 3:2, and Heb 5:12-13). It is not teaching or instruction at all, but the very life of God given in *mercy* (1:3; 2:10b) to those who are reborn, in the same way a mother nourishes her children. "Milk from the breasts of the Lord" later became a striking metaphor in the collection of early Christian hymns known as the *Odes of Solomon* (see, e.g., *Odes* 4.10; 8.14; 14.2-3; 19.2; 35.5; 40.1, in *OTP* 2:725–71). Like babies, Christians need this *pure, spiritual milk* in order to grow. The end of the growth process is *salvation* (v. 2b)—the salvation Peter had said is now *ready to be revealed* in Christ (cf. 1:5). Here as in chap. 1, salvation is the assured and appropriate outcome of a faithful life.

2:4-10. Becoming the people of God. In vv. 4-10, Peter's metaphor shifts from that of growth to that of building under construction (cf. Eph 2:21; 4:12, 16). At the same time his attention shifts from Christians as individuals to their corporate identity as a people. As more and more of them come to Christ in the course of the Christian mission (v. 4)—by "tasting" Christ's mercy (2:3)—they are being built into a kind of temple (*a spiritual house, to be a holy priesthood*, v. 5).

From Isa 28:16, a text Peter assumes is referring to Christ as *a stone, a cornerstone chosen and precious* (v. 6), he draws the implication that Christians too are *living stones* (v. 5) out of which God is building this new "temple." He plays on a contrast almost universal in his time between honor and shame. His text from Isaiah concludes that those who trust in the great cornerstone *will not be put to shame* (v. 6b), and Peter applies this to Christians because they have believed in Jesus (v. 7a). Theirs is the "honor," while "shame" is reserved for those who reject Jesus (vv. 4, 7b; cf. Ps 118:32). God's CORNERSTONE becomes for them *a stone that makes them stumble, and a rock that makes them fall* (cf. Isa 8:14). To this fate, Peter says, God has appointed them (v. 8b), just as surely as God has "appointed" Jesus Christ the cornerstone of faith.

Christian believers, on the other hand, are *God's people*, and the recipients of God's MERCY (v. 10). Although they are gentiles, whatever was true of the Jewish people is now true of them. They are *a chosen race, a royal priesthood, a holy nation*, and *God's own people* destined for vindication (v. 9a; cf. Exod 19:6; Isa 43:20-21). The last of these phrases refers not to the present but to the future, like Peter's references to future salvation in 1:5, 9, and 2:2. Although God has called these gentile Christians "out of darkness" (cf. 1:14, 18) to *marvelous light* (v. 9b), the *marvelous light* of salvation has not quite dawned (cf. *1 Clem* 36.2). They must still undergo suffering for a while longer (cf. 1:6-7). Living as they do between the darkness of their gentile past and the light of God's future, these Christians have the responsibility of praising the God of Israel both with their words and their lives. Like Israel itself (cf. Hos 1:6-9), they were once *not a people* and once *had not received mercy*. Now they are *God's people*, now they have *received mercy* (v. 10; cf. 1:3), and they await their inheritance.

The Responsibilities of the People of God, 2:11–4:11

The expression *Beloved, I urge you* introduces a new section in which Peter will enlarge on his readers' responsibilities to the society in which they live. This section extends all the way to 4:11 (note the repetition of *Beloved* in 4:12 and *I exhort* [lit. "I urge"] in 5:1).

Respect for Everyone, 2:11-17

Building on the designation *exiles* back in 1:1, Peter now focuses on the potential hostility between Christians and a culture where they are *aliens and exiles*. Their struggle is both inward and outward. It is first a struggle between the *soul* of Christian believers (i.e., their new life destined for salvation) and certain *desires of the flesh* within them carried over from their pagan past (v. 11), but it finds outward expression in social conflicts and tensions between Christians and their unbelieving neighbors in the Roman Empire (v. 12). Peter's main concern is with this social dimension of his readers' life in Christ. The conflict in which they find themselves is to be won not by aggressive behavior in society, but by "conducting themselves honorably" among those who ridicule or mistreat them (2:12; cf. 2:15, 20; 3:6, 11, 17).

Peter writes in the spirit of Paul, who had urged Christians in Rome not to "be overcome by EVIL, but overcome evil with good" (Rom 12:21). He also echoes Jesus in the SERMON ON THE MOUNT: "Let your light shine before others, so that they may see your good works and give glory to your Father who is in heaven" (Matt 5:16). Peter has adapted the saying—or one like it—to the social situation of Christians in the empire. Their task in such circumstances is to live in such a way that those who denounce or accuse them will come to appreciate, even worship, the God of Israel. Peter's advice is much like that of the Jewish (or Jewish-Christian) TNaph 8.4: "If you work that which is good, my children . . . God shall be glorified among the Gentiles through you, and the devil shall flee from you." The main difference is that Peter's vision—here as elsewhere—is focused on the coming day *when Jesus Christ is revealed* (cf. 1:7, 13), here understood as a day of judgment or reckoning (v. 12). His hope is that opponents of the Christian movement will see the error of their ways and turn to God, so that on that day they will "give glory to God" and share in the honor in store for those who believe (cf. 1:7, 2:7a). Yet he knows that a different outcome is also possible—not honor but shame (cf. 2:7b)—and he will look more closely at such a scenario later in his argument (cf. 3:16; 4:17-18).

"Good conduct among the gentiles" is defined in vv. 13-17 in relation to Roman imperial authority, and in vv. 18-25 and 3:1-7 in relation to the family or household. For this reason, 2:18–3:7 is commonly viewed as a "household duty code" comparable to other such codes in contemporary Greek and Roman literature (cf. Col 3:18–4:1; Eph 5:21–6:9). Peter does not distinguish sharply between responsibility to the state and responsibility within the family. Both involve a command to defer to the authority of others (vv. 13, 18; 3:1, 5). By giving this command its widest possible application in v. 13 (lit. "every human creature"), Peter makes it clear that he is not urging some kind of abstract subjection to institutional authority (as in the NRSV, *every human institution*), but voluntary deference or respect to individuals simply because God created them. It is in this context that he commands respect for the emperor and the local magistrates who represent him (compare the similar transition in 1 Tim 2:1-2 from "all people" to "kings and all who are in authority").

Unlike Paul in Rom 13, Peter makes no claim that God put the emperor in power or that imperial authority is God's authority. The emperor should be respected *for the Lord's sake*, not because he is divine but because he is human (cf. v. 17, *Honor everyone. . . . Honor the emperor*). His job is to maintain order in society by punishing wrongdoers and rewarding those who do good (v. 14). Peter is confident that the emperor will honor those who honor him, and that if Christians in the provinces "do right," they will silence even their most vocal critics (v. 15). At the same time he insists that they must have their priorities straight. He reminds them that they are "free" in Jesus Christ—not free of all obligation to the empire, but certainly free of its values (i.e., *the futile ways inherited from your ancestors*, 1:18). Because God has set them free, they are at the same time God's *servants* (v. 16). Their reverence for God and their love for each other (cf. 1:22) take precedence even over the respect they owe the emperor and *everyone* (v. 17).

Slaves and Masters, 2:18-25

Peter now shifts attention from all Christians as "servants of God" to those who were actual slaves in Roman households (οἰκέται, lit., "household servants," v. 18), but within a few verses he shifts back again to all the readers of his letter. The household serves as an appropriate context in which to introduce the sobering thought that all Christians may soon have to suffer for their faith in Roman society. Unlike Paul (Col 4:1; Eph 6:9), Peter addresses only slaves, not slaveowners, because he wants to make a point about suffering, and slaves are the ones who suffer. What counts with God is not suffering as such, or even the patient endurance of suffering, but *suffering unjustly* (v. 19) or "doing right and suffering for it" (v. 20). Endurance of suffering is a virtue only when suffering is undeserved, like the suffering of JESUS (vv. 21-23). This is the case when slaveowners are harsh or cruel (v. 18).

It is difficult to specify a point at which Peter widens the application of his words from household servants in particular to Christian believers in general. He allows the former to be stand-ins for the latter because he does not want to temper the optimism about the empire expressed in vv. 13-17. But his readers could hardly miss the point. What could happen to Christian slaves at the hands of a cruel master could happen to any Christian if the mood of the populace took an ugly turn. Christ died for all believers, not just slaves (v. 24). All of them, not just slaves, are called to follow in his footsteps (v. 21). All were *going astray like sheep*, and all have *returned to the shepherd and guardian of your souls* (v. 25).

Because he has all believers in view, Peter puts his emphasis as much on verbal as on physical abuse. Actual physical suffering was not yet widespread among Christians, but they knew what it was to be denounced, ridiculed, and accused of crimes against the social order (cf. 2:12, 15). Peter wants to make sure they do not retaliate in kind. In language drawn from Isa 53, he describes Christ's behavior at his arrest and trial, accenting the fact that "no deceit was found in his mouth" (v. 22; cf. Isa 53:9b). "Deceit" to Peter is not deception, but malice or ill will of any sort (cf. 2:1). He elaborates Isaiah's words with the observation that Christ never denounced his accusers, and never threatened them with divine vengeance, as martyrs were said to have done in the time of the MACCABEES (cf. 2 Macc 7; 4 Macc 9–10). He simply left them to God, and to the prospect of God's righteous judgment (v. 23; cf. 1:17; 4:5).

Still drawing on Isa 53, Peter takes the opportunity to insist that Christ's suffering was more than an example. Adopting the confessional "we" and "our" from Isa 53, he includes himself with his readers (for the first time since 1:3) as sharers in a common salvation. Christ on the cross took "our" sins away (cf. Isa 53:4, 12b). He did not merely atone for sins or secure forgiveness; he actually carried the sins in his body to the cross and left them there (v. 24). With "our" sins gone, "we" are free to live for what is right, even in the face of hostility and slander. Peter quickly shifts back to his customary "you" as he reflects on his gentile readers' "healing" or conversion from paganism (vv. 24b-25; cf. Isa 53:5b-6). Without mentioning Christ's resurrection explicitly, he describes the Christ of the cross as now alive from the dead, carrying out the role of SHEPHERD over his flock (for the risen Christ as shepherd, cf. Mark 14:27-28; John 10:15-17; Heb 13:20-21). Later he will explain how Christ functions as shepherd over his congregations through the ministry of elders (5:2-4).

Wives and Husbands, 3:1-7

3:1-6. Advice to wives. Just as Peter, in addressing slaves, gave special attention to those who served cruel or hostile masters (2:18), so in addressing wives he focuses on those who are married to unbelieving husbands (v. 1). His goal is that husbands might be *won over* not with words but by reverent and pure conduct (v. 2; cf. 2:12). Taking over certain stereotyped denunciations (by Jewish, Greek, and Roman teachers alike) of some women's flamboyant tastes, he adapts them to this purpose. What counts as lavish *adornment* in God's sight is not hairdo or jewelry or clothes (extravagant or otherwise), but rather *the inner self with the lasting beauty of a gentle and quiet spirit* (v. 4). Peter associates flamboyant dress with flamboyant behavior and domestic rebellion, and modest dress with modest behavior and domestic peace. He knows nothing of the Christian "Total Woman" of the 1970s, for whom big hair and excessive makeup became the badge of wifely submission!

Peter does command wives to defer to their husbands' authority, and he does so even when the husband does not *obey the word* (i.e., not a Christian believer, v. 1). But a woman does not carry out this command by denying or concealing who she really is. Her obligation to defer to an unbelieving husband does not extend to adopting his religion—as Roman society expected—for the *conduct* to which she is called includes reverent fear toward her God (v. 2). Her role models are the *holy women* of Israel's past (probably SARAH, REBEKAH, RACHEL, and LEAH) who *hoped in God* (v. 5), and in particular Sarah, who once called Abraham *lord* (v. 6)—even though she laughed when she said it (Gen 18:12)!

Peter is probably aware not only of the irony of Sarah's laughter, but of the deeper irony of using Sarah and the *holy women* as examples in the first place. The women he is addressing here are not married to godly patriarchs like ABRAHAM, ISAAC, and JACOB, or anyone like them. They would have found it truly laughable to call their unbelieving husbands "lord" as they called Jesus "Lord," or "obey" them as they "obeyed" God (cf. the accent on "obedience" in 1:2, 14, 22). Yet by faith they are "Sarah's children." Peter's argument is from the greater to the lesser: if Sarah called Abraham "lord" (even in her laughter), Sarah's children should at least show deference and respect to their less than ideal marriage partners. The real social setting in which these wives lived emerges in Peter's final words of advice: *do what is good, and never let fears alarm you.* The appropriate submission of a wife to her husband is defined by "doing good" (i.e., doing the will of God, cf. 2:15), not the other way around. This means there is always a possibility that the unbelieving husband might not be *won over* by the *purity and reverence* of her life, or even be willing to tolerate her alien religion—hence the comforting but ominous last command to the wives, *never let fears alarm you* (v. 6b; cf. Prov 3:25).

3:7. Advice to husbands. Peter has a few words for husbands as well. If a wife must accept her husband's authority, the husband has a corresponding obligation to *show consideration* and *honor* to his wife—first, because she is physically *weaker* than he, and second, because a Christian husband and wife are together *heirs of the gracious gift of life*. Because society's expectation was that a wife would adopt her husband's religion, the likelihood was that the wife of a Christian husband had become a Christian too. If so, husband and wife are partners in faith and prayer—a kind of church in miniature. If not, the Christian husband must understand and honor his wife simply as God's creature (cf. 2:13, 17a), and as someone weaker than he, knowing that God values weakness above strength (cf. 5:5-6; 1 Cor 1:26-29; 12:22-24).

Seeking Peace, 3:8-12

Peter now generalizes from the advice just given about specific relationships in 2:18–3:7. He urges his readers to show kindness in all their dealings with each other (v. 8), and to seek peace even toward those who do not share their faith, but who ridicule and insult them (v. 9). In particular, he urges them not to trade insults with their oppressors, but always to speak words of kindness and blessing (vv. 9-10; cf.

the appeal to Christ's example in 2:22-23). Drawing on words from Ps 34:12-16, Peter concludes that God will reward such an attitude on the part of his people and punish those who oppress them (vv. 10-12). Like the married couples in the preceding paragraph, they will find that God answers their prayers (v. 12).

The Hope of Vindication, 3:13–4:6

3:13-17. Encouragement "just in case." On the basis of the psalm just quoted, Peter urges his readers to maintain integrity before Christ their Lord in situations where they might have to face opposition and hostile questioning, whether from fellow citizens or the ruling authorities (vv. 14b-15). His confidence in such cases is that those who denounce them will be *put to shame* (v. 16), probably on the day of reckoning (cf. 2:12) when God comes to judge the world (cf. 3:12). Like those "persecuted for righteousness' sake" in the SERMON ON THE MOUNT (cf. Matt 5:10), faithful Christians are *blessed* (v. 14a), for their lot will be infinitely *better* on the day of judgment than that of their oppressors (v. 17).

3:18-22. The victory Christ won. Peter again introduces Jesus Christ as his example, picking up where 2:21-25 left off. There he had spoken of Christ's behavior in his PASSION (2:23), of his actual death (2:24), and (implicitly) of his resurrection (2:25). Now, illustrating the notion of suffering for "doing good" (3:17), Peter refers to Christ's death, RESURRECTION (vv. 18b, 21b), and journey to heaven (vv. 19, 22)—all the "glorious events" the prophets had only partially understood (cf. 1:11). Possibly he and his readers were familiar with a three-part confession of faith about Jesus Christ *put to death in the flesh / made alive in the Spirit / gone into heaven*—a symmetrical expression consisting of three participles in Greek, each with the same ending (-θεις).

The third of these participles (πορευθείς, *gone* in the phrase, *gone into heaven*, in v. 22) is anticipated already in v. 19 with the claim that Jesus *went* (πορευθείς) *and made a proclamation to the spirits . . . who in former times did not obey, when God waited patiently in the days of Noah* (vv. 19-20a). This suggests that throughout vv. 19-22 Peter is elaborating the third element in the three-part confession—Christ's journey to heaven. Building on Jesus' analogy between *the days of Noah* and the present (Matt 24:37 = Luke 17:26), Peter links the evil or unclean spirits Jesus faced in his ministry of exorcism with the state of the world just before the flood. He focuses especially on the illicit union described in Gen 6:1-4 between "sons of God" (usually understood as evil angels) and women on earth. According to some Jewish traditions, this union produced "giants" who would "be called evil spirits upon the earth" (*1 Enoch* 15.8). Peter's point is that the victory over demons which began in Jesus' earthly ministry was completed after his resurrection, in the course of his journey to heaven. This victory established Jesus' lordship over all *angels, authorities, and powers* (v. 22)—even those that are hostile—and so reinforces Peter's assurances to his readers (vv. 13-17) that they have nothing to fear from those who question or denounce their Christian way of life.

One difficulty with the passage is the apparent statement that the disobedient spirits were *in prison* (Gk. ἐν φυλακῇ, v. 19b). If they were in prison, what did Christ announce to them? Their release? This would not have been good news! Their salvation? Nothing here or in any other NT text suggests that evil spirits will be saved. Their subjection to him? If they are already in prison, what would further subjection mean? For these reasons, it is possible that ἐν φυλακῇ should be understood as "in refuge" or "in hiding," rather than *in prison*. According to *1 Enoch* evil angels are said to be chained or imprisoned (cf. also 2 Pet 2:4; Jude 6), but not evil spirits, and the word φυλακή is not used. In Revelation, the only other NT use of φυλακή in connection with evil spirits, Babylon is doomed to be "a haunt of every foul spirit" (Rev 18:2). Such a translation suggests that Peter viewed the "disobedient spirits" as free and very active in the world until Jesus tamed them by his resurrection (vv. 18b, 21b) and journey to heaven (vv. 19, 22). At that point their safe havens (whether on earth, under the earth, or in the air) were no longer safe from his universal lordship, and in the course of his journey he invaded their haunts and announced their subjection.

Within his reflection on Christ's journey, Peter extends the analogy between Noah's day and his own by comparing the waters of the flood to Christian BAPTISM (vv. 20-21). Like NOAH and *a few* others then, Christians are *saved through water* now, not in the sense of being washed clean from their sins, but because they have already been purified through Christ's death and resurrection (cf. 1:2, 22; see also Josephus's explanation of John's baptism, *Ant* 18.117).

4:1-6. Sharing in victory over sin and death. The triumphant tone of 3:22 is at once muted by a reminder that no one can share in Christ's resurrection and victorious journey without first preparing for the same kind of suffering he experienced (cf. 2:21-25). Christ is the one who *has finished with sin* (v. 1b) in that he did away with it *once for all* (3:18a) by his death on the cross (cf. 2:24). Now he has nothing more to do with sin (cf. Heb 4:15; 7:26; 9:28), and the same must be true of his followers (vv. 2-3). They must make an absolutely clean break with the immoral culture out of which they came (cf. 2:1, 11). If they do, they can expect to be ridiculed and slandered (lit., "blasphemed"), just as Christ was before he suffered (v. 4; cf. 2:23a). But like Christ, they too can expect vindication from God, *who stands ready to judge the living and the dead* (v. 5; cf. *the one who judges justly*, 2:23b).

As a postscript to the paragraph, the set phrase *the living and the dead* reminds Peter that God's vindication of the righteous did not begin with Jesus, but embraces many who died long before his coming (cf. Heb 11). They too heard God's *gospel* (cf. Heb 4:2, 6), accepted it, were condemned for it, but have the sure hope of resurrection from the dead. Peter echoes here the thought that "the souls of the righteous are in the hands of God and no torment will ever touch them. In the eyes of the foolish they seemed to have died . . . but they are at peace. For though in the sight of men they were punished, their hope is full of immortality" (Wis 3:1-4, RSV).

Christian Community, 4:7-11

A series of short generalized commands (vv. 7-11a) leading up to a doxology (v. 11b) gives the impression that Peter is now bringing his letter to an end (cf. Paul in 1 Thes 5:12-24). His reminder that *the end of all things is near* (v. 7) follows appropriately the reference to God as *him who stands ready to judge the living and the dead* (4:5). The prospect, however remote, of official persecution requires unity and cohesion among Christian believers, and Peter sees the source of this unity in worshipping and ministering congregations. In contrast to 2:18– 3:7, his focus is on congregations rather than households, and mutuality is at the heart of all his commands: mutual love (v. 8), mutual HOSPITALITY (v. 9), and mutual ministry (vv. 10-11). There are no fixed roles here comparable to slaves and masters or wives and husbands. There are no offices, no clergy-laity distinctions, no leaders or followers. All believers have a responsibility to love, show hospitality, and MINISTER to each other. Precisely who ministers to whom is determined not by status or seniority, but solely by *the manifold grace of God* (v. 10). By repeating the word *God* three times in v. 11a, Peter drives home the point that all ministries are from God, and therefore accountable to *him who stands ready to judge the living and the dead* (4:5).

The Responsibilities of Elders, 4:12–5:11

The address *Beloved* in 4:12, as in 2:11, introduces a new section of the letter. The accompanying appeal, however, does not follow immediately as it does in 2:11, but is deferred until 5:1, where it turns out to be directed to *elders* in particular. The whole section from 4:12 through 5:11 has much the same function as 4:7-11—to build congregational unity in the face of impending trouble—but it does so at greater length, and with a more specific audience in view. Having spoken generally to all the congregations reading his letter, Peter now turns his attention more specifically to those ruled (like his own congregation in Rome) by elders on the basis of seniority. This means that 4:12-19 is something of a digression, laying a basis for the appeal to elders in 5:1-11 by reiterating and reinforcing the themes of 2:11–4:6.

The Fiery Ordeal, 4:12-19

4:12-16. True suffering and true joy. The reiteration carries a new note of urgency, echoing the concern early in the letter about *various trials* testing believers as fire tests gold (cf. 1:6-9). Peter now urges joy in suffering, not because suffering is a good thing in itself or a reason for joy, but because those who suffer for Christ are sharing in Christ's own experience. Consequently, when Christ's glory is revealed, they will rejoice all the more (v. 13; cf. 1:6, 8). Those who are ridiculed for his sake are *blessed* (v. 14a; cf. 3:14), not because they are suffering but because they are suffering for the right reasons (cf. Matt 5:11). At such times the Spirit of God (and the coming glory) rests on them just as Jesus said it would (cf. Luke 12:11-12). Many manuscripts add that if the Spirit is blasphemed (cf. Luke 12:10), the guilt of blasphemy rests not on those who are ridiculed, but on their oppressors (v. 14b KJV).

Such promises do not apply to those who suffer for the wrong reason. Christians who are accused of crimes against Roman society, or even of antisocial behavior that is not explicitly criminal (e.g., as "busybodies" [KJV], or self-appointed guardians of public morality), must make sure that such charges are untrue (v. 15). Only when they have no reason to be ashamed of their actual conduct are Christians free to *glorify God* in the face of hostile questions (cf. 2:12, 15, 19-20; 3:15-16). This, to Peter, is what it means to suffer *as a Christian*.

4:17-19. Judgment at the house of God. Peter's imagery for divine judgment centers on the Christian community as the "house," or temple, of God (cf. 2:5). His point of departure is Ezek 9:6 (LXX), where God orders the judgment on Jerusalem to begin "from my sanctuary" and "from the men who are elders, who are inside the household." Peter refers to the house or sanctuary here and to the "elders" in 5:1-5. To him the judgment of God (cf. 1:17; 2:23; 4:5) is one universal judgment, and is now under way. If a *fiery ordeal* is breaking out even among God's people, how much worse is the fate in store for the "disobedient" (vv. 17-18; cf. 2:8)? This could have led to a kind of vengeful joy in the punishment of the wicked, but it does not. Instead, Peter reminds his readers of the common humanity they share even with their oppressors (cf. 2:13). The judge to whom believer and unbeliever alike are accountable is also the creator who made them all. Peter urges continued trust in that *faithful Creator*, and a renewed commitment *to do good* in the face of unjust suffering (v. 19; again cf. 2:12, 14-15, 20; 3:6, 11-12, 13, 17).

Elders and Their Congregations, 5:1-11

5:1-4. Elders. Peter now resumes the appeal begun in 4:12. For the benefit of congregations ruled by elders, and in keeping with the notion that judgment begins from the elders in "the house of God" (Ezek 9:6), he reminds elders of their responsibilities (vv. 1-4). This he does as an *elder* himself (v. 1), whether as a leader in his own congregation at Rome, or as one of the Twelve chosen by Jesus (cf. 1:1) and therefore an *elder* to all Christians everywhere (cf. v. 9b, *your brothers and sisters in all the world*). He shares with the elders to whom he writes a special responsibility to testify to Christ's sufferings—which he has done repeatedly in this letter (cf. 1:11; 2:21-25; 3:18; 4:1, 13)—and a special hope of reward when Christ's glory is revealed (v. 1b; cf. v. 4). Peter urges elders to be good shepherds over *the flock of God* (v. 2; cf. Acts 20:28), not for financial gain or even "their own satisfaction on the job, but as glad volunteers in God's service" (Kelly, 201). They must lead by example instead of lording it over their respective congregations (lit. "lots" or "assigned portions"), so that *the chief shepherd*, Jesus Christ (cf. 2:25), will reward them when he appears in glory (v. 4).

5:5-11. Their congregations. Peter turns his attention briefly to the *younger* (v. 5a), adapting to his purpose a formalized code of behavior similar to the household codes of 2:18–3:7 (cf. Titus 2:1-6; *1 Clem* 1.3). His actual interest is not in those who are young in age, nor in some subordinate order of ministry, but simply in all who are not elders. He quickly moves from the elder/younger distinction to a strong emphasis on mutuality reminiscent of 4:7-11: *And all of you must clothe yourselves in humility in your dealings with one another* (v. 5b). Such words, like those of 4:7-11, are relevant to all congregations whether ruled by elders or not.

The theme of humility before God continues in the next few verses, as Peter reflects on Prov 3:34 LXX: *God opposes the proud, but gives grace to the humble* (v. 5c; cf. Jas 4:6). The call to humility, with its promise of exaltation or vindication (vv. 6-7, 10-11; cf. Matt 23:12; Luke 14:11; 18:14), frames a related call to resist the devil (vv. 8-9; cf. Jas 4:7-10). Despite Christ's victory over the evil spirits (3:18-22), the devil remains on the loose *like a roaring lion* (v. 8), ready to *devour* those who are unprepared (cf. *JosAsen* 12.9). To Peter, being "devoured" by the devil does not mean persecution as such, or even martyrdom, but APOSTASY or loss of faith. Resisting the devil and trusting God are not two commands but one (cf. Jas 4:7). He reminds his readers that the conflict they face is worldwide (v. 9), and that God's *eternal glory* is their destiny (v. 10; cf. *his marvelous light* in 2:9). Their sufferings are indeed few and brief (v. 10; cf. 1:6) when weighed against that glory to come (cf. Paul in Rom 8:18 and 2 Cor 4:17).

Conclusion, 5:12-14

Peter ends with a word acknowledging *Silvanus*, probably not as scribe or coauthor, but as the bearer of the letter to the Asian provinces (v. 12a). The expression *through Silvanus* is echoed in Ignatius's letters, where the proposition "through" consistently has this meaning (e.g., *Phld* 11.2, *Smyrn* 12.1, Rom 10.1). Playing down the letter's scope (*this short letter*, cf. Heb 13:22), Peter nevertheless claims that it is *true grace of God*, for which those who read it must "stand" (v. 12b). With greetings from a sister congregation *in Babylon* where he resides (probably Rome), and from Mark (cf. Col 4:10, Phlm 24), his associate whom he calls his *son* (v. 13), Peter urges that his greeting (*Peace to all of you*) be passed along through the Asian congregations as through a family, *with a kiss of love* (v. 14; cf. 1:22; 2:17; and 4:8).

Works Cited

Kelly, J. N. D. 1969. *A Commentary on the Epistles of Peter and Jude.*
Michaels, J. Ramsey. 1988. *1 Peter.* WBC.

Second Peter

Edwin K. Broadhead [MCB 1305-1310]

Introduction

Second Peter was accepted into the NT CANON as one of the GENERAL LETTERS—apostolic letters addressed to the CHURCH as a whole. Nonetheless, 2 Peter has proven elusive and problematic. The enigmatic nature of this text was recognized early within church history, and numerous questions remain unanswered. These problems will be identified and addressed by giving attention to the role of 2 Peter in canonical perspective, in historical perspective, and in contemporary perspective.

Second Peter in Canonical Perspective

Origen (ca. 185–254 CE) provides the first written acknowledgement of the existence of 2 Peter (in Eusebius, *EccHist* 6.25.8, 11), yet he also expresses doubts about its authenticity. EUSEBIUS (ca. 260–339 CE) himself was hesitant to accept the letter. Jerome (ca. 346–420 CE) wholly endorsed the letter and assigned it to apostolic authorship. He supposed the difference in style between 1 and 2 Peter could be explained by Peter's use of two different scribes. Probably based on Jerome's endorsement, 2 Peter gained wide acceptance within the Latin and Greek churches. When the canon of the NT was fixed in the fourth-century church, the place of 2 Peter was established.

Second Peter presents itself as an epistle with an apostolic foundation and a postapostolic focus. While other general letters tend to limit apostolic attestation to the opening and closing lines, 2 Peter insists throughout upon its apostolic foundation. In addition to the apostolic address (1:1) the letter recalls the presentation of the apostolic preaching (1:12) and makes plans for its preservation (1:13-15). Peter's role as an eyewitness and his experience of the TRANSFIGURATION are recalled (1:16-18). The continuity and vitality of interpretation are confirmed (1:19). A prior letter is recalled (3:1), and the christological foundation is confirmed on the witness of the apostles (3:2). The witness of PAUL is recalled (3:15-16), and the testimony of scripture is evoked (3:16).

The primary concern of this letter is for the time after the death of the apostles. The departure of the earliest leaders will bring a time of crisis (3:4). This period will be marked by eschatological doubt (3:3-13) and moral failure (2:2, 9-22). The destruction of the world and its judgment lie close at hand (3:5-13). The letter warns against these troubles (2:1; 3:3) and seeks to prepare the reader to face this forthcoming crisis (1:12-15; 3:17-18).

This trauma involves the activity of false teachers from within the Christian tradition (2:1-3, 15; 3:16). They will take advantage of the newly converted and the unstable (2:14, 18-22). The letter prepares its readers for this postapostolic trauma through warning about the future (2:1; 3:3) and remembrance of the past (1:12-15; 3:1-2).

Several issues shape this apostolic challenge. The apostolic faith is foundational. This faith is based upon knowledge of Jesus Christ as Lord and Savior (1:1, 14, 16; 2:1, 20; 3:2, 18). The apostle is an eyewitness to the work of Jesus (1:16-18) and continues to receive REVELATION from Christ (2:14). This apostolic faith is based on the prophetic tradition (1:19-21; 2:3; 3:2, 13). The readers of the letter share in this faith (1:1-2, 12; 3:1-2, 17-18).

The scriptures provide a sure witness and warning for the recipients of the letter. The scriptures are understood as a body of literature which believers hold in common. Among the writings considered as scripture are the prophetic warnings (1:19-21; 2:3; 3:2, 13), the stories and sayings of the OT (2:4-9, 15-16, 22a; 3:5-6, 8), the writings of Paul (3:15-16), and other writings (3:16).

Attention is given as well to the formulation of the faith. The reader is warned against clever myths (1:16) and esoteric interpretation of prophecy (1:21). More importantly, the letter seeks to restore ethical stability (1:3-11; 3:11, 14, 17-18) in the face of moral failure (2:9-22). At the heart of the letter lies a warning against eschatological delusion: the promised judgment and renewal of the earth will not fail (3:4-13).

Second Peter thus presents a strategic approach to the problems at hand. The warning against false teachers is framed as a final letter of challenge from one of the last of the apostles. With prophetic foresight, the apostle warns the readers of the trauma that will engulf believers in the postapostolic age. False teachers practicing corrupt ethics and preaching a failed eschatology are countered by the sure foundation of the apostolic faith, the words of scripture, the consistent righteousness, and the sure hope of the believer.

Within this canonical perspective 2 Peter presents itself as a general epistle based on a final apostolic testimony. From this standpoint, the letter is seemingly addressed to a specific group of Christians by Peter near the time of his death (in ROME ca. 64–65 CE).

Second Peter in Historical Perspective

Second Peter presents a quite different image in historical perspective. Current knowledge about language, theological development, and church history raise serious questions about the relationship of 2 Peter to the apostolic era and to the other writings of the NT.

Second Peter is only formally related to 1 Peter. The greeting (1:1), the blessing (1:2), and the benediction (3:18) are on the same model as those of 1 Peter. Beyond this, 2 Peter is framed as the second letter from the apostle (3:1). This formal framework does not bear up in the substance of the letter. Differences in language and style were noticed as early as Jerome (*Ep* 120.11), and modern statistical analysis confirms this. The style of 2 Peter tends to be more formal and grandiose than 1 Peter. The two letters share few themes or concerns in common.

In reality, the epistle closest to 2 Peter is JUDE. Indeed, large parts of Jude are found in 2 Peter:

2 Pet 1:2	=	Jude 2
2 Pet 1:12	=	Jude 5a
2 Pet 2:1-3	=	Jude 4
2 Pet 2:6	=	Jude 7
2 Pet 2:10b-15	=	Jude 8–12a
2 Pet 2:17	=	Jude 12b–13
2 Pet 2:18	=	Jude 16
2 Pet 3:2-3	=	Jude 17
2 Pet 3:14	=	Jude 24
2 Pet 3:18b	=	Jude 25

Beyond this, various elements of organization and numerous themes are shared in common between Jude and 2 Peter.

This common ground has been explained through three theories: (1) Jude is a reduction of 2 Peter; (2) Second Peter is an expansion of Jude; (3) Jude and 2 Peter are two different applications of one traditional work. The third opinion is the most likely. The relatively low level of precise verbal agreement in the common material speaks against direct dependence of one letter upon the other. Both works may be based on an apostolic testimony that circulated in a variety of forms. The letter of Jude, employing a midrashic approach with various allusions to the OT and to apocryphal writings, represents a more Jewish form of the tradition. Second Peter shows less interest in the Jewish traditions and structures and represents a more Hellenized form of the apostolic testimony.

Of primary concern for most interpreters is the relationship of 2 Peter to the apostolic era and to Peter. The language and conceptualization of the letter seem far removed from the world of a Galilean fisherman. The desire to escape the corruption of the world and participate in the divine nature (1:4) is more akin to Hellenistic thought than to the Palestinian world of Peter. Common authorship of 1 and 2 Peter is unlikely. Various images in the letter point to a postapostolic period. While the crisis is foreseen as a future event (2:1; 3:3), it is addressed as a present reality (2:10; 3:4, 16). The death of the earliest leaders is seemingly acknowledged (3:4). The apostolic experience of faith is now expressed in more fixed and formulaic terms (1:1; 3:2). The tension between Paul and Peter is absent

(3:15). A fixed body of scripture is assumed, and includes Paul's writings (3:16). The proper interpretation of scripture has become an issue (1:20-21). The remembrance of JESUS has been framed primarily as *power* and *majesty*, and it has been focused in one event—the Transfiguration (1:16-18). Second Peter is almost unknown in the first and second century, and its apostolic origin is questioned from the beginning. The letter first emerges in the manuscripts from Egypt, and it is accepted last among the Syrian church.

Second Peter also stands at a distance from the major lines of NT thought. The experience of faith has been formulated as apostolic commands (3:2). The CHRISTOLOGY posed here tends to focus on formal titles (1:11; 2:20; 3:18), to be docetic in outlook (1:1, 3), and to emphasize power and glory (1:3, 16-17). FAITH is framed as revelation (1:14) and recognition (1:3, 8, 12; 2:20; 3:18). Missing are the teachings of Jesus, the cross and the resurrection, and the experience of GRACE and RECONCILIATION. The outlook is closer to Hellenism than to Palestinian Judaism. The moral demands likely reflect the virtues of Hellenistic Judaism. The expected collapse of the universe is similar to Stoic thought. The heresy addressed sounds similar to the developing gnostic tendencies of the late first and early second centuries. This outlook is also evident in the language of 2 Peter. There are fifty-seven words in 2 Peter not found elsewhere in the NT; thirty-two of these are not found in the Greek OT (i.e., LXX) either. Fifteen of these thirty-two words are found in other Jewish Hellenistic writings. Three words in 2 Peter have no parallel in Greek literature. Thus, the historical perspective makes doubtful the identity of 2 Peter as an epistle from the apostolic age.

A more likely framework for 2 Peter is the literary form known as the "Testament" (see TESTAMENTS, APOCRYPHAL). In this literature a heroic figure gives words of instruction and warning before departing. Without exception, these texts are composed after the death of the hero to recall and preserve the impact of the leader. Often these texts are used to address particular problems faced by a later generation. The pattern for Peter's Testament may be drawn from the story of MOSES in Deuteronomy. Told that his death is imminent, Moses ascends the mountain to see what lies ahead (Deut 3:23ff.). Moses' mountaintop experience with God is remembered (Deut 4:9-14). The earlier COMMANDMENTS are recalled (Deut 4:13). Warnings to OBEDIENCE are issued, and the people are instructed in how they should face the trials of the future without their leader. This Mosaic model is taken up in the writings of Josephus (*Ant* 4.8.2) and in the *Testament of Moses*. Examples of the Testament form may be found in the OT, in Jewish literature, and in the NT.

Seen from a historical perspective, 2 Peter belongs to the postapostolic stage of church history in which the teaching and authority of the apostles was brought to bear against contemporary controversies. From this historical perspective, 2 Peter is a Testament framed in the form of a letter. It seeks to draw upon the apostolic era to address a postapostolic situation, likely between 90 and 110 CE. Likely addressed to a general audience, the author and place of composition are unknown.

Second Peter in Contemporary Perspective

Second Peter continues to hold value in a contemporary perspective. Second Peter provides key historical insights into the postapostolic age and the development of the institutionalized church. Seen in terms of its own context and purposes, this letter provides crucial information about the controversies which underlie the formation of the CHURCH.

Beyond this, 2 Peter offers a theological contribution. This epistle provides a primary example of how the Christian church handled the literature and the traditions which it inherited. The traditions of the OT, of Judaism, and of apostolic Christianity converge within this text. Of key interest is the manner in which the early church appropriated these traditions for its own age and task. Beyond this, the interaction of the church with the world is modeled. The ongoing dialogue of Judaism and Christianity with the Hellenistic environment echoes through this epistle. Second Peter also demonstrates the in-house arguments that form the matrix of early church history. The definition of scripture, the naming of heresy, and the fixing of church patterns are all underway in this letter.

Thus, 2 Peter provides information on how early Christianity handled its heritage, articulated its identity, and found its way in the world. The church, which lives yet between the age of the apostles and the day of judgment, has much to learn from this work.

For Further Study

In the *Mercer Dictionary of the Bible*: EPISTLE/LETTER; ESCHATOLOGY IN THE NT; GNOSTICISM; JUDE, LETTER OF; LORD IN THE NT; PAROUSIA/SECOND COMING; PETER; PETER, LETTERS OF; SAVIOR IN THE NT; TESTAMENTS, APOCRYPHAL.

In other sources: R. Bauckmam, *Jude, 2 Peter*, WBC; C. Bigg, *A Critical and Exegetical Commentary on the Epistles of St. Peter and St. Jude*, ICC; J. Calvin, "2 Peter," *Calvin's Commentaries*; L. Johnson, *The Writings of the New Testament*, 442–52; E. Käsemann, "An Apologia for Primitive Christian Eschatology," in *Essays on New Testament Themes*, 169–95; K. Schelkle, *Die Petrusbrief, der Judasbrief*, HTKNT 13/2; W. Schrage and H. Balz, *Die katholischen Briefe: Die Briefe des Jakobus, Petrus, Johannes, und Judas*, NTD; R. Summers, "2 Peter," *BBC*; D. F. Watson, "The Second Letter of Peter," *NIB*.

Commentary

An Outline

I. Salutation, 1:1-2
II. Theological Exposition, 1:3-11
  A. The Gift, 1:3-4
  B. The Demand, 1:5-7
  C. The Result, 1:8-11
III. The Author's Situation and Purpose, 1:12-15
IV. The Apostolic Foundation, 1:16-21
  A. The Certainty of the Witness, 1:16-18
  B. The Certainty of the Message, 1:19-21
V. The Coming Crisis: Ethics, 2:1-22
  A. The Appearance of False Teachers, 2:1-3
  B. Old Testament Lessons, 2:4-10a
  C. The Character of the False Teachers, 2:10b-22
VI. The Coming Crisis: Eschatology, 3:1-13
  A. The Appearance of Scoffers, 3:1-4
  B. The Apostolic Answer, 3:5-13
VII. The Challenge to Endure, 3:14-18a
VIII. Final Benediction, 3:18b

Salutation, 1:1-2

Typical of ancient letters, 2 Peter opens with mention of the sender and the receiver and with a word of greeting. The apostolic nature of the letter is established from the beginning in the titles associated with the author: *servant and apostle of Jesus Christ.* The author names himself as *Simeon Peter.* Simeon represents an unusual spelling based on the Hebrew form and is found elsewhere in the NT only in Acts 15:14. Many interpreters see here an attempt to convince the reader of the ancient and apostolic nature of the letter.

The recipients of the letter are specified only as fellow believers. Later they are identified as the recipients of a prior letter (3:1). The word of greeting is framed upon 1 Pet 1:2b, and it enhances the apostolic appearance of the letter. Three elements within the salutation, however, point to a postapostolic period: faith is understood more as a possession than an experience (v. 1); Jesus is seemingly addressed as *God* (v. 1); and the title of *Savior* is applied to Jesus. While these elements have parallels within the NT, they typify the later, more marginal stages of NT thought.

The reference to the believer's *knowledge* (ἐπίγνωσις) *of God and of Jesus* may be a subtle rebuke of the false teachers. They are, perhaps, among those who claim a special knowledge (γνῶσις) of the divine, later known as Gnostics. If so, the greeting already sets the true knowledge of believers over against that of false teachers (see KNOWLEDGE IN THE NT).

Theological Exposition, 1:3-11

The Gift, 1:3-4

The body of the letter opens with a brief theological exposition that sets the background for the apostolic challenge. The reader is first reminded of all that has been given to believers. The knowledge and the promises of Christ provide life and deliverance. The gift is understood primarily in terms of knowledge. While the basis of this message is primitive Christianity, the language and concepts are those of Hellenism.

The Demand, 1:5-7

Demand is built upon gift. The believer is to support the gift of faith with a life of virtue. This list combines normative biblical values (*faith, mutual affection, love*) with ethical categories common to popular Greek philosophy (*knowledge, goodness, self-control, endurance*). Again, a basic NT pattern is expressed in the concepts of Hellenism.

The Result, 1:8-11

The result is focused, both in its positive and its negative aspects. At the center of this discussion echoes the theme of knowledge. Depending on how one practices morality, the *knowledge of . . . Jesus Christ* may be cultivated or lost. The discussion alternates between gift and demand. BAPTISM, calling, and ELECTION form the basis of the Christian life; these may be lost through moral neglect. Entrance into the kingdom is a gift; it may be forfeited. The reduction of the kingdom of God wholly to the kingdom of Christ is further evidence of a later stage of Christian thought.

The Author's Situation and Purpose, 1:12-15

The situation of the author clarifies the purpose of the letter. The apostle has received revelation of his imminent death (v. 14). While the apostle remains, his purpose is twofold: to remind the readers of the apostolic faith (v. 13) and to prepare them for the postapostolic period (v. 15). These two goals shape the remainder of the letter.

The Apostolic Foundation, 1:16-21

The Certainty of the Witness, 1:16-18

The author assures the readers of the validity of the tradition they have received. Not *cleverly devised myths*, but the apostolic message provides the foundation of their faith. Perhaps the author seeks to counter the timeless mythical structures of Hellenistic thought with a salvation-history focus on God's activity. Here the authority of the entire apostolate is confirmed through the use of the plural (*we* is used twice in v. 16; in v. 18; and in v. 19). This authority is based on eyewitness experience, and the TRANSFIGURATION of Jesus is recalled as an example. Those who preach the future coming of Christ are qualified to do so by their experience of his past revelation in honor and glory. The faith of the postapostolic church is founded on its sure witness to God's saving activity within history.

The Certainty of the Message, 1:19-21

Further confirmation is provided by the certainty of the message. Behind the prophetic and apostolic word stands the activity of the HOLY SPIRIT. As God spoke on the mount of Transfiguration, so God speaks through the prophecy that the church possesses. This tradition is confirmed over against all alternatives as the message for the church.

The Coming Crisis: Ethics, 2:1-22

The apostolic heritage is now applied to the postapostolic situation. Apostolic instruction is set against false teachers in two specific areas: ethics and eschatology.

The Appearance of False Teachers, 2:1-3

Emphasizing the continuity between OT and apostolic tradition, the *false prophets* of the OT reemerge within the postapostolic church. Their leadership is set against that of apostolic tradition—*the way of truth* (v. 2). Their teaching will be marked by subtlety, destructiveness, immorality, heresy, and deceptive words. Both their appearance and their judgment have been prophesied.

Old Testament Lessons, 2:4-10a

The continuity of OT and apostolic traditions is filled out through three examples: the fallen angels (drawn from apocryphal sources such as *EthEnoch* 20:2; *SibOr* 4:185); Noah's generation (Gen 6:6-8; 8:18); *Sodom and Gomorrah* and *Lot* (Gen 19:16, 24, 29). The point of these examples becomes clear in 2:9-10a: God is able to preserve the godly and to judge the unrighteous. Second Peter applies this truth directly to the situation of the postapostolic church.

The Character of the False Teachers, 2:10b-22

A full range of vocabulary and imagery describes the opponents' moral failure. Evocative similes are employed: irrational animals, cursed children, waterless springs, storm-driven mists, and slaves of corruption. Numerous descriptions clarify their immorality: bold, willful, slanderous, revelers, blots, blemishes, adulterous, insatiable, greedy, cursed, bombastic, and licentious. The OT story of BALAAM (vv. 15-16) and two graphic proverbs describe those who follow their path (v. 22).

The Coming Crisis: Eschatology, 3:1-13

The second heresy addressed by the letter is the failed eschatology of the false teachers. A similar pattern of argument is followed.

The Appearance of Scoffers, 3:1-4

The warnings of 2 Peter are grounded upon four foundations: the word of *the holy prophets*, the commandments of Jesus, the teaching of the apostles, and a previous letter. The specific threat addressed in the remainder of this epistle is the loss of faith in the return of the Lord. In this threat both ethical and eschatological failure are combined (v. 3). The death of the fathers (v. 3) points to the end of the apostolic era. Historically, this transition meant that expectation of the return of Christ faded into the distance and with it the threat of imminent judgment. The author of 2 Peter fights against this tendency.

The Apostolic Answer, 3:5-13

The early church sought in various ways to deal with the delayed PAROUSIA of Christ. A unique approach to this problem is given in 2 Pet 3:5-13. Four arguments are given against those who have abandoned the apostolic tradition of the imminent parousia. First, the word of God does not fail. Upon the dynamic of God's word the ancient world was both founded and judged by water. Upon the same divine word, the present world will undergo a judgment of fire. A second answer, based on Ps 90:4, argues that God's time is relative. A third response sees purpose behind the delay: God has allowed time for REPENTANCE and salvation. The fourth reply focuses the unexpected nature of the judgment; the lack of present signs is no indication of its failure or its lack of intensity. The apostolic reply concludes with an appeal that again unites ethics and eschatology: the certainty of judgment should produce lives of holiness and godliness. As with the OT models, both destruction and renewal are envisioned. Here the renewal extends beyond the interests of the individual or even of the church to include the entire creation.

The Challenge to Endure, 3:14-18a

In view of the coming trauma, believers are challenged to wait with upright behavior. The delay is to be seen as a particular moment of grace within God's salvation history. The reader is warned that attempts to twist the apostolic message are not new: Paul's letters and other scripture suffer the same abuse. In light of the ethical and eschatological crisis, the believer has received an apostolic warning. Rather than fall away or turn back, the believer is to *grow in the grace and knowledge of . . . [the] Savior Jesus Christ.*

Final Benediction, 3:18b

Even the final words of the apostolic message recall its focus. Over against the unstable ways of the false teachers, believers are to give glory to Jesus Christ, both in their present living and until the day of judgment.

First, Second, and Third John

John B. Polhill [MCB 1311-1318]

Introduction

The three Johannine Epistles can be classified in two ways. Along with the Petrine Epistles, James, and Jude, they belong to the category of "general" or "catholic" epistles. They have also traditionally been grouped with the Gospel of John and Revelation in the "Johannine corpus." Their affinity with the fourth Gospel is unmistakable. The relationship to Revelation is more remote.

Literary Form

In form, all three have traditionally been denoted epistles. This is most accurate for the latter two. Second John follows the standard conventions of first-century epistles and is addressed to a Christian congregation. Third John is a private epistle from a church leader to an individual. The writer of both identifies himself as *the elder* (2 John 1; 3 John 1).

First John is anonymous. It does not have the usual form of an epistle: no address, no conclusion, none of the conventions of a Greek letter. It is still probably best described as general epistle—a written communication, probably to a group of churches by a church leader concerning matters of mutual concern. The language and thought are so close to that of the other two that it was probably also written by "the elder."

Authorship and Date

Who was this *elder*? Tradition identifies him with the apostle JOHN, who is said to have lived to a ripe old age, ministering in Ephesus. This view identifies John with the BELOVED DISCIPLE and sees him as author of the Gospel and Epistles of John. A second view builds upon a tradition from POLYCARP that there were two Johns in Ephesus, the apostle and a disciple of the apostle known as the Elder John (EUSEBIUS, *EccHist* 3.39.4-6). Many would see this "elder John" as "the elder" of the three epistles. A third view emphasizes the communal aspect in the Johannine Epistles and sees the entire Johannine corpus as coming from a "Johannine School" of thought. The traditions in which this community grounded itself are taken back ultimately to the beloved disciple of the fourth Gospel.

Although some argue otherwise, the majority of scholars place the epistles in a Johannine milieu according to one of these three views. They are usually placed in Asia Minor around the last decade of the first century. Throughout this commentary, the writer will be designated as John or the elder with no distinction implied between the two.

Life Setting

All three epistles depict a CHURCH in conflict. False teachers have separated from the church. The elder accuses them of three errors. First, they have an inadequate view of the INCARNATION, failing to give full due to the humanity of Jesus (1 John 2:22; 2 John 7). Second, they have a deficient view of SIN, failing to keep God's commandments while at the same time claiming to be above sin (1 John 1:8, 10; 2:4). Finally, they have a failure in FELLOWSHIP, not loving their Christian brothers and sisters (1 John 2:9; 4:20).

These separatists have often been identified with GNOSTICISM, and more specifically with Cerinthus, a Gnostic precursor whom IRENAEUS depicts as an opponent of John in Ephesus. There are problems with this identification, however, since Cerinthus does not seem to have held all the views applied to the false teaching in 1 John, nor are all Cerinthus's main views attacked in the epistles. That the elder was fighting some sort of incipient Gnosticism seems likely. Later Gnostics often maintained a spiritual perfectionism that saw itself as above sin. They were elitist and tended to disdain others (lack of love), and they held a docetic CHRISTOLOGY, denying the humanity of Jesus.

For Further Study

In the *Mercer Dictionary of the Bible*: ATONEMENT/EXPIATION IN THE NT; BELOVED DISCIPLE; EPISTLE/LETTER; GNOSTICISM; INCARNATION; JOHN; JOHN, GOSPEL AND LETTERS OF; LIGHT/DARKNESS IN THE NT; LOVE IN THE NT; RIGHTEOUSNESS IN THE NT.

In other sources: C. C. Black, "The First, Second, and Third Letters of John," *NIB*; R. E. Brown, *The Epistles of John*, AncB; R. A. Culpepper, *1 John, 2 John, 3 John*, Knox Preaching Guides; I. H. Marshall, *The Epistles of John*, NICNT; S. S. Smalley, *1, 2, 3 John*, WBC.

Commentary

An Outline: First John

I. Prologue, 1:1-4
II. Part One: God Is Light, 1:5–3:10
  A. Dealing with Sin, 1:5–2:2
  B. Keeping His Commandments, 2:3-11
  C. Shunning Worldliness, 2:12-17
  D. Making the True Confession, 2:18-27
  E. Living as Children of God, 2:28–3:10
III. Part Two: God Is Love, 3:11–5:12
  A. Loving in Deed and Truth, 3:11-24
  B. Testing the Spirits, 4:1-6
  C. Being Perfected in God's Love, 4:7-21
  D. Finding Life in the Son, 5:1-12
IV. Epilogue, 5:13-22

Prologue, 1:1-4

With its reference to *what was from the beginning* and *the word of life*, the prologue to 1 John is reminiscent of the fourth Gospel's prologue (John 1:1-18). There are differences, however. In 1 John *the beginning* probably refers to the tradition of the Christian witness to Christ rather than to the preexistence of the Word. There is also a stronger emphasis on the eyewitness TESTIMONY to the real humanity of Christ: *what we have seen with our eyes, what we have looked at and touched with our hands* (v. 1). Already John focuses on the false teachers. In response to the innovations of the false teachers, John calls his readers back to their roots—to the original apostolic testimony to Christ, to the word of the gospel they first heard. He especially concentrates on the false teachers' inadequate CHRISTOLOGY, as he expands on the "word made flesh" of the fourth Gospel's prologue (John 1:14).

Of particular concern to John is the unity of his community. It is a triangular fellowship—among Christians with both *the Father* and *Son* (v. 3). This emphasis persists throughout 1 John, particularly in the motif of "abiding." John expresses his personal purpose for writing in verse 4—*that our joy may be complete*. John is concerned with restoring the joy of the fellowship, which has been threatened by the withdrawal of the false teachers from the community.

Part One: God Is Light, 1:5–3:10

First John is difficult to outline, because its themes are constantly repeated. The division followed here is based on the recurrence of the phrase *this is the message* in 1:5 and 3:11. In 1:5 the message is defined in terms of light, in 3:11 in terms of love.

The Johannine Epistles are marked by dualistic language. There is either darkness or light, no in-between. One belongs either to the realm of light or to that of darkness. Darkness is marked by sin, falsehood, hate, and death. Life is characterized by righteousness, TRUTH, love, and life. The first main division contrasts these two realms. The contrast is explicit in the first two subdivisions: those who walk in light are cleansed from sin (1:5–2:2); they keep the commandments (2:3-11). The light and darkness imagery is not explicit in the following sections but is implicit in the dualistic contrasts. The world is to be shunned as the world of darkness (2:12-17). The true confession in the Son is contrasted with the lie of the false teachers (2:18-27). Finally, *the children of God*, children of light, are contrasted with the children *of the devil* (2:28–3:10).

Dealing with Sin, 1:5–2:2

John's first subject is the place of sin in the believer's life. His basic premise is that God is wholly light (v. 5). Since sin is darkness, there is no room for sin in the lives of those who have FELLOWSHIP with God. Yet, sin is a reality even for believers, and God has provided means for dealing with it.

This section is constructed in a series of six antitheses, expressed in conditional sentences ("if anyone should . . . "). There are three negative statements describing those who walk in the darkness of sin (1:6, 8, 10). Alternating with these are three positive statements, treating the believer's relationship to sin (1:7, 9; 2:1-2).

The negative statements are best seen as describing the false teachers. They are not walking in the light but continue to sin (v. 6). This is so because they claim to have no sin, and this is sheer self-delusion (v. 8). They even claim to have never sinned (v. 10), and this makes God a liar, who throughout scripture asserts the sinfulness of all humanity (cf. Prov 20:9; Ps 14:2-3). Much like later Gnostics, John's opponents seem to have claimed a spiritual perfection in which they either viewed themselves as above sin or considered moral behavior a matter of indifference. John did not agree with this spirit/flesh DUALISM, but rather saw one's behavior in the flesh as indicative of one's spiritual state.

In three positive antitheses, John presents his readers with a realistic program for dealing with sin. His conviction is that sin has no place for those who walk in the light. The atoning blood of Christ has cleansed them of sin (1:7). If they do sin, however, they should confess it, and God will forgive and cleanse them (1:9). In such a case, the believer has an ADVOCATE to intercede with the Father (2:1). (Note the term "paraclete" applied to Jesus in his intercessory role. In the Gospel of John, the term is used of the Spirit.) The word "just" refers to the righteousness of Christ which qualifies him as intercessor for our unrighteousness. Christ is further described as the atonement (*hilasmos*) for our sins, a term with sacrificial overtones (cf. *blood* in 1:7). John is a realist. The goal of every Christian is to have fellowship with God, to walk in his light, to be free of sin (2:1). But we still live in an imperfect world where temptation is a reality. When we do sin, we have forgiveness through Christ.

Keeping His Commandments, 2:3-11

This section can be divided into two subsections. The first (vv. 3-6) is closely related to the previous treatment of sin, as it deals with keeping the commandments. The second (vv. 7-11) moves the thought forward to the supreme command to love. In both sections the argument is built around a recurring participial construction ("the one who says, loves . . . ").

Verse 3 begins with the theme of "being known" by God. This is an experiential knowledge, closely related to the theme of "abiding" that permeates this section: the truth is *in* a person (v. 4); we are *in him* (v. 5); one claims to *abide in him* (v. 6). For John, salvation is a relationship—to be personally known by God; to live in him and in the Son; to live in a community of love with fellow Christians. In this section John depicts the keeping of the commandments as a mark of this relationship to the Father. Probably he has in mind the whole moral tradition of the Johannine community. Verse 6 focuses on the specific example of Christ. In contrast to the false teachers, who seem to have put little stock in Christ's human life, John presents it as a model for Christian living.

Verse 7 moves to a particular COMMANDMENT—that of love. It is both old and new. It is old because the Christians have heard it from the beginning of their Christian life (v. 7). It is also the *new commandment* that Christ gave (John 13:34; 15:12). Verses 8-11 reflect the close relationship of light and love. Because God is both light and love, to walk in his light is also to walk in his love. John again looks to the false teachers. They are likely the ones who *hate* (v. 11). Johannine dualism allows no in-betweens: To fail in love is to hate. Throughout the epistle love applies to love between Christian brothers and sisters. John is concerned with the conflict in his own community and does not address the Christian's relationship to outsiders—except, that is, the false teachers. Once they belonged to John's community; now they have left (2:19). They have no love for their former sisters and brothers in Christ.

Shunning Worldliness, 2:12-17

With vv. 12-14 one comes upon the address that was lacking at the epistle's beginning. The section raises many questions. Who are the *little children, fathers,* and *young people*? Elsewhere in 1 John *little children* addresses the whole community, and indeed the things said about the little children (forgiveness of sin, knowledge of the Father) apply to every Christian, but who are the fathers and young people? Do these terms designate age, or office, or stages in Christian maturity? Why does v. 14 virtually repeat vv. 12-13? For emphasis? The main function of the section seems clear. These are words of assurance to the Johannine Christians that they need not shrink from the disdain of those who have left nor doubt their own status with God. Their roots are firm: their sins are forgiven, they know the Father and the Son, and they have conquered the devil (*evil one*).

Verses 15-17 link up with the reference to conquering the devil in v. 14. In Johannine thought the devil holds sway over the world (John 12:31; 16:11). To *love the world* is to place oneself under his dominance. John does not depict the world as EVIL in itself; on the contrary, Christ died for the world, God sent his Son to save it (1 John 2:2; John 3:16). In the Johannine dualism, however, one cannot live within the world's sphere of POWER and God's at the same time. Verse 16 aptly summarizes the world's enticements—physical appetites, things which please the eye, boasting in self-achievement. To center oneself on these rather than on God is to invest in the transient.

Making the True Confession, 2:18-27

The reference to the world's *passing away* in 2:17 serves as a transition to the announcement that it is the *last hour* in v. 18. The term *antichrist* seems to have originated in Johannine circles, but the idea of false prophets and messiahs coming in the last days before Christ's return was well established in early Christianity (cf. Mark 13:22; 2 Thes 2:8). Usually ANTICHRIST is depicted as a single figure, but John speaks of many of them because he identifies antichrist with those who separated from his community (v. 19). For John the separation proves they never really belonged in the first place. They are guilty of the cardinal lie, denying that JESUS is the Christ (v. 22). This is the primary doctrinal error of the separatists. They held an inadequate view of the INCARNATION, emphasizing Christ's divinity and neglecting his humanity. The example of his life (2:6), his mediatorial role (2:1f.), and his atoning death (5:6) held no importance for them. Because they did not have the Son, neither did they have the Father nor the *eternal life* which is in him. It is not so for John's *little children.* They have the anointing of the Spirit (v. 20). They make the true confession and have both Son and Father (v. 23). Theirs is the life eternal (v. 24). John was concerned lest the separated group lead his community astray (v. 26). He thus assures them they need no experience in the Spirit that they had not already received, no teaching other than what they had been given from the beginning (v. 27).

Living as Children of God, 2:28–3:10

John returns to the theme of the last days, continuing his note of assurance in v. 28. His *little children* will have boldness to appear before the Lord at his return because they abide in him. The mark of their abiding is their righteous living. Since God is righteous, their righteousness is a sign that they have been begotten by God and are his true children (v. 29). The style of this section is again antithetical, constructed with the phrase "everyone who. . . ." It is interrupted in 3:1-2 by an encomium on being a child of God. Because God has begotten us in his love, we are now his children (3:1). Our final state does not yet appear, but John assures us we will be like Christ, *for we will see him as he is* (3:2).

Returning to the "everyone who . . . " style, 3:3 urges that those who share this hope of glory maintain their conformity to Christ even now by sharing in his purity. This links with the reference to doing righteousness in 2:29 and contrasts with the reference to *commits sin* in 3:4. Those who live in sin and iniquity will not share in Christ's coming. Christ came to take away sin (cf. John 1:29). Sin finds no place in him, and the sinner has neither seen nor known him (3:6). In fact, those who sin are the children of sin's originator, the devil (3:8, 10). Here again John's dualistic treatment of sin appears. The one abiding in Christ does not sin (3:6). The one begotten of God *cannot sin* (3:9). One must bear in mind John's treatment of sin in the life of the believer (2:1-2). He was well aware of that reality and faulted those who claimed to be sinless (1:8, 10). Many have noted that John used the present tense throughout this section, indicating a continual state of sinning: the one who abides in Christ does not "live in" sin. One must be careful not to water down John's point. Christ and sin are incompatible. The one who abides in Christ must seek to perfect that relationship by conquering sin.

Part Two: God Is Love, 3:11–5:12

The same themes recur in 1 John 3:11–5:12 that are found in 1:5–3:10—right living, the right confession of Christ, love. The balance differs. Whereas God's righteousness dominates the first part, God's love commands the last half of the epistle. The word used for love throughout 1 John is *agape*, a rather bland word in secular

Greek, which often meant little more than "like, prefer." The NT writers seized the word and filled it with new meaning in the light of God's gift of love in Christ. No one does this more profoundly than John.

Loving in Deed and Truth, 3:11-24

Using his normal antithetical style, in vv. 11-18 John contrasts love and hate. CAIN's murder of ABEL is held up as the archetype of all hatred. Cain's disposition is traced to the devil, and his motivation is linked to his jealousy over his brother's righteous deeds (v. 12). Thus, in dualistic fashion, John makes of a single piece hatred, unrighteousness, murder, and the devil. Ultimately, death is added to the fabric. To hate is to murder, and no murderer has a share in eternal life (v. 15). This is the way of the unrighteous world which, like Cain, abhors the righteous. Christians should thus not be surprised when they encounter the world's hatred (v. 13; cf. John 7:7; 15:18, 19).

If the way of hatred is death, the way of love is life, life in God's own Son who laid down his life for us. This is how we *know* what love is (v. 16). How we *demonstrate* that love abides in us is in concrete deeds of charity to needy brothers and sisters (v. 17). Love is not a feeling or a profession for John. It is active, expressed in concrete deeds (v. 18; cf. Jas 1:22). Perhaps such lack of concern for the needy was the clearest evidence of the lovelessness of those who had separated from John's community.

Verse 19 introduces the theme of confidence before God's judgment. It is closely connected to v. 18, because it is this active, charitable love that gives such confidence. John assures his readers that even should they experience qualms of GUILT at their own imperfection in love and righteousness, God knows the hearts of those who truly abide in his love (v. 20). Indeed, because we abide in him, God hears our prayers and grants our requests (v. 22). Verses 22b-23 summarize the three main traits of the one who abides in God, the three which run like a thread throughout the epistle: keeping God's commandments, loving one another, and believing in the Son. There is also a witness that God abides in his children—the HOLY SPIRIT (v. 24). The mention of the Spirit serves as a transition to the next section.

Testing the Spirits, 4:1-6

The early CHURCH was alive with spiritual experience, but it soon became apparent that not all such experience came from God. It became necessary to *test the spirits* (v. 1). Much like PAUL (1 Cor 12:3), John laid down the basic confession of Jesus Christ as the main test (v. 2). But John adds a qualifying clause: they must confess Jesus Christ as having *come in the flesh*. He has the Christology of the separatists in mind, their failure to acknowledge the significance of Jesus' humanity. Theirs is not God's Spirit, but the spirit which opposes God, that *of the antichrist* (v. 3; cf. 2:18, 22).

Verses 4-6 contrast *the Spirit of God* and *the spirit of the antichrist* (vv. 2-3). John's *little children* may take assurance that the victory is theirs, because God's

Spirit is more powerful (v. 4; cf. 2:14). One certain contrast is that *the world* listens to the message of false spirits; it does not heed God's Spirit (vv. 5-6a). This is perhaps indicative that the separatists who had *gone out* into the world (2:19) were having more success in spreading their message than John. It certainly reflects John's conviction that *the world* is under the sway of the evil one and naturally heeds the spirit of deceit rather than *the spirit of truth* (v. 6).

Being Perfected in God's Love, 4:7-21

First John 4:7-21 is the most profound treatment of God's love in the NT. Verses 7-11 depict the priority of God's love. Verse 12 is transitional, introducing the main themes of the following verses: abiding in God's love (13-16), and being perfected in God's love (17-21).

True love, perfect love, begins with God (v. 7-11). The main thrust of this section is that John's readers should *love one another*. This exhortation begins and ends the treatment (vv. 7, 11). In between John establishes the basis of all love—God's love. It is significant that throughout this section John addresses his readers not as *little children* but as *beloved* (3:21; 4:1, 7, 11); that is, as those who have received God's love. Within the Christian community all love begins with God. *God is love* (v. 8). The evidence of God's love is his sending his Son into the world to die as a sacrificial atonement (*hilasmos*; cf. 2:2) for our sins so that we might have life (vv. 9-10; cf. John 3:16). Through acceptance of God's sacrificial love in Christ, the believer is begotten of God and comes truly to know him (v. 7). It is not a matter of the believer's striving after God and finding him but of God reaching down in love; he loved us first (v. 10; cf. v. 19). There is thus a triangle of love which begins with God's love, is manifested in the love of Christ, and comes to life in the believer who accepts God's sacrifice of love in Christ. But this love is not genuine until it becomes a quadrangle, reaching out to others (vv. 7, 11).

The theme of abiding in God (vv. 13-16) is closely related to that of being "begotten" by (*born of*) God and "knowing" him in v. 7. "Abiding" is a favorite Johannine term. It describes the intimate, mystical relationship between Father, Son, Spirit, and believer. The evidence of this relationship is the presence of the Spirit in the believer's life (v. 13; cf. 3:24). The basis of the relationship for the believer is confessing that Jesus is the Son of God sent to save the world (vv. 14-15; cf. vv. 9-10). The stuff of the relationship is love—God's active love in the believer's life. God is love; abiding in love and abiding in God are one and the same (v. 16).

Verses 17-20 treat the "perfection" or "completion" of God's love in the believer. The very concept of perfection points to the relational character of love. It grows in proportion to the depth of one's abiding in God. It models itself after the example of Christ's sacrificial love (v. 17). As it deepens, fear is dispelled, for there is *no fear* in a genuine relationship of love (v. 18). Abiding in God's love, the believer has no room for fear, only for confidence on the day of judgment (v. 17). This confidence is only justified when love is perfect, and love is perfect only when it reaches out to others. Just as God loved us first and reached out to us, so must his love in us reach out to others (v. 19). Love is tangible (cf. 3:17-18). To claim love for an invisible God, a love that cannot be visibly demonstrated, is a sham. The arena for showing one's love for God is the visible world of the brother or sister in need (v. 20). As John has said before, none of this is new (2:7-8). It is *the commandment* of the Lord (v. 21; cf. John 13:34, 15:12).

Finding Life in the Son, 5:1-12

The concluding section of the body of 1 John is a final word of ASSURANCE to John's readers that they have obtained life in the Son (v. 12). Three characteristics in them demonstrate this (vv. 1-5), and three witnesses confirm it (vv. 6-12).

Verses 1-5 are a final summary of the three traits that mark one as begotten of God. First, they *love God,* and because they love the Father they love his children as well (v. 1). Second, they keep God's *commandments,* and this is not burdensome because God gives them the power to conquer the world (vv. 3-4; cf. Matt 11:30). Finally, they have the right faith, believing and confessing Jesus as the Christ, *the Son of God* (vv. 1, 5).

Verses 6-12 point to the witnesses that confirm that there is life in the Son. Verse 6 is a crux of interpretation: the proper confession of Jesus affirms that he came through *the water and the blood.* Do these refer to the INCARNATION, the water and blood of childbirth? Do they refer to his atoning death, the water and blood that flowed from his side at the CRUCIFIXION (John 19:34)? Or does the water refer to his BAPTISM and the blood to his atoning death? The last seems the more likely. The separatists from the community may have held a view much like that of Cerinthus, who maintained that the divine Spirit descended on the man Jesus at his baptism and departed before the crucifixion. It was the coming of the Spirit that counts, not the life of the man nor his death. No, replies John. He came by water and by blood, by his divine Spirit and by the outpouring of his human blood in his atoning death. The Spirit associated with his baptism and the blood of his crucifixion are thus two witnesses to who Christ is. The inner testimony of the Spirit is a third (v. 8). Finally, there is a fourth witness, *the testimony of God* (vv. 9-12). What is this witness of God? Is it his giving of his Son, as v. 11 seems to indicate? Or, is it his raising him from the dead and thus assuring the life that is in the Son?

Epilogue, 5:13-21

In vv. 13-21 John brings together themes which have run throughout the epistle. Verses 13-15 are words of assurance. Verse 13 gives John's main purpose in writing—that his readers might fully know that they *have* ETERNAL LIFE through their faith in the Son (cf. John 20:31). The false teachers may have raised doubts for some. John assures they need not fear for their salvation—they already have life in Christ. (Note the Johannine "realized eschatology.") Verses 14-15 give the further assurance that God answers their prayers. There is a qualification: the petitions must be *according to his will* (3:22 should also be read with this qualifier).

Verses 16-17 treat intercessory prayer of one Christian for another. John's readers are assured that God hears and grants such requests. But there is a sin for which John does not recommend intercession—the sin "unto death" (*mortal sin*). It is not altogether clear what he had in mind. Perhaps it was the sin of those who had left the community and rejected the significance of Christ's atoning death.

In vv. 18-19 John returns a final time to the subject of sin in the Christian. The one *born of God* does not live in the realm of sin, the world dominated by the evil one. Instead, children of God belong to God and Christ (the most likely referent for *gennetheis* in v. 18) keeps them from the devil's clutches.

The false teachers may have claimed special knowledge. John assures his readers that the SON OF GOD has come and given them insight into the truth (v. 20). He is himself the truth (John 14:6) and the only way to knowledge of the one true God (cf. John 1:18, 17:3).

Why John concludes with an abrupt command to shun idols is anybody's guess. The warning may be quite literal. The Greek world, and Ephesus in particular, was filled with idols. The reference may be figurative, as it often is in the NT. The error of the separatists with their proud claims to sinless perfection was itself a form of self-idolatry.

An Outline: Second John

I. Salutation, 1-3
II. Body of the Letter, 4-11
  A. Reminder of Love Commandment, 4-6
  B. False Teachers Described, 7-9
  C. Warning Not to Receive False Teachers, 10-11
III. Conclusion, 12-13

Salutation, 1-3

Second John follows closely the customary Greek letter form. The sender is *the elder*. The recipient is *the elect lady,* which most likely refers to a sister CHURCH. The church is one within the Johannine community, as the elder's implicit authority and the customary Johannine language would indicate (e.g., *all who know the truth . . . that abides in us*). In place of the usual Greek word of salutation, *chairein*, the NT writers characteristically substitute *grace* (*charis*) and add the Hebrew greeting *peace*. John adds a third greeting *mercy* (cf. 1 Tim 1:2; 2 Tim 1:2). At the end he tacks on two more distinctly Johannine blessings—*truth and love.*

Body of the Letter, 4-11

Reminder of Love Commandment, 4-6

The main body of 2 John is divisible into three parts: vv. 4-6, 7-9, and 10-11. In the first part (vv. 4-6) John reminds the sister church of the Lord's *new* commandment of love. John's main concern in the letter is to warn the congregation of the false teachers, and as is clear from 1 John, one of their primary faults was their lack of love. Another was their moral deficiency; so John reminds the congregation that genuine love for God is demonstrated by living according to the *commandments* (v. 6).

False Teachers Described, 7-9

In vv. 7-9 John focuses on the false teachers more directly. Once a part of the community, they have now *gone out* into the world (cf. 1 John 2:19). They belong to the deceiver, *the antichrist* (cf. 1 John 2:18, 26). They do not confess that Jesus Christ has come in the flesh; that is, they have a deficient view of his humanity (cf. 1 John 2:22f.; 4:2f.). John describes them as "progressives." They have gone out into the world and "gone ahead" in their theology, departing from the true teaching of Christ (v. 9). Johannine theology could itself be described as "progressive" in the sense of "advanced." The trouble with the separatists was in having gone too far in their accommodation to the world.

Warning Not to Receive False Teachers, 10-11

The false teachers do not yet seem to have reached the *elect lady*, and in vv. 10-11 John advises the congregation to shun them altogether should they arrive. They are not to accept them in their homes, not even to greet them. This should be understood in light of early Christian HOSPITALITY. Itinerant missionaries depended on local Christians to provide their basic needs as they traveled. In the case of false teachers, to show them the customary hospitality would only further their cause.

Conclusion, 12-13

As with the salutation, the conclusion to 2 John closely follows conventional letter form with its exchange of greetings. Even in the note that he had more to write but hopes to share it in person, the elder is following literary convention.

An Outline: Third John

I. Salutation, 1-2
II. Body of the Letter, 3-12
  A. Gaius's Hospitality, 3-8
  B. Diotrephes' Opposition, 9-11
  C. Commendation of Demetrius, 11-12
III. Conclusion, 13-15

Like 2 John, 3 John is quite brief, the length of a single PAPYRUS page. It too follows customary epistolary form. Unlike 2 John, it is written to an individual. It makes no mention of false teachers, but it does have an ironical relationship to 2 John. The refusal of hospitality *the elder* recommended to the "elect lady" (2 John 1) is now experienced by the elder himself.

Salutation, 1-2

The writer again identifies himself as *the elder* and addresses *Gaius*. We know nothing else of GAIUS. He may have been a member of Diotrephes' church (v. 9) or, as is more likely, one nearby. The prayer that all be well and the recipient *in good health* (v. 2) is a standard feature of private letters in John's day.

Body of the Letter, 3-12

The body of the letter falls into 3 parts: Gaius's hospitality (vv. 3-8), Diotrephes' opposition (vv. 9-11), and a commendation of *Demetrius* (vv. 11-12).

Gaius's Hospitality, 3-8

Verses 3-4 commend Gaius for the good report "the brothers" have given him, that he is walking in the truth. Most likely, this refers to his giving hospitality to "the brothers" (vv. 5-8). These were probably co-workers of John, itinerant missionaries who had been provided for by Gaius while they were working in his region. On returning to John's church, they had reported Gaius's generosity to the congregation. The passage reflects the early Christian practice of providing for traveling missionary workers. They were given food and lodging and on their departure enough provision to take them to their next stopping place. They refused help from non-Christians, depending wholly on the Christian community. Verse 8 states a basic principle of Christian missions—those who give support to missionaries participate in the ministry.

Diotrephes' Opposition, 9-11

Verses 9-11 reflect a breakdown in this arrangement. John had written a letter to *the church*, presumably regarding the provision of hospitality for his co-workers, but an individual in the congregation named *Diotrephes* had opposed him. Diotrephes' opposition was expressed in four ways: he spoke idle, gossipy words against John; he refused hospitality to the traveling Christian workers; he forbade others to give them hospitality; he expelled any member who did offer them support. We know nothing else of Diotrephes. John does not accuse him of any doctrinal or moral failure; so he doesn't seem associated with the separatists. We don't know from what he derived his POWER over the CHURCH, whether from office or personal prestige. John accuses him of liking *to put himself first* (v. 9).

The whole situation betrays a power struggle. Diotrephes may have been exerting the autonomy of his congregation against the authority of the elder John. The situation may reflect a transition stage in church organization. The old order of centralized apostolic authority was dying out. Whatever the situation, the irony is that Diotrephes was following the elder's own advice (cf. 2 John 10). The elder's emissaries were certainly not false teachers, but Diotrephes may have turned John's prohibition of supporting false teachers into a blanket principle covering all itinerant workers. Verse 11 is best understood in this connection. For John there is no greater work than loving one's fellow Christian. Refusing hospitality was an unloving, evil work, and evil workers have *not seen God*. Here John comes close to linking Diotrephes with the separatists.

Commendation of Demetrius, 11-12

The commendation of *Demetrius* (v. 12) is probably linked to the problem with Diotrephes. DEMETRIUS may have been the bearer of 3 John, and Gaius's accepting him and furnishing hospitality the whole purpose for John's writing.

Conclusion, 13-15

Third John's conclusion follows conventional epistolary form. The claim to have more to write and the desire to talk face-to-face are literary conventions (cf. 2 John 12). In this instance, however, John's desire for a visit may have been substantive. The problem with Diotrephes may have urged the elder to come *soon* (v. 14) and deal with the matter personally (cf. v. 10).

Jude

Watson E. Mills [MCB 1319-1323]

Introduction

Along with 2 and 3 John, Jude ranks among the most neglected and least well known of the twenty-seven books of the NT. The neglect of Jude is especially deplorable since Jude is a crucial document from a period of Christian history when rigid lines were being drawn between orthodoxy and heresy. In the strongest terms, the book of Jude posits a definite relationship between belief and practice.

Jude is included in a division of the NT CANON known variously as the GENERAL LETTERS or sometimes the "apostolic epistles" (James, 1, 2 Peter, 1, 2, 3 John, and Jude). These letters are said to be "catholic" (or universal) in their appeal since the letter opening does not name a single, specific recipient as do most of Paul's letters. The universal letters rather are addressed to all Christians everywhere (cf. 1 Pet 1:1). Yet despite this tradition, it would appear that the words of warning in Jude are directed to a very specific, though unnamed, community of Christians. In fact, the author appears to know the specific situation so well, that he is even aware of the movements of the "opponents" (see below, Opponents).

Authorship

The JUDE referred to in v. 1 is almost certainly JUDAS, the brother of Jesus, whose brother JAMES is James "the Just," a leader of the Jerusalem church. Both names were common in the early Christian community. For instance, the two disciples Judas Iscariot and Judas son of James; Judas Barsabbas (Acts 15:22-33); and, in the Maccabean era, Judas Maccabeus.

Jude is the short form for Judas (and is used only here in the NT for Ἰούδας, otherwise translated Judas) and James is the English form for Jacob. In the NT there are several men by each name. There is only one combination of brothers by those names, however—the James and Jude who are listed as two of the four brothers of Jesus (Matt 13:55; Mark 6:3). While most modern commentators agree on the referents, they disagree as to whether the author was the Jude referred to, or someone who used his name. The hypothesis that the author used the name of Jude has prevailed in many recent commentaries (Barnett, Grundmann, Reicke, Schelkle,

Sidebottom), if only because arguments for a date too late for Jude's lifetime are held by the commentators.

We know little about Jude the brother of Jesus. He was one of four brothers of Jesus (with James, Joseph, and Simon), probably younger than James (Matt 13:55; Mark 6:3). Apparently, like Jesus' other brothers, Jude did not become a follower of Jesus during Jesus' earthly ministry (John 7:5) but only after the resurrection (Acts 1:14). According to 1 Cor 9:5, the brothers of the Lord became traveling missionaries, and, presumably, Jude is included in that reference. His missionary work was probably among the Jews, but not necessarily limited to PALESTINE. Julius Africanus (Eusebius, *EccHist* 1.7.14) says that the relatives of Jesus spread the gospel throughout Palestine, starting from Nazareth and Cochaba (in TRANSJORDAN). According to the *Acts of Paul* (*NTApoc* 2:388), Judas, the Lord's brother, befriended Paul in DAMASCUS—a tradition based only on identifying the Judas of Acts 9:11 with the brother of the Lord.

The fact that the writer refers to himself as Jude the *brother of James* (v. 1) and not the brother of Jesus could be a telling argument against the hypothesis of pseudonymity. Such a description is much more easily explicable on the hypothesis of authenticity. The humility that prompted this description must in itself be regarded as a mark of genuineness, matched by his more eminent brother's similar behavior (Jas 1:1).

Date, Relationship to 1 Peter, Recipients

Many of the scholars who doubt the traditional authorship do so on the grounds that the content of the letter suggests it is of a late composition. Bo Reicke (1964), for example, settled on a date of 90 CE. Verse 3 supposes that the faith is already becoming a systematic body of doctrine, and vv. 17, 18 speak as if the generation of the apostles has died out. If Jude was indeed the younger brother of Jesus then is it not impossible that he was alive well into the latter part of the first century. J. A. T. Robinson argues that if *James* (v. 1) had already died, the author would have given some epithet such as "blessed" or "good" or "just" in referring to him. In the absence of any such reference Robinson holds that Jude must be dated before James's death in 62 CE.

The date of the writing is inevitably related to the question of the relationship between Jude and 2 Peter. Except for a few opening and closing words, virtually all of Jude is included in 2 Peter:

JUDE		2 PETER
2	=	1:2
3	=	1:5
5a	=	1:12
5b-19	=	2:1–3:3
24	=	3:14

Not only is the material common to the two letters, but each reflects a similar organizational approach. Both letters (1) warn against false teachers; (2) use three illustrations of God's judgment, two of which are identical (*angels* and *Sodom and Gomorrah*; (3) use BALAAM as an example of false teachers; (4) characterize the false teachers as those who are defiant toward divine authority; (5) use materials from apocryphal writings; and (6) use the same strong metaphors to characterize the false teachers (i.e., irrational animals, doomed to eternal darkness; spots and blemishes; arrogant boasters, etc.).

These literary similarities may be explained in one of three ways: (1) Second Peter borrowed heavily from Jude; (2) Jude borrowed heavily from 2 Peter; (3) both 2 Peter and Jude used a common source either oral or more probably written, but in either case no longer extant.

Since the early nineteenth century, a majority of scholarly opinion has favored the priority of Jude (option 1 above). Essentially the evidence is that (1) it is far more likely that the writer of 2 Peter would incorporate Jude into 2 Peter than that Jude would have lifted one chapter out of 2 Peter and presented it as a separate epistle; (2) the unknown writer of 2 Peter made use of the epistle from Jude, the brother of James and Jesus, to lend authority to his letter; (3) the writer of 2 Peter removed from Jude the explicit references to apocryphal books (*1 Enoch* in Jude 6, 14, and 2 Peter 2:4) and the identifiable materials of apocryphal books (the *Assumption of Moses* in Jude 9 and 2 Peter 2:11) to make his letter more acceptable to Christian readers.

There is nothing to indicate to whom the letter was written, or where the writer was situated, except that the author is addressing Christian people (v. 1) who are apparently beset by the same kind of problems that have plagued the recipients of 2 Peter. This reality may well suggest an identity of the two groups, but in no way proves it.

Opponents

The most universally held opinion is that these false teachers were Gnostics. Indeed, GNOSTICISM was a very widespread threat to the mainstream of Christian thought by the late first and early second centuries. By that time it was firmly entrenched in the Mediterranean world—Palestine, ASIA, Africa, and ROME. Some scholars, however, contend that this letter comes too early for it to contain specific refutations of a fullblown Gnosticism such as that found in the second century. Moreover, if it were a refutation of Gnosticism, it is surprisingly timid in its denunciation. Bauckham (1983) suggests the opponents were itinerant charismatics who have caused trouble for the Christian community elsewhere (Matt 7:15; 2 Cor 10-11; 1 John 4:1). Whoever they were, the "opponents" were not just casual passersby, but rather active members of the Christian community who were involved directly in its various functions, and thus had a fertile ground and opportunity to promulgate their heretical teachings.

Purpose and Structure

The purpose of the letter is to demonstrate how these false teachers pose a threat to the Christian community and how the readers must carry on the fight for the faith.

The statement of the theme (vv. 3-4) contains two parts: (1) an appeal to Jude's readers to carry on the fight *for the faith* and (2) the background to this appeal, that is, specific references to the false teachers, their character and their judgment. Similarly the body of the letter contains two parts that correspond to this division: (1) the background (vv. 5-19) establishes that these false teachers are condemned and that their judgment has been prophesied in the Hebrew Bible since the days of Enoch. Thus these false teachers constitute a genuine and serious threat to the churches. Thereby the way is prepared for the second, and central, part the of body of the letter; (2) the appeal (vv. 21-23) calls on his readers to fight for the faith.

Jude cites a series of four "texts" although they are not actual quotations so much as textual allusions. The arrangement is such that each text is followed by an interpretative section:

TEXT	INTERPRETATION	LOCATION	DRAWN FROM
one		vv. 5-7	three types
	one	vv. 8-10	from the Hebrew Bible
two		v. 11	three types
	two	vv. 12-13	from the Hebrew Bible
three		vv. 14-15	the Book
	three	v. 16	of Enoch
four		vv. 17-18	the
	four	v. 19	Apostles

The first two "texts" are summary references to two sets of three OT types (vv. 5-7, 11). It is evident from the way he quotes the material in two of these instances (Prov 25:14 and Isa 57:20) that here Jude is depending upon the text of the Hebrew Bible and not that of the LXX as has been often supposed. The writer then quotes a prophecy of *Enoch* (vv. 14-15) and a prophecy *of the apostles* (vv. 17-18). Each is followed by a passage of interpretation (vv. 8-10, 12-13, 16, 19) which, by pointing to the character and behavior of the false teachers, identifies them as those to whom this type of prophecy applies. In text one, a secondary text (v. 9) is introduced in the course of the passage of interpretation.

Ellis (1978) has demonstrated that vv. 5-19 are actually cast in the form of a midrash. The term "midrash" is used in this instance to describe Jude's exegesis of the scriptures and other ancient materials and his application of these results to a specific historical situation. The term does *not* imply that Jude's midrash bears any close resemblance to the highly developed and stylized forms of later rabbinic midrashim.

The function of this section is to provide the background for the ultimate purpose of the letter: the appeal for its readers to *contend for the faith* (v. 3).

The midrash demonstrates the clear danger that these false teachers bring to the church, and prepares the way for the clarification and expansion of the purpose of the letter (vv. 20-23) already hinted at in v. 3.

In vv. 20-23 the author brings his readers to a dramatic conclusion, the urgency and relevancy of which has been heightened. Jude issues the call for his readers to fight to keep the faith.

For Further Study

In the *Mercer Dictionary of the Bible*: ENOCH, FIRST; ENOCH, SECOND; GENERAL LETTERS; GNOSTICISM; JAMES; JUDE, LETTER OF; PETER, LETTERS OF.

In other sources: R. J. Bauckham, *Jude, 2 Peter*; J. D. Charles, "Jude's Use of Pseudepigraphical Source-Material as Part of a Literary Strategy," *NTS* 37 (1991): 130–45; J. N. D. Kelly, *A Commentary on the Epistles of Peter and Jude*; B. Reicke, *The Epistles of James, Peter, and Jude;* E. M. Sidebottom, *James, Jude, and 2 Peter*; D. F. Watson, "The Letter of Jude," *NIB*.

Commentary

An Outline

I. Greeting, 1-2
II. Purpose, 3-4
  A. Appeal, 3
  B. Background, 4
III. Development of the Background, 5-19
  A. Description of the False Teachers as Sinners, 5-10
  B. Description of How These False Teachers Are Leading Others into Sin, 11-13
  C. A Prophecy Adapted from Enoch, 14-16
  D. A Prophecy Adapted from the Apostles, 17-19
IV. The Appeal, 20-23
V. Closing Doxology, 24-25

Greeting, 1-2

This section follows the form of the Jewish letter with the parties formula (from sender "X" to recipient "Y") and salutation or greeting. The authority rests upon the term "servant" (δοῦλος) not upon identification of the writer with Jesus' blood line. *Those who are called* reflects the fact that "the called" (κλητοῖς) has become a technical term within the Christian community, indicating those who have responded to the gospel. The tripartite formula *called, beloved,* and *kept* could possibly reflect an understanding of the servant songs of Isaiah (41:9; 42:1; 42:6). Jude omits "grace" (χάρις) in the salutation. The *mercy, peace, and love* offered here is also found in 1 and 2 Timothy.

Purpose, 3-4

The present less-finished treatise has been substituted for the one planned because of the danger of the present situation, that is, there are those present who refuse to follow the teachings of the faith and are ready to lead others in this heretical vein. The writer is thinking not so much of any creed or dogma, but rather an erroneous and unacceptable mode of conduct. There is a contemptuous ring in the phrase *certain intruders* who *have stolen* their way into the community. This threat is real; the author calls his readership to their responsibility to face up to this threat.

Development of the Background, 5-19

Description of the False Teachers as Sinners, 5-10

Next, the author describes the certainty of the judgment upon any who fail to live out the faith. Examples from the Hebrew Bible make it abundantly clear that status alone is no guarantee of a saving relationship with God. These false teachers, and any who follow them, are sinners and must face the consequences of their actions.

Description of How These False Teachers Are Leading Others into Sin, 11-13

Here the author points out, rather graphically, how as in the cases of CAIN, BALAAM, and KORAH, these false teachers are trying to lead others into immorality and away from their calling. These false teachers are motivated by jealousy and pride—a pride so great that it cannot tolerate any knowledge or power greater than its own.

A Prophecy Adapted from Enoch, 14-16

Jude quotes Enoch's prophecy as dramatic evidence of the impending punishment upon the false teachers. Apparently the Book of Enoch was well known in the first century, and Enoch himself was remembered as one "who walked with God" (Gen 5:22, 24). Here the Lord has come to bring judgment upon the ungodly, their character, their behavior. *Grumblers* (see Exod 16:2, 9) calls to mind the experience of the Israelites as they wandered aimlessly in the wilderness. These false teachers are chronic faultfinders, who, while incessantly complaining about others, follow their own lustful desires without regard for others.

A Prophecy Adapted from the Apostles, 17-19

Taken from the words spoken earlier by the apostles (though the specific tradition quoted remains unknown), this apostolic prophecy is expressed as a warning. That such persons as these would appear among the faithful is itself a sign that the "end times" are near. These false teachers cause serious divisions within the community by setting themselves up as superior to ordinary Christians. Jude maintains it is *these ungodly people* who are *devoid of the Spirit*.

The Appeal, 20-23

All that has come before has pointed the reader to this final appeal. Here Jude offers an exhortation to the faithful, a kind of "Christian antidote" to countermand the work of the false teachers. This appeal to action begins *But you, beloved* to heighten the contrast between the faithful and the false teachers. The contrast is further sharpened when he adds praying *in the Holy Spirit* as a quantifier for the faithful. This theme calls to mind a similar note found in the writings of Paul (Rom 8:26; 1 Cor 12:3; Gal 4:6; Eph 6:18). The referent here is in no way equivocal since the false teachers are without the Spirit. Jude offers these specific ingredients for his "antidote": (1) *build yourselves up on [the] most holy faith*; (2) *pray in the Holy Spirit*; (3) *keep yourselves in the love of God*; (4) *look forward to the mercy of our Lord Jesus Christ.*

Verses 22-23 abruptly shifts the focus to the way in which in the readers should respond toward those have been taken in, to greater and lesser degrees, by the false teachers. The text here is uncertain and it is not immediately clear whether Jude refers to two or three groups of individuals. The NRSV follows א and A (three groups) while the NEB follows B and Clement of Alexandria. If we are to understand three groups, Jude's advice becomes progressively more drastic: (1) those who have not made up their minds—they must be convinced by argument; (2) those who are already involved with the false teachers—spare no effort in trying to rescue these (*save others by snatching them out of the fire*, v. 23); (3) those who have strayed so far they are only to be pitied—these must be feared by the faithful so as to avoid contamination.

Closing Doxology, 24-25

Beyond the responsibilities of the recipients is the sure presence of God's support and protection that in effect guarantees that their efforts to avoid spiritual heresy will not be in vain. These closing words call to mind an eschatological celebration of worship. The believers celebrate the final consequence of God's purposes, that is, they are found to be a suitable sacrifice before God.

Works Cited

Barnett, A. E. 1962. "The Epistle of Jude. Introduction," *IB*.

Bauckham, Richard J. 1983. *Jude, 2 Peter*. WBC.

Ellis, E. Earle. 1978. *Prophecy and Hermeneutic in Early Christianity*.

Grundmann, W. 1974. *Der Brief des Judas und der zweite Brief des Petrus*. THKNT.

Robinson, J. A. T. 1976. *Redating the New Testament*.

Reicke, Bo. 1964. *The Epistles of James, Peter, and Jude*. AncB.

Schelkle, K. H. 1980. *Die Petrusbriefe, der Judasbrief*. HTKNT.

Sidebottom, E. M. 1967. *James, Jude, and 2 Peter*. NCB.

Revelation

Mitchell G. Reddish [MCB 1325-1347]

Introduction

Few writings have captured the imagination of as many people as has the Book of Revelation. Artists, musicians, and writers have been intrigued by its rich imagery and symbolism and have mined its treasures as inspiration for their own works. Examples include Olivier Messiaen's musical composition *Quartet for the End of Time* and Handel's *Messiah*; Dürer's woodcuts and Michelangelo's *Last Judgment* in the Sistine Chapel; William Blake's *America, a Prophecy*; and Ernesto Cardenal's *Apocalypse*. People in despair and in crisis situations have turned to Revelation for comfort and hope, finding assurance in the book's confident assertion that God is in control of the universe and that good will ultimately triumph over EVIL. Its hymns, prayers, and words of praise have greatly enriched the church's liturgy.

In spite of its tremendous influence, Revelation remains for many readers a mysterious, enigmatic, even frightening work. The bizarre symbolism and repetitive structure of the book have caused many readers to abandon hope of making sense of John's message. On the other hand, some people claim to possess the key to unlocking the mysteries of this work, viewing it as a book of predictions of soon-coming world events. Armed with fanciful interpretations often more bizarre than the images of the book itself, these individuals transform John's writing into a propaganda sheet for their own futuristic views. Both reactions to the book—bewilderment and sensationalism—need to be avoided. Properly understood, Revelation contains a message of hope and comfort, as well as a call to faithfulness, that is still as valid to the CHURCH of today as it was to the church of the first century.

Literary Form

The Book of Revelation exhibits characteristics of several literary types. The work contains the major elements of ancient letters: greeting (1:4-5a), blessing or thanksgiving (1:5b-6), body (1:7–22:20), and closing (22:21). Embedded within the work are also seven messages to local churches, each cast in a form similar to a letter. Some scholars have argued that Revelation should be understood as prophetic literature. Indeed the author calls his writing a *prophecy* (1:3; 22:7, 10, 18, 19) and refers to the prophets as his brothers (22:9, NRSV *comrades*). Other scholars have viewed Revelation as modeled after the form of ancient Greek drama.

As valid as these insights may be, most scholars agree that Revelation is best understood as belonging to the literary form of an apocalypse, a type of writing popular in certain Jewish and Christian circles. The name of the genre is derived from the opening words of Revelation in which the author calls the contents of his work an *apocalypsis* (revelation). Ancient apocalypses were writings that purported to contain revelations of cosmic secrets, mediated to human recipients by supernatural beings either directly or in visions or dreams. The contents of the revelations usually consisted of both eschatological and otherworldly information. Although the social setting for many of the ancient Jewish and Christian apocalypses is unclear, apocalypses seem to have been produced in response to some sort of crisis situation (political, military, social, theological), either real or imagined. APOCALYPTIC LITERATURE was written to offer its readers a message of hope and comfort by providing an alternative view of reality from that dominant in the current sociohistorical setting. Apocalyptic writings assured their readers that, in spite of how the situation appeared, God was in control of history and the universe. Eventually God would triumph, rewarding the faithful and destroying evil.

Several literary and theological characteristics, while not definitive of the genre, are commonly found in apocalypses. Among the literary characteristics are pseudonymous authorship, historical reviews in the form of *ex eventu* prophecy ("prophecy" after the event has happened), mythological and symbolic language, visionary and auditory revelations, and rapture experiences. Theological characteristics include a dualistic theology (God versus the powers of evil), a dualistic view of history (two ages: the present, evil age and the glorious age to come), expectation of the imminent end of this age, and a deterministic understanding of world events.

Provenance and Social Setting

Evidence from Revelation indicates that the author and his audience were residents of Asia Minor, located in present day Turkey. The author states that he received the revelation contained in the Apocalypse while he was on the island of PATMOS, located off the coast of Asia Minor in the Aegean Sea. In addition, churches in seven cities of Asia Minor are recipients of special messages in Revelation.

John states he is on Patmos *because of the word of God and the testimony of Jesus* (1:9). Whereas this could mean John went to the island to share the Christian faith with the people there, the usual understanding is that John was banished by the Roman authorities to Patmos for being a Christian. Some islands in this area were used by the Romans as penal colonies, although there is no evidence that Patmos was ever so used. Similar phrasing elsewhere in the book supports the understanding that John's presence on Patmos was due to persecution (cf. 6:9; 12:11; 20:4).

The social and political setting reflected in Revelation is one of persecution and even martyrdom. Not only has John been banished because of his faith, but he also knows of other Christians who have been killed, even singling one out by name, *Antipas* (2:13; see also 2:9-10; 6:9-11; 16:6; 17:6; 18:24; 19:2; 20:4). Martyrdom is a major interpretive key for Revelation, with martyrs receiving special praise and reward. Calls to faithfulness and endurance resound throughout the book. Whereas some persecution seems to be based on Jewish hostilities (2:9-10), the majority derives from the Roman government. Enforcement of emperor worship and punishment of those who refuse is a major cause of the persecution (chap. 13).

This sociopolitical setting of suffering and persecution has been questioned by scholars who correctly point out that evidence for such persecution is meager or even nonexistent. No empire-wide persecution against Christians occurred in the first century. Furthermore, the portrayal of the emperor Domitian as a cruel despot by Roman and early Christian writers is likely due more to bias and imagination than to historical fact. Yet even if this is true, the author of Revelation was aware of some cases of persecution and martyrdom, no matter how limited in scope or duration. From his vantage point as a recipient of such persecution, the situation did indeed seem perilous. Reality is a matter of perspective, and from the perspective of John and his audience persecution was a present experience and a future threat. Although all Christians in Asia Minor might not have viewed the social and historical situation as life-threatening, John certainly did. Thus the setting for Revelation can be correctly labeled a persecution setting, even if that persecution was not widespread.

Date and Authorship

The writing of Revelation is commonly placed during the time of Domitian, emperor of Rome 81–96 CE. The statement of IRENAEUS (ca. 140–ca. 202 CE) that the VISION of the Revelation was seen at the end of the reign of Domitian is the earliest external evidence attesting the date of Revelation (*AdvHaer* 5.30.3). Several writers in the following centuries also support a Domitianic dating for the book. Other early writers mention the reigns of Claudius, Nero, and Trajan as the setting for Revelation. Internal evidence lends additional support to the claim of Irenaeus. In Revelation *Babylon* (14:8; 16:19; 17:5; 18:2, 10, 21) is used as a symbolic name for ROME, a practice that would be appropriate only after 70 CE. As Babylon had destroyed Jerusalem in the sixth century BCE and had persecuted the people of God, Rome had also destroyed Jerusalem (70 CE) and was now persecuting God's people. A further indication of dating appears in the use of the Nero *redivivus* myth in chaps. 13 and 17. This belief in the return of Nero was popular during the last half of the first century, following the death of Nero in 66 CE. Since the internal evidence coheres with Irenaeus's dating of the book during the time of Domitian, most scholars place its composition around 95 CE.

The author of Revelation identifies himself as *John* (1:9). Christian writers as early as the second century identified this John as the disciple of Jesus. This identification is almost certainly ruled out, however, by the way in which the author refers to *the twelve apostles* as the *foundations* of the new Jerusalem (21:14). The writer is looking back on a venerated group of heroes of the faith. Furthermore, the author never claims apostolic authority for his writing. He describes himself simply as *your brother who share with you in Jesus the persecution and the kingdom and the patient endurance*" (1:9). Whereas the majority of Jewish and Christian apocalypses were written pseudonymously, such does not seem to be true of Revelation. The writer of the Apocalypse apparently does not claim to be anyone other than who he is: John, a Christian leader who has received a revelation from God while on the island of Patmos. John was obviously well known to the Christians in Asia Minor and knew the churches and their backgrounds intimately (2:1–3:22). Since he referred to his message as a *prophecy* (1:3), he viewed himself as a Christian prophet and had possibly functioned in this role among the Christians in Asia Minor. His extensive use of the Hebrew Bible and the many semitisms in his Greek suggest that he was a Jewish Christian, likely originally from Palestine.

Literary Structure

The literary structure of Revelation has been the focus of much debate among interpreters. All commentators recognize the importance of the number seven as a structuring device in the book—seven messages, seven seals, seven trumpets, seven bowls. How are these series of sevens related? The seven messages in 2:1–3:22 have sometimes been viewed as disconnected to the remainder of the work. A close examination, however, reveals otherwise. The clearest example of such connections occurs in the introductions to each of the seven messages, which borrow phrases from the description of the exalted Christ in chap. 1. Furthermore, the themes of persecution, faithfulness, endurance, rewards for the righteous, and the new Jerusalem, which are prominent in the seven messages, are also the major themes in the remainder of the book.

Some interpreters see the four series of sevens as consecutive series; that is, John presents in chronological order his vision of coming events. A progression is certainly intended in the events described, as evidenced by the opening of the seventh seal that introduces the seven trumpets. Yet the progression is not strictly linear. Rather, later events sometimes recapitulate earlier events. For example, the plagues and calamities of the seven trumpets describe in a new way the punishments and judgments of the end times depicted by the seven seals. Instead of a straight linear progression, the structure of Revelation presents a movement that is spiral. Earlier events are presented in different forms and use different images. As in certain musical pieces, a theme is played, then variations of that theme occur, each variation moving the piece forward. In Revelation, the movement of the work is from John's historical situation to the arrival of the new Jerusalem, the fulfillment of God's ultimate plan for creation. Within that overall forward movement, however, are numerous instances of overlapping and parallel scenes.

Interpreting Revelation

Fascinated and intrigued by the often bizarre imagery in Revelation, interpreters throughout the centuries have attempted in various ways to understand this writing. One of the more popular approaches today understands the book as a catalogue of unfulfilled prophecies of the final days of history. Proponents of this view believe that they are now living in the last days and that informed readers can see predictions in Revelation being fulfilled in current world events. Wars, natural disasters, societal ills, and economic catastrophes are all interpreted as signs of the end times. The beasts and other symbols of evil are identified as actual persons and institutions now in existence or soon to appear. According to this view, John was not addressing the concerns of his own time and situation, but was speaking about the events unfolding today. One of the major problems with this method of interpreting Revelation is that it divorces the work from its first-century historical context. The message of Revelation would have been virtually incomprehensible and meaningless to the Christians of Asia Minor to whom it was addressed. Another problem with this approach is that it fails to take seriously the apocalyptic genre of Revelation with its extensive use of ancient myths and symbols.

A proper interpretation of the Apocalypse must take account of the sociohistorical context and the literary genre of the work. In addition, the function of the language of Revelation needs to be understood. The language of the book is primarily pictorial and symbolic. It is not propositional language. The message of Revelation cannot be condensed into neat, concise theological statements. The language of Revelation is evocative, powerful, emotive language, more akin to poetry than to prose. The Book of Revelation should overwhelm the reader (or hearer) with visual and auditory symbols. Revelation needs to arouse the imagination. It must be experienced, not deciphered. A skilled exegete can explain the origin of many of John's symbols and images by pointing to the Hebrew Bible, Jewish APOCALYPTIC LITERATURE, and ancient myths as the sources for much of the writing. A scholar can also help us understand how John's original readers may have understood the book's message in their sociohistorical context. As helpful and necessary as these insights are, however, they do not exhaust the meaning of the Apocalypse. The symbols in the book are multivalent and open-ended. They continue to speak to new generations of perceptive readers who realize that the monstrous evils of pride, idolatry, abuse of power, and dehumanization represented by the beasts of Revelation continue to appear in ever new forms, manifesting themselves in individuals and institutions. Likewise, the images of hope and assurance that empowered and comforted John's first-century audience still function in that manner for modern readers.

For Further Study

In the *Mercer Dictionary of the Bible*: APOCALYPTIC LITERATURE; CHURCHES OF REVELATION; LAMB OF GOD; MYTH; NT USE OF OT; REVELATION, BOOK OF; PERSECUTION IN THE NT; SYMBOL; VISION.

In other sources: G. R. Beasley-Murray, *The Book of Revelation*, NCB; I. T. Beckwith, *The Apocalypse of John*; J. L. Blevins, *Revelation as Drama*; M. E. Boring, *Revelation*, Interp; G. B. Caird, *The Revelation of St. John*, HNTC; A. Y. Collins, *The Apocalypse, N.T. Message*, *Crisis and Catharsis: The Power of the Apocalypse*, and "Revelation, Book of," *AncBD* 5:694-708; E. Schüssler Fiorenza, *The Book of Revelation*, and "Revelation: Vision of a Just World," *Procl*; C. J. Hemer, *Letters to the Seven Churches*; R. L. Jeske, *Revelation for Today*; C. C. Rowland, "The Book of Revelation," *NIB*; J. P. M. Sweet, *Revelation*, WPelC; L. L. Thompson, *The Book of Revelation*.

Commentary

I. Prologue, 1:1-8
II. The Commissioning of John, 1:9-20
III. The Messages to the Seven Churches, 2:1–3:22
IV. The Heavenly Throne Room, 4:1–5:14
V. The Seven Seals, 6:1–8:5
  A. The First Six Seals, 6:1-17
  B. Interlude, 7:1-17
  C. The Seventh Seal, 8:1-5
VI. The Seven Trumpets, 8:6–11:19
  A. The First Six Trumpets, 8:6–9:21
  B. Interlude, 10:1–11:13
  C. The Seventh Trumpet, 11:14-19
VII. The Great Conflict, 12:1–14:20
  A. The Vision of the Great Dragon, 12:1-18
  B. The Two Beasts, 13:1-18
  C. Interlude, 14:1-20
VIII. The Seven Bowl Plagues, 15:1–16:21
  A. The Martyrs on the Heavenly Shore, 15:1-4
  B. The Seven Angels with Bowls, 15:5-8
  C. The Pouring of the Seven Bowls, 16:1-21
IX. The Fall of Babylon, 17:1–19:10
  A. The Great Whore, 17:1-18
  B. Laments on Earth, 18:1-24
  C. Celebration in Heaven, 19:1-10
X. The Final Victory, 19:11–20:15
XI. The New Jerusalem, 21:1–22:5
  A. New Heaven and New Earth, 21:1-8
  B. The Holy City, 21:9-27
  C. The River of Life, 22:1-5
XII. Epilogue, 22:6-21

Prologue, 1:1-8

The first two verses serve as a title to the work and describe it as a revelation (Gk. *apocalypsis*) from God mediated to John by a heavenly messenger, dealing with soon-occurring events. This description contains many of the elements of the literary genre of an apocalypse as defined by scholars. Indeed, the genre derives its name from the opening word of v. 1 in the Greek text. Although God is the ultimate source of the revelation, it comes to John from Jesus through an ANGEL. John is described as one *who testified to the word of God and to the testimony of Jesus Christ* (v. 2). Testifying, or bearing witness (*martyreō*), is an important theme in Revelation (cf. 1:5, 9; 2:13; 3:14; 6:9; 11:3; 12:11, 17; 17:6; 20:4). One of the purposes of the writing was to call all Christians to be faithful witnesses. The benediction in v. 3 (the first of seven benedictions in the work) indicates that John intended his work to be read aloud to the Christians in Asia Minor as they gathered for worship. Like other apocalyptic writers, John saw himself as living in the final days of history.

These verses comprise an epistolary introduction, describing both the sender and the recipients of the message. *The seven churches* (v. 4) refer to the churches in the Roman province of Asia mentioned in 1:11 and 2:1–3:22. Although addressed to these seven churches specifically, the work is intended for all Christians because the number seven often symbolized completeness or totality. The description of God as the one *who is and who was and who is to come* (vv. 4, 8), an adaptation of Exod 3:14, affirms the continuing presence of God in the lives of believers. Note the change in structure at the end of this trilogy. John does not describe God as the one "who will be" but uses a more dynamic phrase, the one *who is to come*. God is active, not static. *The seven spirits* before God's throne symbolize the power and presence of God active throughout the world (cf. 5:6; Zech 4:1-14), later expressed in Christian theology by the doctrine of the HOLY SPIRIT. The titles attributed to Christ—*the faithful witness, the firstborn of the dead, and the ruler of the kings of the earth*—would have been especially appropriate to John's first-century readers who were faced with persecution and martyrdom. If they too are faithful witnesses, refusing to concede to the divine claims of earthly rulers, they will share in Christ's resurrection.

After the doxology to Christ in vv. 5b-6, John, in language borrowed from Dan 7:13 and Zech 12:10, delivers a prophetic pronouncement of the coming of Christ. The coming, or PAROUSIA, of Jesus Christ, which symbolizes the fulfillment of God's goal for the universe, is portrayed in the subsequent visions (19:11-21), is divinely promised (22:7, 12, 20), and is the final plea of the book (22:17, 20). The prologue closes with a threefold declaration from God, giving divine assurance of the authenticity of John's revelation. This is one of only two places in the book where God speaks directly (cf. 21:5). The ascription *the Alpha and the Omega*, the first and last letters of the Greek alphabet, identify God as the beginning and the end of all history. God is the creator and the consummator of the universe.

The Commissioning of John, 1:9-20

Like many of the Hebrew prophets, particularly ISAIAH and EZEKIEL, John relates a dramatic experience of being commissioned as a PROPHET. *In the spirit* means overcome by the Spirit of God, perhaps in a trance. This phrase identifies John's experience as a visionary experience. *On the Lord's day* probably refers to Sunday, the day of Christ's resurrection. The selection of these particular seven churches to be recipients of the revelation to John is not clear. Perhaps they were the churches with which John was most familiar.

John's vision of the SON OF MAN combines features from the "Ancient One" in Dan 7:9 and the mighty figure of Dan 10 (cf. also Ezekiel's vision of God in 1:26-28). The phrase *one like the Son of Man* (v. 12, lit. "one like a son of man," i.e., one in human form) is also drawn from Daniel (7:13). The exalted Christ stands among the churches, a symbol of power, majesty, and judgment.

Overwhelmed by the spectacle, John falls to his feet (cf. Dan 10:8-9). Both the description of the Son of Man and his first words to John (*I am the first and the last*) indicate his unity with God. He is the resurrected Christ who has conquered death and the place of the dead (*Hades*). For John's readers faced with the possibility of death, that claim would indeed be comforting. The imagery of *the seven stars* in Christ's right hand is perhaps drawn from contemporary depictions of the emperors holding the seven planets or stars in their hands, symbolizing their power over the world. For John, Christ and not the emperor is sovereign. Christ identifies the stars as *the angels of the seven churches*. These angels are the guardian angels of the churches, but even more, they are the heavenly counterparts of the churches. (Cf. the assertion in Dan 10 that nations have such heavenly guardians/counterparts.) When the angels receive the message, the churches do also. The imagery of *the seven lampstands* is derived from Zech 4 where a seven-branched lampstand represents the presence of God (cf. Exod 25:31-40). For John *the seven lampstands are the seven churches* (v. 20), in the midst of whom Christ stands to strengthen and uphold them.

The Messages to the Seven Churches, 2:1–3:22

Often called letters, these messages are cast more in the form of court decrees or proclamations. With slight variations, the messages follow a typical pattern: address to the angel of the church, description of Christ (in terms borrowed from the attributes of the Son of Man in chap. 1), words of praise and/or admonition and condemnation, exhortation, a call to hear, and a promise to the ones who conquer. The information stated or implied about each of the churches bespeaks John's deep familiarity with each of the cities (see Hemer 1986; see also CHURCHES OF REVELATION).

2:1-7. Ephesus. EPHESUS, a seaport and major trading center, was the most important city in Asia Minor. The city was renowned for its temple to the goddess ARTEMIS (cf. Acts 19:21-41), and was also one of the centers of the imperial cult in Asia Minor. Christianity had been established early in Ephesus and had prospered (cf. Acts 18:24–19:41). Christ praises the church at Ephesus on two accounts: its patience and endurance, apparently in the face of some sort of persecution, and its faithfulness in discerning good from evil, truth from falsehood. The latter commendation includes the church's wisdom in rejecting the works of the NICOLAITANS, a group mentioned more fully in the letter to the church at Pergamum. The Ephesian church, apparently in its zeal to preserve the integrity of its faith and root out evil, has become overzealous and forgotten that love is the first responsibility of Christians. The church is admonished to repent of this error or Christ will come in judgment on the church. To *remove your lampstand from its place* means that the people will no longer be a part of the body of Christ. As in all the letters, a closing promise is given to those who conquer, that is, the faithful believers. The promises in all the letters are variations of the same theme—the faithful are assured of participation in the kingdom of God. The *paradise* imagery in v. 7 is found in many apocalyptic writings. The world to come will be a restored and transformed Garden of Eden where the faithful will enjoy a blessed existence.

2:8-11. Smyrna. Like Ephesus, SMYRNA was an important seaport, located approximately thirty-five miles north of Ephesus. It was a city loyal to Rome. In 195 BCE the city erected a temple to the goddess Roma and in 26 CE was given the right to build a temple in honor of the emperor TIBERIUS. Nothing is known of the beginnings of Christianity in Smyrna. During the reign of Trajan (98–117 CE), IGNATIUS, bishop of ANTIOCH, was martyred. On his way to Rome to be executed, Ignatius stayed in Smyrna, and later on the journey wrote a letter back to the church there and one to Polycarp, bishop of Smyrna. Around 156 CE Polycarp himself suffered the fate of martyrdom (see POLYCARP, MARTYRDOM OF). Christ issues no criticisms of the church at Smyrna, only encouraging and extolling the Christians there. Although outwardly poor and afflicted, they are rich in faith and in spirit. The church is suffering persecution from Jews in Smyrna, who because of their attacks on God's people no longer deserve to be called Jews but *a synagogue of Satan*. This statement should not be generalized to mean that John condemns all Jewish people. His harsh words here are aimed only at those who were persecuting the church. John warns the church at Smyrna that more persecution is to be expected. They are to remain faithful, however, even if martyrdom is required. The faithful will receive eternal life, symbolized by the *crown of life*. In Greek athletic contests, the victors were awarded a crown or wreath. To be exempted from *the second death* is another metaphor for ETERNAL LIFE (cf. 20:6, 14).

2:12-17. Pergamum. The capital of the Roman province of Asia, PERGAMUM was home to numerous temples, among them the spectacular temple to ZEUS and the famous ASCLEPION, devoted to Asclepius, the god of healing. Pergamum was an important center for the imperial cult also, having been the first city in the province of Asia to erect a temple to the deified Augustus. The references to *Satan's throne* and *where Satan lives* (v. 13) likely refer to the imperial cult, although some commentators see them as references to the temples of Zeus or Asclepius. The Christians in Pergamum are commended for their faithfulness even in the face of martyrdom. Strong in resisting this external threat, they have been weak in resisting internal threats to their faith. Some in their group have accepted the false teaching of BALAAM, a Mesopotamian diviner who was blamed for leading the Israelites into idolatry and sexual immorality (see Num 22–25, 31). The Nicolaitans at Pergamum are accused of a similar heresy. They eat food sacrificed to idols and practice FORNICATION. They were likely libertine Christians, similar to those in CORINTH (1 Cor 8–10), who believed it was acceptable to eat meat that had been ritually slaughtered and offered to pagan gods or even to the emperor. Whether fornication here is to be understood literally as sexual immorality or figuratively for participation in pagan cults (as often in the Hebrew Bible) is unclear. The faithful will receive MANNA and a white stone. In some Jewish traditions the miracle of the manna in the wilderness (Exod 16:13-36) was expected to be repeated in the messianic age. White stones were used to indicate acquittal in a jury trial and also served as admission tickets to certain events. Either meaning could apply here.

2:18-29. Thyatira. THYATIRA was the least important of the seven cities whose churches are sent messages in Revelation. LYDIA, the dealer of purple cloth whom PAUL met in PHILIPPI (Acts 16:11-15), was originally from Thyatira. The city was home to a large number of trade and craft guilds, organizations that served both social and religious functions. The church at Thyatira is praised highly for its works and for its increasing faithfulness. Like the church at Pergamum, the Thyatirans have not been diligent enough, however, in resisting false teachings and practices. A woman referred to as *Jezebel* (cf. the stories of JEZEBEL in 1–2 Kings) was serving as a prophet and teacher in the church. Her practices were similar to those of the Nicolaitans at Pergamum. Perhaps she was claiming that Christians could participate in the religious rituals and practices of the trade guilds without compromising their faith. Having been warned previously, perhaps by John, she has persisted in her practices. Now she and her followers will be punished by God. The *bed* upon which the woman is to be thrown (v. 22) is likely a sickbed. *Adultery* here is almost certainly figurative. The woman and her followers may have claimed to be so "spiritual" and so in touch with the supernatural world that they could fathom even *'the deep things of Satan'* (v. 24). On the other hand, this phrase may be John's sarcastic parody of their claim to be in touch with the deep mysteries of God. In language borrowed from Ps 2, the faithful are promised that they will triumph over evil and rule with Christ, *the morning star* (v. 28; cf. 22:16).

3:1-6. Sardis. The city of SARDIS had once been the capital of the ancient kingdom of Lydia and a wealthy city. Under Roman rule it was still a prosperous commercial center but did not match its former glory. Sardis was located on an almost impregnable acropolis. On two occasions in its history, however, the city had been conquered due to the lack of diligence on the part of its defenders. John may be alluding to these events in the city's past when he tells the church that it must *wake up* (vv. 2-3) and be diligent in its work. The church in Sardis receives only mild praise (v. 4). The majority of the message to the church is an admonition to wake up and be more alive. The church suffers from lethargy and apathy. Outwardly it appears vital, but its inward condition is critical. The church is on the point of death. If the church does not change, then Christ will come in judgment on them. Their lack of watchfulness will prove disastrous, for Christ *will come like a thief* (cf. Matt 24:42-44; 1 Thes 5:2). The faithful at Sardis will be clothed in white garments, a symbol of purity, and their names will not be removed from *the book of life*. Ancient cities kept registries of their citizens. The book of life is the list of heavenly citizens (cf. Exod 32:32; Dan 12:1). The promise of Christ to confess the name of the faithful before God echoes a similar saying in the Gospels (cf. Matt 10:32; Luke 12:8).

3:7-13. Philadelphia. Founded in the second century BCE by either Attalus II Philadelphus or his older brother Eumenes II (who succeeded one another as kings of Pergamum), the city of PHILADELPHIA and the surrounding area were subject to frequent earthquakes. In 17 CE Philadelphia (as well as Sardis) suffered major destruction from an earthquake. Philadelphia, like Smyrna, was visited by Ignatius on his way to martyrdom and the church there received a letter from Ignatius. The *key of David* imagery is borrowed from Isa 22:22. Here, Christ, as the holder of the key, grants or withholds entrance into the KINGDOM OF GOD. The church at Philadelphia receives no condemnation, only commendation, exhortation, and promise. The *open door* (v. 8) provided by Christ leads to God. Access to God is at the heart of the struggle for this church. The local Jews were perhaps denying the validity of the Christians' approach to God and excluding them from the synagogues (v. 9). The words of Christ offer them assurance that they do indeed have access to God, an access that cannot be denied. Even their Jewish opponents will eventually have to admit that the Christians are indeed beloved by God. The faithful will be preserved from the *hour of trial that is coming*, a reference to the eschatological woes that will come in judgment upon the earth. These cataclysmic events are described in detail in the remainder of the book. The conqueror will become *a pillar*, that is, will have a secure place in the presence of God.

3:14-22. Laodicea. Located in the Lycus River valley, the city of LAODICEA was founded by Antiochus II around the middle of the third century BCE and named after his wife Laodice. Because of its location at an important crossroads, Laodicea became a major commercial center. The church at Laodicea is mentioned in Col 4:13-16. Nothing worthy of praise is found among the Laodicean Christians. They receive only criticism from Christ, who condemns them for being ineffective, describing them as neither cold nor hot. This imagery was likely suggested by the beneficial hot springs at nearby Hierapolis and the pure, cold water at COLOSSAE. Laodicea, on the other hand, was plagued with a bad water supply that was both lukewarm and foul. The emetic quality of the water at Laodicea provides the background for the description of Christ who is nauseated by the Laodiceans and spits (or vomits) them from his mouth (v. 16). Although the Laodiceans think they are successful and self-sufficient, they are in reality *wretched, pitiable, poor, blind, and naked* (v.17). To correct their bankrupt spiritual condition, the Laodiceans must turn to Christ. The offer of white robes, symbols of PURITY, is particularly appropriate at Laodicea for the city was famous for its clothing industry, and particularly for its black wool. The salve for their eyes likewise draws upon local information. Laodicea was famous for an eye salve manufactured there. The memorable image of Christ knocking at the door and inviting those inside to eat with him is a promise of Christ's presence, both now and particularly at the messianic BANQUET in the coming age. Those who conquer are promised a share in Christ's reign in the coming kingdom (cf. 22:5).

The Heavenly Throne Room, 4:1–5:14

Chapter 4 begins a new section in the Apocalypse. Whereas chaps. 2 and 3 dealt primarily with the immediate concerns of John's readers, the remainder of the book, while still addressing the first-century situation, is more eschatological in orientation. A characteristic of many apocalypses is the otherworldly journey in which the author claims to have been taken away to another domain (heaven, the under world, the extremes of the earth) and shown the secrets of those places. Chapter 4 begins in that fashion, but the motif of a journey is not carried through. John's "visit" to the heavenly regions is a visionary experience and not a physical journey.

4:1-11. The throne of God. The open door (cf. 3:8) leads to God's dwelling place. God and his throne are described in images drawn from Ezekiel's vision of the throne-chariot of God (Ezek 1–2; cf. Dan 7 and Enoch's vision of God's throne room in 1 Enoch 14:8-24). The vision is intended to overwhelm and awe the reader with a sense of the majesty and mysteriousness of God. The scene serves as a forceful reminder that God, and not the Roman emperor or any other power, is sovereign over the universe. God, and God alone, is worthy of worship. The *twenty-four elders* seated on thrones constitute the heavenly council. Who they represent is not clear. The most popular suggestion is that they represent the twelve patriarchs of Israel and the twelve disciples of Jesus. The *sea of glass, like crystal* (v. 6) likely draws from the mythological imagery of the sea as representative of chaos, the untamed part of creation, threatening to overcome the created order. Here the sea is still a potential threat, but it has been subdued (the sea is smooth like crystal, instead of turbulent). In the *new heaven* of chap. 21, the sea no longer exists. The *four living creatures* (John has creatively transformed Ezekiel's imagery) lead the heavenly entourage in continual worship of God. Liturgical elements are prevalent in Revelation.

5:1-14. The lamb and the scroll. John then sees *a scroll* in the hand of God. The SCROLL is sealed to guarantee its authenticity and to keep secret its contents. The scroll contains the destiny of the world, the purposes and plans of God for all creation (cf. Ezek 2:9-10; Dan 10:21). As in many apocalyptic writings, in Revelation the course of history is already determined. The heavenly council is at an impasse because no one in the universe has been found who is able to break the seven seals and open the scroll. The dramatic tension of the scene is heightened by the reaction of John, who begins to weep because no one is *worthy to open the scroll*. Then one of the elders informs him that indeed there is one who can open the scroll—the Messiah, described as the Lion of the tribe of JUDAH (Gen 49:9) and the Root of David (Isa 11:1, 10).

Christ stands among the elders as a slain *Lamb.* Whether the specific referent for this metaphor is the sacrificial lamb of the Jewish cultus, the PASSOVER lamb, or the imagery of Isa 53, sacrifice is certainly a part of the message of this slaughtered Lamb figure. But there is a deeper meaning in the imagery. The slain Lamb is the crucified Christ, that is, the martyred Christ. This Lamb is more than victim, however. He is also a powerful, conquering Lamb, similar to the great horned sheep in *1 Enoch* 90:9-42. In fact, as the book of Revelation emphasizes, martyrdom is the means of conquering for both Christ and his followers. The *seven horns and seven eyes* on the Lamb emphasize his strength and wisdom—all-powerful and all-knowing. When the Lamb takes the scroll, the twenty-four elders and the four living creatures fall down in worship before him and once more break forth in song, praising the Lamb for the redemption he has effected for those *from every tribe and language and people and nation* (v. 9). Like the Israelites in Exod 19:6, the redeemed community is to be *a kingdom and priests serving our God* (v. 10). Soon the twenty-four elders and four living creatures are joined by a countless multitude of angels singing in full voice a resounding chorus of praise to the Lamb. Next the whole universe joins in the doxology of adoration and praise, not just for the Lamb but for *the one seated on the throne* as well. Christ is not just the agent of God, but is one with God. For that reason the worship and honor that are due God are appropriate for the Lamb as well.

The Seven Seals, 6:1–8:5

The Lamb proceeds to open the seals on the scroll one by one, unleashing a series of destructive events on the earth. Series of cataclysms such as these are a stock element of many apocalyptic writings (cf. 2 Esdr 4:51–5:13; 6:11-28; 8:63–9:13; 2 Bar 27:1-15; *TMos* 10:4-6; Mark 13:3-27 par.). Often called the eschatological woes, these events are presented as signs of the end times and serve as a part of God's punishment of the earth. As mentioned earlier, the events associated with the seven seals, as well as the other calamities in the book, should not be taken literally, nor assumed to be presented in chronological order. The destructive punishments unleashed by the seven trumpets and seven bowls are different representations of the same eschatological occurrences.

The First Six Seals, 6:1-17

6:1-8. The first four seals. The opening of the first four seals lets loose on the earth the four horsemen of death and destruction, one of the most memorable of the images in the entire Apocalypse. The symbolism of the riders on four different colored horses (*white, red, black,* and *pale green*) is adapted from Zech 1:8-11 (four horsemen are sent out by God to patrol the earth) and Zech 6:1-8 (chariots with four different colored horses are sent out over the earth). The first four seals are opened with a dramatic flourish—the seal is opened and one of the four living creatures cries, "*Come!*" The first rider, on *a white horse,* symbolizes warfare and conquering. White is an appropriate color, since victorious military commanders often rode a white horse in a triumphant procession. "Wars and rumors of wars" (Mark 13:7) are often associated with the end times. When the second seal is opened, a rider on *a red horse,* symbolizing violence and bloodshed, marches across the stage of history, leaving in its path disorder, violent death, and the absence of peace. The opening of the third seal brings forth the rider on *a black horse,* representing famine. The prices for the wheat and the barley are so exorbitant that the average person could not afford to buy food. Luxury items, olive oil and wine, would not be affected however. While the poor starve, the wealthy can continue their indulgent, selfish lifestyle. The fourth rider appears on *a pale green horse.* He is identified as *Death* (the Gk. word can also mean "pestilence") and is accompanied by *Hades,* the place of the dead. Together they wreak destruction upon the earth in a variety of forms (cf. Ezek 5:15-17; 14:21). Their destruction is not complete, however, for they kill only a fourth of the inhabitants of the earth.

6:9-17. The fifth and sixth seals. The opening of the fifth seal reveals to John the souls of the martyrs under the heavenly altar. Their location under the altar derives from their lives having been poured out as a sacrifice. The cry of the martyrs (*How long?*) is a cry for justice, for divine vindication. The cry is both one of personal vengeance and a cry for God to avenge the cause of justice and righteousness. How long will the forces of evil continue to dominate? How long will God allow the people of God to suffer? In outward appearances, the death of the martyrs seemed in vain. Their God was powerless to save them. The forces of evil had conquered. The prayer of the martyrs is that God will reverse the judgment of the world so that the purpose of their dying, as well as the sovereignty of God, might be revealed. The martyrs are each given *a white robe,* symbols of purification and victory, and told to wait until the number of martyrs would be complete. This idea of a predetermined number of righteous who must die before the end arrives is found in other apocalyptic writings (cf. *1 Enoch* 47:3-4; 2 Esdr 4:33-37). The deaths of the martyrs are not meaningless. Their deaths help fulfill the predetermined number and thus hasten the coming of the end when God's justice will be established.

A series of new cataclysms breaks forth when the sixth seal is opened. Described in traditional apocalyptic language, the cosmic disturbances and catastrophes bring judgment upon all the earth, particularly upon the rich and the powerful (v. 15). The punishment is so severe that the people cry out for mercy, asking who is able to withstand such judgment.

Interlude, 7:1-17

Before the seventh seal is opened, the action pauses. In the midst of all the punishment and judgment, John stops to give a word of assurance to God's people. The two visions that comprise this interlude reassure the faithful that they will be saved from the punishments that will affect the earth.

7:1-8. The sealing of the 144,00. vision John sees four angels hold back the winds that are set to unleash destruction on the earth. Another angel commands them to delay their punishment until God's servants have been given a mark on their foreheads for protection. Ezekiel 9:3-4 is the source for this imagery of a mark on the forehead for protection (cf. also the mark on the doorposts that saved the people of God from the plague of the death angel in Exod 12:21-32). Those who are thus protected comprise a throng of 144,000, with 12,000 taken from each of the twelve tribes of Israel. The number 144,000 should be understood figuratively. As a multiple of 12 and 10, both of which often symbolized completeness, 144,000 also represented completeness. But who comprises this complete group? Although some interpreters have argued that the 144,000 are Jews or Jewish Christians, in Revelation neither of these groups receives preferential treatment. Just as the numerical size of the group should not be understood literally, neither should the description of the group as being drawn from the twelve tribes. Instead the imagery depicts the church as the new people of God, the new Israel (cf. Jas 1:1). Although it is possible that the groups in the two visions both symbolize the complete number of God's people, the 144,000 more likely represent a complete subgroup—the martyrs (see the further descriptions of this group in 14:1-5). John gives special attention to them because they must bear the ultimate witness to their faith.

7:9-17. The great multitude. In contrast to the 144,000 in the first vision, the people who comprise the group in the second vision are too numerous for anyone to count. Whereas the first group was solely martyrs, the second group includes all the people of God, *from every nation, from all tribes and peoples and languages* (v. 9). They have *come out of the great ordeal* (v. 14), that is, the persecution that precedes the end. In a paradoxical metaphor, John says that they have washed their robes *in the blood of the Lamb* and made them white. Christ's sacrificial death has purified the people and rendered them righteous. This innumerable crowd of the faithful is in heaven, where they wave palm branches, symbols of joy and celebration, and sing a song of praise to God. Once more the heavenly chorus composed of the angels, the twenty-four elders, and the four living creatures join in with their doxology to God. The interlude ends with a comforting description of the existence awaiting the faithful. Neither hunger, nor thirst, nor scorching heat will afflict them for the Lamb will care for them. The Lamb, paradoxically, will be their shepherd who provides for their needs. Suffering and pain will be absent, for *God will wipe away every tear from their eyes* (cf. 21:3-4).

The Seventh Seal, 8:1-5

A climactic moment has been reached. The seventh seal is opened. One expects a final vision of what is to come. Instead, a short period of silence follows the opening of the last seal. The silence is not only for dramatic effect, but also indicates reverence, awe, and anticipation. The opening of the seventh seal does not yield the expected end but inaugurates a new series of woes, the seven trumpets. Before the trumpet series begins, another angel appears. Standing before the heavenly altar, the angel mixes incense with the prayers of the people and offers them on the altar. Although not restricted to them, the prayers of the martyrs under the altar in 6:9-11 would certainly be included in this offering. The prayers of the people are prayers for justice and the coming of the kingdom of God. *The smoke of the incense, with the prayers of the saints, rose before God* (v. 4), indicating that

God hears the people's prayers. The angel takes fire from the altar and casts it down upon the earth, resulting in thunder, lightning, and an earthquake. The prayers of the people have been effective. The judgment on the earth has begun, as the blowing of the seven trumpets will make clear.

The Seven Trumpets, 8:6–11:19

The blowing of *the seven trumpets* sets forth a new series of eschatological woes on the earth. What was begun with the opening of the seven seals is portrayed here in a different set of images. The two series overlap rather than succeed one another. There is a progression from the seals to the trumpets, however. Whereas the destruction wrought by the opening of the seals was basically limited to humanity, the destruction from the trumpet blasts affects the entire universe: the earth (8:7), the oceans (8:8-9), fresh water (8:10-11), the heavenly bodies (8:12), and persons (9:1-20). A further advance is noted in the extent of the destruction of human lives. When the fourth seal is opened, Death and Hades kill one-fourth of the population. In contrast, the trumpet punishments affect one-third of the world. Again, one must remember that this is poetic, not mathematical, language. The numerical statements convey that the destruction is not yet complete. The trumpet judgments are dependent on the Egyptian PLAGUES in Exod 7–10. Plagues of hail and fire (8:7), water turning to blood (8:9), darkness (8:12), and locusts (9:1-11) match the Egyptian plagues.

The First Six Trumpets, 8:6–9:21

8:6-11. The first three trumpets. The first trumpet blast sends fire that scorches the earth, affecting a third of the plant life. The second trumpet causes *something like a great mountain* (8:8) to fall into the sea, turning the water to blood. Not only are the fish in the sea killed but ships are also destroyed. The plague from the third trumpet blast is an extension of the second one. Whereas the second trumpet blast affected only the salt water, the third affects fresh water, turning them poisonous. *Wormwood,* the name of the star that poisons the water, is a popular name for any of several related plants. The wormwood mentioned several places in the Bible is probably a small shrub with hairy, gray leaves that was known for its extremely bitter taste. This latter characteristic explains why in the Bible "wormwood" is used figuratively for bitterness and sorrow. The plant is not actually poisonous, but John intensifies its effect.

8:12-13. The fourth trumpet. The results from the blowing of the fourth trumpet provide a good example of why the imagery in Revelation cannot be taken at face value. If a third of the sun and moon were darkened, then the length of a day and a night would not correspondingly be shortened by one third. John's imagery is not limited by reality or scientific accuracy, however. Between the sounding of the fourth and fifth trumpets, an announcement is made by an eagle flying through the sky. The announcement serves as a preview of what is to come and as a warning to the inhabitants of the earth. The first three trumpets have unleashed their punishments, but even more terrifying are the calamities yet to come. This announcement is a dramatic technique that heightens the suspense of John's vision.

9:1-11. The fifth trumpet. After the eagle warning, the fifth angel blows his trumpet and a fallen star takes a key and opens the bottomless pit. The star is an angel, as is often the case in APOCALYPTIC LITERATURE (cf. *1 Enoch* 86, 88). *The bottomless pit,* or abyss, is the place where demons or fallen angels were imprisoned. (Cf. *1 Enoch* 1–36, known as the "Book of the Watchers." This work, elaborating on the tradition in Gen 6:1-4, describes the rebellion against God of a group of angels. As punishment they are consigned to the abyss, described as a desert place and a place of burning fire.) The pit is the reservoir of EVIL. When the shaft to the pit is opened, smoke billows out and blocks the sun. Out of the smoke comes a swarm of locusts who look *like horses equipped for battle* (v. 7). The imagery of destructive horse-like locusts is drawn from Joel 1:1–2:11. The plague of locusts in Joel is also accompanied by darkness throughout the land. Locusts were (and still are) a devastating terror in the Near East. Swarms of locusts can destroy an entire region due to their numbers and their voracious appetite. John is even more creative than Joel in his description of the locusts. Not only do they have the appearance of horses, they wear

> *what looked like crowns of gold; their faces were like human faces, their hair like women's hair, and their teeth like lions' teeth; they had scales like iron breastplates, and the noise of their wings was like the noise of many chariots with horses rushing into battle.* (vv. 7-9)

The surreal locusts of John's vision are told not to harm the vegetation. Instead their task is to torture the wicked of the earth, those *who do not have the seal of God on their foreheads* (v. 4). They do not kill, but only inflict agonizing torture with their scorpion tails for five months, a limited amount of time. These demonic locust figures are grotesque and frightening representations of evil. They symbolize war, destruction, and chaos, but on a much grander scale than anything seen before. These evil forces, released in the last days, serve God's purposes by inflicting pain and punishment on the wicked. Evil itself, however, after this final resurgence will eventually be defeated by God. The idea of the last assault of evil is given in a different form in 19:11–20:15. The name of the leader of the locust monsters is given in Hebrew (*Abaddon*) and in Greek (*Apollyon*). The word *Abaddon* means "destruction" and is used figuratively in the Hebrew Bible for death or the place of the dead (see Job 26:6; 28:22). *Apollyon* is from a Greek word meaning "to destroy." (Some scholars have seen here a reference also to Apollo, whose symbol was a locust and of whom Domitian claimed to be an incarnation. See Beasley-Murray 1974, 162–63.)

9:12-21. The sixth trumpet. The sixth trumpet, which is the second woe foretold by the eagle, brings forth another invading army, cavalry from the *river Euphrates*. This woe is set in motion by the command of a voice from the heavenly altar, the place where the prayers of the people have been poured out (8:3-5) and from underneath which the cries of the martyrs have been heard (6:9-11). The sixth trumpet, then, is in part a response to the prayers of God's people. It is part of God's punishment of the wicked and the vindication of the righteous. As with the earlier punishments, this one is limited. Only a third of humankind is killed. The EUPHRATES River was the eastern boundary of the ROMAN EMPIRE. On the other side were the Parthians, the dreaded enemy of the Romans. The Parthian cavalry may have provided the rudimentary image for John, but John's army is no earthly force. Like the locust plague of the fifth trumpet, the cavalry is a grotesque, supernatural force that will wreak destruction. Their appearance is frightening; their effect is devastating. John envisions God using these demonic agents to carry out God's will. The angels who lead the destruction are *bound* (v. 14), that is, they are part of the fallen angels who were bound and thrown into the pit according to apocalyptic writings (see comment on 9:1).

The EXODUS motif that is so prevalent in Revelation explains the statement that, even after these plagues, the remainder of the people do not repent. The people of the world will follow in the footsteps of the PHARAOH. They will continue their idolatrous and rebellious ways.

Interlude, 10:1–11:13

As was the case between the sixth and seventh seals, so between the sixth and seventh trumpet blasts John inserts an interlude to provide reassurance to the faithful that they will not be harmed by the eschatological woes. This interlude, like the earlier one, contains two visions.

<u>10:1-11. The mighty angel with the little scroll.</u> John sees a mighty angel coming down and standing with one foot *on the sea* and one *on the land*. The physical description of the angel owes much to the description in Dan 10 of a similar heavenly being and the description of God in Ezek 1:26-28. This scene draws also upon the vision in Dan 12 in which two angels appear to Daniel, "one standing on this bank of the stream and one on the other" (12:5). The angel speaks like a roaring lion, causing the seven thunders to break forth. The seven thunders deliver a message that John is able to understand and that he is about to write down when he is told to seal up the message, that is, keep it secret. The reader is left puzzled and curious about the contents of the message from the seven thunders. The secrecy motif heightens the drama, but it plays a more important role. The refusal to reveal the message of the seven thunders is a way of saying that even such revelatory visions as John experienced and wrote down for his readers are incomplete. God's purposes and plans are not all revealed, because God is beyond full comprehension by mortals. The ineffable MYSTERY of God remains intact.

The angel *raised his right hand to heaven and swore by him who lives forever and ever* (vv. 5-6; cf. Dan 12:7) that there would be no more delay. The time for the fulfillment of God's purposes is near. John believed that he and the church of his time were living in the last days. The final onslaught of evil was breaking forth upon the world. Soon God would act decisively and would triumph over the evil forces. This word would have been a message of great comfort to John's readers who were facing persecution and perhaps martyrdom. The cry "How long?" has been answered: "No more delay!"

The voice from heaven speaks once more to John, commanding him to take the open scroll from the angel's hand and *eat it.* A similar episode is reported by Ezekiel as part of his experience of being called to be a prophet (2:8–3:3). For John, eating the scroll is a reinforcement of his commissioning to the role of the prophet. The scroll is *sweet as honey,* but makes his *stomach . . . bitter* (v. 10). This scroll, like the scroll in chaps. 4–5, contains God's plan for all creation, the message John is to make known as a prophet of God. Eating the scroll is symbolic of taking in the message, of "consuming" God's word, so that God's message is now John's message. The scroll is both bitter and sweet, because both judgment and mercy, punishment and blessing, are a part of the divine plan. A close parallel with the scroll is found in Dan 12. There Daniel is told to keep the book sealed "until the time of the end" (12:4). Now, however, the book is unsealed because *there will be no more delay* (v. 6). The long-awaited time of God's vindication has arrived.

11:1-13. The measuring of the Temple and the two witnesses. The second vision of the interlude begins with John being given a measuring rod and told to go and measure the Temple. Only the inner courts are to be measured. The measuring is a sign of protection. Whereas the inner court is preserved, the outer court will be trampled by the nations. Many scholars have postulated that this was an earlier prophecy that was put forth by ZEALOT defenders of Jerusalem prior to its destruction by the Romans in 70 CE. After the outer part of the Temple was captured by the Romans, the defenders barricaded themselves in the inner courts. If the suggestion by some interpreters is correct, this prophecy would have been a prediction by the Zealot defenders that even though the Romans might trample the outer courts, God would not allow the inner sanctuary to fall to them. Sadly, they were in error. John has perhaps taken this earlier prophecy and adapted it for his purposes. The Temple has already been destroyed by the time John writes, so his concern is not with the actual Temple in Jerusalem. Rather, for John the people of God are now the Temple. The church is what is marked for protection. This vision then serves as a word of encouragement and assurance to the faithful. The unrighteous will be "trampled" (v. 2) during the time of the eschatological woes, but God's people will not be harmed. The period of the trampling will be forty-two months, three and one-half years. In Daniel three and a half years (or "times") is the predicted length of time before the end arrives (7:25; 12:7). The figure should not be pressed. As half of seven, a number for completeness or totality, three and one half represents incompleteness, a short period of time.

The introduction of the *two witnesses* (v. 3) seems disconnected to the vision of the Temple. The abruptness of their appearance supports the contention that the measuring of the Temple is an earlier tradition that John has reworked. The two witnesses are given authority to prophesy for 1260 days (three and one half years), the same amount of time mentioned in v. 2. To prophesy is to proclaim God's message to the world, to be faithful witnesses of God and Christ. The content of their message is likely indicated by their garb, *sackcloth.* Since sackcloth was worn as a sign of penitence, the prophecy of the two witnesses is a call to repentance. The two witnesses are further described as *the two olive trees and the two lampstands that stand before the Lord* (v. 4). In Zech 4 the image of two olive trees is used for ZERUBBABEL the governor and JOSHUA the high priest, both of whom are viewed as messianic figures. The two olive trees provide oil for the lampstand. John applies both images, the olive trees and the lampstands, to the two witnesses. For John, however, the two witnesses are not messianic figures. They are further described in terms reminiscent of ELIJAH and MOSES (11:6; cf. 1 Kgs 17:1; Exod 7:8–11:10).

The two witnesses must give the ultimate testimony—their lives—when they are attacked and killed by the beast *from the bottomless pit.* This beast John will describe more fully in the coming chapters. The place where they are killed is *prophetically called Sodom and Egypt, where also their Lord was crucified* (v. 8). Jerusalem, like Sodom and Egypt, has become for John a symbol of rebellion against God. Jerusalem is representative of the entire world that rejects God and the prophets of God. John's portrayal of Jerusalem as the place where the prophets are killed is not an anti-Jewish statement. In the Hebrew Bible, Jerusalem is often condemned for its disobedience to God and its rejection of God's spokespersons. John is simply adapting that tradition here. Of course, for him that condemnation of Jerusalem is even more pointed because Jerusalem was the place of Jesus' martyrdom. Even after death, the two witnesses are treated shamefully, their bodies allowed to lie on the streets to be the subject of taunts and ridicule.

God will not allow his prophets to die in vain, however. After a short span of time (*three and a half days*), they are resurrected and ascend into heaven in the sight of their enemies. Following their ascension, a great earthquake strikes the city, killing seven thousand people. Those who are left *were terrified and gave glory to the God of heaven* (v. 13). The witness of the two martyrs produces results. Their testimony in word and in blood leads to repentance by the people.

The Seventh Trumpet, 11:14-19

Verse 14 serves as a reminder of the action of the work prior to the interlude. The lengthy interlude had interrupted the three woes that were announced by the eagle (8:13). Verse 14 ties the earlier section with what is to follow. The third woe, though announced, is not described. It is hinted at in the first part of v. 18 (*the nations raged, but your wrath has come*). The seventh trumpet blast brings the action to an end. God's purposes have been fulfilled. The heavenly voices declare the completion of God's plan when they announce, *The kingdom of the world has become the kingdom of our Lord and of his Messiah* (v. 15). God's reign no longer lies in the future, but is a present reality. In a way, the seventh trumpet blast is anticlimactic. After all the destruction and punishment leading up to the last days,

John provides no description of God's new order. It is completed. Instead of a picture of the kingdom of God, John lets his readers hear the celebration that takes place over God's victory. The twenty-four elders sing a song of triumph, saying, *We give you thanks, Lord God Almighty, who are and who were, for you have taken your great power and begun to reign* (v. 17). God is no longer described as the one who is and who was and who is to come. The last element is no longer needed. God has already come; the future has become the present. John could have ended his message here. The consummation of the kingdom has been achieved. John has more to reveal, however. He will present new images of punishment and salvation, eschatological woes and eternal reward.

Chapter 11 ends with a brief glimpse into the heavenly Temple in which the ark of the covenant is seen. The ARK had sat in the Holy of Holies in Solomon's Temple, a visual reminder of the presence of God in the midst of the people. The ark of the covenant was probably carried away or destroyed when the Babylonians captured Jerusalem in the sixth century BCE When God's kingdom has arrived in its fullness, John sees the ark in the heavenly Temple, a symbol of God's presence with the people.

The Great Conflict, 12:1–14:20

Chapters 12–14 portray the life-and-death struggle of the church with the evil forces aligned against it. For John and his readers, evil is incarnated primarily in the Roman emperor and his claims to divinity. This confrontation with the imperial cult is the major focus of this section. But John realizes that the conflict he and other Christians are facing is larger than what it appears. John sees this struggle in the context of the great cosmic conflict between the forces of good and evil. The evil powers have always rebelled against the sovereignty of God and attempted to thwart God's purposes. The suffering of the Christians of John's day was not isolated or insignificant. John paints their trials on a cosmic canvas, one that stretches back in history to primeval times. The struggles in which the church is engaged is simply another chapter in the ancient story of chaos versus order, obedience versus disobedience, rebellion versus loyalty. By giving his readers a new perspective on their ordeal John gave meaning to their suffering. Their persecution and martyrdom were not in vain. By their patient endurance and faithful witness, they were contributing to the overthrow and defeat of the powers of evil. John also offers assurance to his readers by revealing to them the ultimate outcome of this cosmic conflict of which they are a part.

The Vision of the Great Dragon, 12:1-18

Chapter 12 draws heavily upon ancient mythology for its images, adapting a popular cosmic combat MYTH found in many cultures of the ancient world. The closest parallel to the story told by John is the Greek version of the myth which tells of the birth of Apollo, son of Zeus and Leto. Python, the great dragon, pursues the pregnant goddess Leto, seeking to kill the unborn Apollo and his mother. Leto is carried away to safety to an island where Poseidon, god of the sea, hides her by sinking the island under the sea. When Python's search is unsuccessful, he finally gives up and goes away. The island is raised and Leto gives birth to Apollo, who goes and kills Python. John adapts this universal myth to convey the story of the defeat of the forces of evil by Jesus. John's use of this myth may have been particularly significant for his readers who were confronted with the claims of the imperial cult. Several of the Roman emperors used this myth for their own propaganda purposes, presenting themselves in the role of Apollo, the destroyer of evil. John and his readers know otherwise, however. Christ, not the emperor, is the real victor over the malevolent forces of chaos, darkness, and wickedness. As such, Christ and not the emperor is the one worthy of obedience and worship.

12:1-6. The woman, the dragon, and the child. The woman is presented as the cosmic queen, *clothed with the sun, . . . the moon under her feet, and . . . [wearing] a crown of twelve stars* (the zodiac). The *great red dragon* has *seven heads and ten horns, and seven diadems on his heads* (v. 3). In the Babylonian story of creation TIAMAT, the monster of the deep, also has seven heads. LEVIATHAN, the serpent-like monster of chaos in Hebrew folk-lore, also had many heads (cf. Ps 74:14). The *ten horns* (cf. Dan 7:7) symbolize the monster's power, the crowns his dominion. He is a powerful figure, as evidenced by his knocking a third of the stars out of the heavens (a traditional motif in many of the ancient myths). The application of Ps 2:9 to the child—he *is to rule all the nations with a rod of iron* (v. 5)—identifies him as the Messiah. The dragon fails in his attempt to kill the child, who is snatched away and taken to God. In John's story the birth and ascension of Christ are compressed into a single event. The woman escapes to the wilderness and is protected there by God for 1,260 days, the same three-and-a-half-year period John has mentioned before (see 11:2-3).

12:7-12. Michael and the dragon. Verses 7-12 appear to be an insertion into the cosmic combat myth. In reality they contain simply another version of the same struggle. That John is adapting a Jewish story here is evidenced by the role played by MICHAEL. He is the hero of the story, the one who defeats the dragon and his angels. The story of the ouster from heaven of rebellious angels is found in several Jewish sources (cf. *1 Enoch* 6–16) and has been popularized in John Milton's *Paradise Lost*. The great dragon is identified as *that ancient serpent, who is called the Devil and Satan, the deceiver of the whole world* (v. 9). In the Hebrew Bible Satan (literally the "accuser" or "adversary") is not the leader of the forces of evil who are arrayed against God. Rather Satan is the accuser of the righteous, the "prosecuting attorney" who brings charges against God's people. In later nonbiblical Jewish writings, likely due to the influence of the Zoroastrian religion of Persia, Satan (or Belial, or Beliar, or Azazel, or Semyaza) begins to be seen as the leader of the demonic forces of evil. Satan is portrayed as the archenemy of God. That understanding of the role of Satan was taken over by NT writers and is evident in Revelation also (see SATAN IN THE NT).

The ancient Jewish myth that John is using would have portrayed Michael as the one who defeats Satan and casts him out of heaven. John alters that story. Satan has been overthrown *by the blood of the Lamb and by the word of their testimony* (v. 11), that is, the testimony of the martyrs. For John the defeat of Satan is not a primeval event, but one that occurs in the death and exaltation of Christ and continues in the faithful witness of the martyrs who give their lives for the sake of God. John is saying to the persecuted church that their deaths have meaning. The faithful are contributing to the overthrow of the forces of evil. Their deaths may look like defeat, but John gives them a new vision in which death is victory.

12:13-18. The pursuit of the woman. Thrown out of heaven, Satan turns his attack upon the woman on earth. The woman, however, is given divine protection. She is *given the two wings of the great eagle* and carried off to the wilderness where she is protected during the coming period of trouble (cf. Exod 19:4, "I bore you on eagles' wings and brought you to myself"). Unable to defeat the woman, the dragon then goes off to make war on her children, the faithful witnesses (v. 17). The woman is a multivalent image. She is at the same time Mary (mother of Jesus), Israel (from whom the Messiah comes), the church, and the people of God of all ages, whose "children" are still being persecuted. John is adapting a universal myth here for his Christian message. Exact correspondence between the characters in the myth and the Christian story is not possible. One should not press for consistency in the role of the woman in the story.

The Two Beasts, 13:1-18

Whereas chap. 12 depicted the heavenly battle with Satan, chap. 13 reveals the earthly counterpart of that struggle. Thrown down to earth, the dragon stands poised to unleash his fury against God's faithful.

13:1-10. The beast from the sea. The first beast arises from the sea, the primordial realm of chaos and rebellion. The description of the beast is dependent on the four beasts from the sea in Dan 7, whose characteristics are merged into this one beast. John makes clear the source of this beast's power: *the dragon gave it his power and his throne and great authority* (v. 2). In awe and fear of this great beast, the people follow after the beast and worship him. Who is this beast? Even though the term is not used in Revelation, he is the ANTICHRIST, the eschatological opponent of Christ and his followers (see Reddish 1990, 34.) The Antichrist has taken on a particular identity for John. As the clues John gives elsewhere make clear, the beast is the ROMAN EMPIRE, and particularly the emperors themselves (see chap. 17). The many heads symbolize the various emperors who have ruled over the empire. The statement that one of the heads of the beast *seemed to have received a death-blow, but its mortal wound had been healed* (v. 3) is a reference to the Nero *redivivus* myth. Nero occupied a special place in the minds of the Christians, for Nero had instigated the first persecution against Christians when he blamed the fire in Rome on them in 64 CE. Later, Nero committed suicide by stabbing himself in the throat. The rumor soon spread, however, that Nero was not really dead or that he would come back to life and rule over the people again. By saying that this mortal wound had been healed, John is warning the church that Nero's persecution has returned in the present emperor, Domitian.

For forty-two months (three and a half years) the beast wages war against God's people. Without attributing evil to God, John states that the beast *was allowed to make war on the saints* (v. 7). Satan and his cohorts may have the upper hand at the moment, but ultimately God will assert control and the beast will be allowed to persecute the saints no longer. Those who succumb to the lures of the beast and worship it are the ones whose names are not written in *the book of life*, the register of the citizens of heaven (cf. 3:5). The last part of v. 10 is a refrain that sounds throughout the Apocalypse: *Here is a call for the endurance and faith of the saints.*

13:11-18. The beast from the earth. The second beast, also called *the false prophet* (19:20), is a beast from the land who deceives the people and enforces worship of the first beast. He performs SIGNS AND WONDERS like prophets of God, but he is a *false* prophet. Those who refuse to worship the first beast are killed. Those who comply, who pay homage to the first beast, receive a mark on their right hands or on their foreheads. This "mark of the beast," a parody of the sealing of the 144,000 in chap. 7, allows them to buy and sell in the marketplace. The mark of the beast requires wisdom, John says, for the number of the beast is the number of a person. That number is 666. The ancient practice of *gematria*, the assigning of numerical values to words, is at work here. In the ancient world, letters were used for numbers. (In our alphabet, A=1, B=2, C=3, etc.) One could easily convert a person's name into a number. Since the numerical value of several names could equal 666, the identification of the person John had in mind is not certain. The most likely referent for John's 666 number code, however, is Caesar Nero, whose name in Hebrew equals 666. The beast is not Nero, for he is dead. But Domitian, the current emperor, is a reincarnation of Nero. (Some commentators have argued for the symbolic meaning of 666. Since six is one less than seven, the perfect number, then 666 represents triple imperfection or evil.)

The background for this chapter is obviously emperor worship. The first beast who is worshiped represents the Roman emperor. Who, then, is the second beast? He represents everyone who encourages and supports emperor worship (local magistrates, imperial priests, provincial councils). By depicting the emperor and the promoters of the imperial cult as beasts who operate under the authority of the great dragon, John pulls back the curtain and reveals to his readers the true identity of those who are persecuting them. The imperial cult is an instrument of Satan, for it usurps the worship that belongs only to God.

Interlude, 14:1-20

Once more John pauses in the midst of scenes of suffering to offer words of encouragement and assurance. Twice already John has reassured his readers that the faithful will receive divine protection during the coming trials. This protection is protection from the effects of God's punishment, not protection from persecution and death. John is fearful that many of his Christian comrades may have to bear witness through death. Even if that happens, however, they can be assured that God will not abandon them. They will still share in God's new kingdom. That is the assurance that the marks of protection convey.

14:1-5. The Lamb and the redeemed. These verses reveal the ultimate destiny of the faithful. Chapter 13 portrayed the apparent defeat of God's people who died a martyr's death. The opening section of chap. 14 reverses that judgment, depicting the faithful not as defeated but as triumphant. John sees Christ (the Lamb) standing on Mt. Zion, the center of the messianic kingdom. With him are the 144,000 that were introduced in chap. 7. Like the heavenly chorus in 5:8-10, the 144,000 sing a new song of praise to God, a song that no one else could learn. While it is tempting to interpret the 144,000 as symbolic of all the redeemed of humanity, a closer reading of the description of them suggests that they are specifically the martyrs, the ones who have been the victims of the beasts in chap. 13. These with the Lamb *have not defiled themselves with women, for they are virgins* (v. 4). This description is figurative, not literal. One of the regulations for HOLY WAR required sexual abstinence before battle (cf. 1 Sam 21:4-5). John uses this requirement for ceremonial purity to symbolize moral and religious purity. The 144,000 have not been defiled by idolatry or by the enticements of the great whore of Babylon (chap. 17). They *follow the Lamb wherever he goes*, even unto death. They are described as *first fruits*. This is sacrificial language, appropriate for those who have sacrificed their lives for God. Finally, *in their mouth no lie was found*. The martyrs maintained their witness even under persecution, refusing to proclaim Caesar as lord.

14:6-13. The message of three angels. The central section of this chapter presents three angels who move across the stage, each proclaiming the coming judgment of God. The message of the first angel is a call to repentance and a warning of the impending judgment. The second angel issues a proleptic announcement of the fall of Babylon (Rome). The third angel pronounces judgment upon those who have succumbed to the power of the beast and its cult. Once more a call for the endurance of the saints is sounded (v. 12). The second beatitude of Revelation pronounces blessings upon those *who from now on die in the Lord* (v. 13). Those who are called to die as martyrs can face their ordeal with the knowledge of the glorious rest that awaits them. After death, they will no longer have to endure trials and persecutions.

14:14-20. The final judgment of God. This section depicts the final judgment of God in imagery that is borrowed from Joel 3:13. The first scene shows the harvesting of the earth, like wheat that is cut with a sickle (cf. Matt 13:24-30). John does not make clear whether this harvesting is a complete gathering of all people, the wicked for punishment and the righteous for rewards, or whether, like the second scene, this one portrays only the judgment of the unrighteous. Either of these options is preferable to the attempt by some commentators to argue that the first scene depicts only the ingathering of the faithful, whereas the second scene (vintage), portrays the punishment of the wicked. In Joel both images are used to show God's judgment against the wicked. In both scenes in chap. 14 an angel from the presence of God (*the temple . . . the altar*) gives the comand for the divine judgment to begin. The imagery of blood flowing *as high as a horse's bridle, for a distance of about two hundred miles* (v. 20) conveys the magnitude and severity of God's punishment on the wicked.

The Seven Bowl Plagues, 15:1–16:21

The seven seals and the seven trumpets have already disclosed the eschatological woes that are to strike the earth. John now introduces a different series, this one composed of seven bowls, that will present a different perspective on these calamities. Like the seven trumpet plagues, the bowl plagues are modeled after the PLAGUES on Egypt in the book of Exodus.

The Martyrs on the Heavenly Shore, 15:1-4

Verse 1 gives a brief announcement of the new series of seven plagues that are soon to break forth. These will be the last plagues, *for with them the wrath of God is ended* (v. 1). Before beginning the bowl plagues, John presents another vision of the faithful whom he sees standing beside *a sea of glass mixed with fire* (v. 2). This is the sea that stands before the throne of God (4:6). Here the sea also connotes the RED SEA of the Exodus tradition. As the Israelites traveled safely through the Red Sea and arrived in the Promised Land, so the faithful in John's vision have passed through their Red Sea (persecution and martyrdom) and now stand on heaven's shore. Moses and the Israelites sang a song of THANKSGIVING and praise after reaching the distant shore (Exod 15:1-18.) Likewise the victorious martyrs now sing *the song of Moses . . . and the song of the Lamb* (v. 3).

The Seven Angels with Bowls, 15:5-8

John sees seven angels who are to inflict the seven plagues come out of the heavenly Temple. Each is given a bowl containing the wrath of God that is to be poured out on the earth. The imagery of the bowls is likely a composite of two ideas from the Hebrew Bible. Bronze basins or bowls were used by the priests to carry away the ashes from the altar after sacrifices were offered (Exod 27:3). In John's vision the angels who are given the bowls have just exited the Temple where the heavenly altar is located (cf. the angel with the censer at the altar in 8:3-5). The bowls are *full of the wrath of God* (v. 7). Several passages in the Hebrew Bible speak of the cup of God's wrath (Isa 51:17; Ps 75:8; Jer 25:15-29; 49:12) that God's enemies drink, symbolizing God's punishments on them.

The Pouring of the Seven Bowls, 16:1-21

16:1-7. The first three bowls. In response to a command by a voice from the Temple, the seven angels pour out their bowls of judgment on the earth. The bowl plagues are very similar to the trumpet plagues, both of which draw upon the plagues inflicted on Egypt. The pouring out of the first bowl results in painful sores on *those who had the mark of the beast and who worshiped its image* (v. 2). This plague is similar to the sixth Egyptian plague (Exod 9:8-12). The second and third bowl plagues, like the second and third trumpet plagues, affect first the sea and then the fresh water. Here both are turned to blood, which is seen as fitting because the wicked had *shed the blood of saints and prophets* and now they must drink blood (v. 6). John proclaims that God is a God of justice. The people deserve the punishment they receive. The altar (the angel attending the altar, or the souls of the martyrs under the altar?) agrees in the assessment that God's judgments are true and just. The result of the second bowl plague is more severe than the result of the second trumpet plague. With the latter, only one-third of the earth is affected. With the former, *every living thing in the sea died* (v. 3).

16:8-11. The fourth and fifth bowls. The pouring of the fourth bowl on the sun brings about a scorching heat on the earth. Like the Egyptian PHARAOH, the people are obstinate in their rebellion against God and refuse to repent. The first four plagues have already affected all parts of the cosmos (land, waters, sea, and the sun). The focus of the fifth plague is narrower than that of the previous four plagues. The fifth bowl is poured *on the throne of the beast*. The ROMAN EMPIRE receives special punishment because it is responsible for leading many people into idolatry. Reminiscent of the ninth plague on Egypt (Exod 10:21-29), the fifth bowl plague produces an agonizing darkness over the whole land. Once more John states that the people do not repent of their evil ways. Some people are so hardened against God that nothing is able to bring them to repentance.

16:12-16. The sixth bowl. The sixth bowl plague has many similarities with the sixth trumpet plague in 9:13-19. Both describe invading armies from across the Euphrates who invade the west. In both scenes John is making use of the Roman fear of a Parthian invasion. John sees *three foul spirits like frogs* (v. 13) coming out of the mouths of the dragon, the beast, and *the false prophet* (that is, the second beast). The imagery of the frogs comes from the second Egyptian plague (Exod 7:25–8:15) in which the land is overrun by an abundance of frogs. John has greatly modified the imagery, however. These are no ordinary frogs. They are demonic spirits who gather together the kings of the earth for the great eschatological battle. The place where they are assembled *is called Harmagedon* (v. 16, or, ARMAGEDDON). The name Harmagedon is likely derived from Hebrew words meaning "mountain of Megiddo." Megiddo was an important city guarding the pass through the JEZREEL Valley in Israel. Several important battles had been fought at Megiddo throughout Israel's history. Thus the name Megiddo would have connoted a battlefield for people familiar with Israel's past. John is not predicting a literal battle that is to take place at Megiddo. *Harmagedon* is figurative language. It symbolizes the final attempt by the forces of evil to defeat God. John does not give any description here of the confrontation. He will do that in a later chapter (19:11-21). Instead, he gives an admonition from Christ: *"See, I am coming like a thief! Blessed is the one who stays awake and is clothed, not going about naked and exposed to shame"* (v. 15). This call to watchfulness is a warning about being unprepared for the coming of Christ which will occur unexpectedly. The wise person will live in anticipation and preparedness.

16:17-21. The seventh bowl. The emptying of the seventh bowl into the air brings down the curtain on the eschatological drama. A loud voice from the Temple announces, *"It is done!"* (v. 17). A cataclysmic earthquake, accompanied by lightning and thunder, rips through the earth, destroying *the great city . . . and the cities of the nations* (v. 19). The great city is called *Babylon,* but in reality is Rome. It is singled out for special mention because of its role in the persecution of God's servants and its idolatrous and blasphemous claims. The following chapters will present a fuller description of the downfall of Rome. The plague of hail that also occurs when the seventh angel pours his bowl is a part of the Exodus motif that is so strong in this section of the Apocalypse.

The Fall of Babylon, 17:1–19:10

For John, Rome represented the ultimate rebellion against God. The divine claims of the emperor, the imperial cult, and the persecution of God's people were all components of Rome's sinfulness and resistance to God. John goes to great lengths in this section to expose the true character and identity of this "great city" and to show reactions both on earth and in heaven to the city's demise.

The Great Whore, 17:1-18

Invited by an angel to see the judgment that befalls the great city, John is carried away *in the spirit* (in a vision) into a wilderness. John introduces a new imagery for Rome. The city is portrayed as a *great whore* who rides on a scarlet beast *full of blasphemous names* who has *seven heads and ten horns.* The beast is the same as the one John described in 13:1-10 and represents the Roman Empire. The blasphemous names refer to the divine claims made for the emperors. The woman riding on the beast is dressed in luxurious clothes and adorned with expensive gold and jewels. In her hand she holds a golden cup full of filth, representing her idolatry and wickedness. To the world, Rome appeared to be a dazzling, enticing city. John unmasks the true identity of the city. It is a repulsive, drunken prostitute. Like prostitutes in ancient Rome who wore their name on a headband, the woman bears her name stamped on her forehead. The use of sexual imagery for IDOLATRY is prominent in biblical traditions (cf. Rev 2:20-22). The most damning indictment of the city is the statement that the woman is *drunk with the blood of the saints and the blood of the witnesses to Jesus* (v. 6).

The angel describes the beast as the one who *was, and is not, and is about to ascend from the bottomless pit and go to destruction* (v. 8). This description is a parody of God, *who is and who was and who is to come.* In addition, the description is a reference to Nero who lived, then died, and was expected to return to lay claim to the throne once more (see 13:3). Through the voice of the angel, John tells his readers that the vision of the woman and the beast has more than a surface meaning for those who are wise enough to understand. As the woman represents Rome, the beast upon which she rides symbolizes the Roman Empire. The seven heads of the beast have a dual meaning. They represent seven mountains (Rome was known as the city of seven hills) and seven kings (the emperors). John's explanation of the beast has intrigued commentators for centuries. Who are the specific emperors John has in mind when he says that *five have fallen, one is living, and the other has not yet come; and when he comes, he must remain only a little while* (v. 10)? What about the beast who *is an eighth but it belongs to the seven* (v. 11)?

Scholars have given various answers to these questions. The problem is that by the time of John there had been more than seven emperors. Where does John start? Whom does he omit? Rather than attempt to decipher the listing of emperors, one should interpret the number seven as symbolic. The number seven is derived from the ancient myth of a seven-headed monster. That myth, not the actual number of emperors, controls John's imagery. The seven-headed beast symbolizes all the emperors up to and including Domitian. *Five have fallen*, meaning that Rome has already seen the majority of its rulers; *one is living* (Domitian); and the seventh will last only a short time (because the end is near). The claim that the beast is the eighth, but also part of the seven, is another reference to the Nero myth. Domitian (one of the seven) is, figuratively, the reincarnation of Nero.

The ten horns represent the rulers of other nations who are cohorts of the beast. They will join forces in the war against the Lamb. Their power is limited (*for one hour*), however. They will meet their defeat at the hands of Christ and his faithful followers (cf. 19:11-21). Verses 15-18 present a surprising development. The beast and the ten kings turn on the great whore and destroy her. They unwittingly become agents of God in inflicting punishment on Rome for its arrogance, idolatry, persecution, and greed.

Laments on Earth, 18:1-24

Chapter 18 is similar in form to a funeral dirge. It is composed of several laments over the fall of Babylon (Rome). Examples of these abound in the writings of the prophets in the Hebrew Bible, from which John has freely borrowed in constructing the present songs of doom (cf. Isa 13; 23–24; 34; Jer 50–51; Ezek 26–27). An angel first announces the fall of the city, an event John narrated earlier in 17:15-18. The destruction of the city will be complete. It will become a place haunted by demons and foul animals. Not only has Rome committed evil itself, but it has lead astray other nations, kings, and merchants who have drunk her wine and committed fornication with her.

In this chapter, the chronological perspective shifts. In vv. 2-3, Babylon has fallen. In vv. 4-8, the fall has not yet occurred and the people of God are given advance warning to leave the doomed city before its destruction occurs. Even though for John the destruction is future, he is so certain of God's ultimate triumph that he can speak of it as an accomplished fact. A similar chronological shift occurs several times in the following verses. The command to come out of the doomed city, modeled after Jeremiah's words in Jer 51:45, has a figurative meaning as well as perhaps a literal one. The people are to come out, or separate themselves, from the idolatry and wickedness of the city. God's people are called to reject the values and lifestyle of Rome and its followers. Rome's arrogance and pride are aptly stated in v. 7, *"In her heart she says, 'I rule as a queen; I am no widow, and I will never see grief'."*

Verses 9-20 report the laments of three groups of people who witness the fall of the great city (cf. Ezek 26–28). Each of these groups (kings, merchants, and mariners) has profited from its association with Rome. They weep and mourn because the fall of Rome means economic and political ruin for them. The wealth and extravagance of Rome is indicated by the vast amount of goods sold by the merchants. The last item in the list of v. 13 is rather jarring and indicates the depth of Rome's depravity: *cattle and sheep, horses and chariots, slaves—and human lives.*

After the laments are finished, an angel takes up a huge millstone and throws it into the sea, stating that such will be the fate of Babylon. This imagery of destruction is adapted from Jer 51:63-64 where the prophet is told to take the scroll on which his oracle against Babylon is written, tie a stone to it, and throw it into the Euphrates River, saying, "Thus shall Babylon sink, to rise no more." The totality of Rome's destruction is expressed in vv. 21-23. No music will be heard, no artisans will be found, no sounds of millstones or bridal parties will be heard, and no light will shine any longer. The city will be desolate. Rome has deserved this punishment, for in the city *was found the blood of prophets and of saints, and of all who have been slaughtered on earth* (v. 24). The destruction of the city is divine retribution for the suffering and persecution that Rome had inflicted on God's people.

Celebration in Heaven, 19:1-10

Strictly speaking, this section is an audition, rather than a vision. Each part of this section describes what John has heard. The fall of Rome brings about a reaction of celebration in heaven. The heavenly multitude sings praises to God because God has exacted judgment on Rome. Their song is a song of victory. The cry of the martyrs (6:10) has been answered and God has avenged *the blood of his servants* (v. 2). The songs of the heavenly chorus are not primarily songs of gloating, but celebrations of justice and vindication. The *twenty-four elders and the four living creatures* join in the worship and praise of God. Then a heavenly voice invites all God's people to join in the celebration. Heaven and earth are united in glorious peals of praise to God as Hallelujahs! reverberate throughout all creation. (This chapter is the only place in the NT where the word HALLELUJAH occurs.)

The final hallelujah song in this section offers praise not for the destruction of Rome but for *the marriage of the Lamb* (v. 7). The bride of the Lamb is the church. In the Hebrew Bible the metaphor of Israel as the bride of God is found often (see esp. Hos 1–3). Since Christians saw themselves as the new Israel, the application of the bride imagery to the church was a natural one. In the NT the author of Ephesians gives an extended application of this metaphor (Eph 5:23-32; cf. 2 Cor 11:2). The bride is dressed in *fine linen, bright and pure*, which is interpreted as the righteous deeds of the saints. The contrast between the church and Rome is unmistakable. Rome is the great prostitute, drinking from a cup of abominations and impurities. The church, on the other hand, is the pure bride of Christ, adorned in fine, bright linen.

The fourth beatitude of Revelation (v. 9) declares: *Blessed are those who are invited to the marriage banquet of the Lamb.* Who are the guests? They too are the church. One cannot press John's imagery for consistency. John's language is poetic, imaginative language, not analytical or scientific language. In John's creative presentation, the church can be both the bride and the wedding guests. The imagery of a wedding and a wedding feast convey the mood of the kingdom of God. God's kingdom is filled with joy and celebration, happiness and intimacy.

In response to all that he has heard, John falls down in worship before his angel guide. The reaction of the angel is quick and decisive: *"You must not do that! I am a fellow servant with you and your comrades who hold the testimony of Jesus. Worship God!"* (v. 10). The words of the angel were apt words for John's readers as well. Tempted to compromise their faith and participate in emperor worship, they should hear these words as a warning. No one, not even the angels and certainly not the beastly emperor, is worthy of worship. Worship belongs to God alone.

The Final Victory, 19:11–20:15

Several times John has either intimated or directly stated that the decisive victory over evil has been accomplished. In this section he gives the final and most complete portrayal of the defeat of all the forces aligned against God. Like all of the Apocalypse, the scenes here are not literal predictions of coming events, arranged in chronological order. Instead, John presents the reader with powerful images of judgment, punishment, and the righteousness of God.

19:11-16. The triumphant Christ. This passage portrays the coming of Christ as judge and warrior. Heaven opens and John sees a rider on *a white horse.* (This horse and rider should not be confused with the one that appeared at the opening of the first seal in 6:1-2.) The rider is Christ, *called Faithful and True* (cf. 3:14, *the faithful and true witness*). His eyes are *like a flame of fire* (cf. 1:14; 2:18). His many diadems are evidence of his royal position. His name *that no one knows but himself* (v. 12) signifies the mystery of Christ who surpasses all human understanding. His robe is dipped in blood, like that of God the Divine Warrior in Isaiah 63 whose robe is stained with the blood of his enemies. *His name is called The Word of God* (cf. John 1:1, 14; and esp. Wis 18:14-16). The sword from his mouth, his ruling with a rod of iron, and his treading the wine press (v. 15) are all images of judgment upon the earth. In case any doubt exists concerning the identity of this splendid figure, emblazoned on his robe and on his thigh are the words *King of kings and Lord of lords*. Christ is accompanied by the armies of heaven, also riding white horses. Although some commentators understand the heavenly armies to be composed of angels, the forces here are probably identical with the *called and chosen and faithful* of 17:14, the martyrs. They do not engage in actual combat (notice they wear festal garb, not battle vestments), but they accompany Christ to share in his victory. They are witnesses of their own vindication.

19:17-21. The final battle. An angel calls to the birds and invites them to *the great supper of God* to eat the bodies of God's enemies who will be killed (cf. Ezek 39:17-20). This is a grotesque counterpart to 19:9. Like the redeemed who are invited to the marriage supper of the Lamb, the wicked of the earth will also participate in a great feast. The difference is that they will be the main course! In the final battle the beast and false prophet are captured and thrown into *the lake of fire that burns with sulfur* (v. 20). The lake of fire is GEHENNA, the place of torment for the wicked. The remainder of the forces arrayed against Christ are killed *by the sword that came from his mouth* (v. 21). The identification of Christ's weapon as the sword of his mouth (i.e., the word of God) should be a caution to anyone who is tempted to interpret the battle imagery of Revelation literally.

20:1-6. The millennial reign. As a result of the battle, Satan is bound by an angel and thrown into *the bottomless pit* (see 9:1; cf. Isa 24:21-22). There he is to remain for a thousand years. The imprisonment of Satan is certain, for he has been bound with a chain, locked in the pit, and a seal placed over the door. All the evil forces have now been removed from the earth.

The millennial reign of Christ and his followers now begins. The concept of an interim earthly rule prior to the consummation of the KINGDOM OF GOD in heaven is found in several apocalyptic writings. The idea apparently developed from the attempt to combine the older prophetic idea of a this-worldly kingdom of God centered in Israel that would occur in the last days with the apocalyptic notion of a new heaven and new earth as the locale for God's kingdom. The interim reign of the messiah, followed by the otherworldly kingdom of God, preserves both concepts. The length of this interim reign varies in different traditions. John pictures it lasting for *a thousand years*; in 2 Esdr 7:28 the messianic reign lasts 400 years. Among the many other limits set for this reign are 4,000 years, 600 years, 60 years, 365 years, or even 365,000 years.

According to v. 4 the millennial reign is not for all believers, but only for the martyrs. This interim period is a special reward for those who have given their lives for the sake of God's kingdom. The rest of the dead (righteous and unrighteous) will not be raised until the end of the millennium. The first resurrection is only for those who have paid the ultimate price for their witness. They are the *firstfruits* (14:4) of the harvest. The remainder of the faithful will be united with them after the second resurrection. The millennium should not be taken literally. Instead it should be seen as powerful imagery offering reassurance that God knows and values the tremendous sacrifices that some believers are called upon to make for the sake of God's kingdom.

20:7-10. The final conflict. Satan is loosed from his imprisonment after the millennium is ended and mounts one last assault on the people of God. Why, in John's scheme, Satan must be released after he has been bound is not clear. Perhaps it is John's way of emphasizing the formidable power of evil. Even when it appears that evil has been contained and is no longer a threat, it has the capacity to rebound and wreak havoc in one's life. A more mundane reason for having Satan released is so John could introduce one more image in his apocalyptic drama, the figures of *Gog and Magog*. Satan is joined by Gog and Magog, representing *the nations at the four corners of the earth* (v. 8). The symbolism of Gog and Magog is taken from Ezek 38–39 where Gog, the leader of the land of Magog, leads a group of nations in an attack on Jerusalem. John adapts that tradition, making Gog as well as Magog the names of nations. Satan and his army attack the people of God, described as *the camp of the saints and the beloved city* (v. 9). God intervenes, however, destroying the rebellious forces of Satan. Satan is thrown into the lake of fire, there to be *tormented day and night forever and ever* (v. 10), along with his cohorts, the beast and the false prophet. Finally, and definitively, Satan is defeated.

20:11-15. The last judgment. The final judgment takes place in front of the *great white throne* of God. The earth and heaven flee from God's presence because as part of the old, rebellious order no place exists for them anymore. A new heaven and new earth will be needed. All people stand before the throne, while two types of books are brought and examined. In one book, *the book of life* (cf. 3:5; 13:8; 17:8), are recorded the names of all the people of God. It is the heavenly register of the redeemed. In the other books are recorded all the deeds of humanity. The imagery here appears in conflict. If one's name is in *the book of life,* how can one also be judged by works? If one's name is not in the book of life, can one be saved by works? The resolution of this tension lies in the creative juxtaposition of these two images. John is reminding his readers that salvation is a matter of God's grace, not their achievement (the book of life). On the other hand, one's actions do matter. They are an indication of the seriousness of one's commitment to God. Grace and works are held together in this scene in creative tension. No one escapes God's judgment. Even Death, the last enemy and the destroyer of life, is not exempt. *Death and Hades* (the place of the dead), along with *anyone whose name was not found written in the book of life*, are cast into the lake of fire, the second death.

The New Jerusalem, 21:1–22:5

All of John's visions have been leading up to this final section. The eschatological woes, the punishments, the words of assurance, the last judgment, all are left in the shadows of this final spectacular scene of God's glorious kingdom. As has been the case throughout the Apocalypse, John draws heavily upon motifs and images from the Hebrew Bible and apocalyptic traditions. The reader must keep in mind that John's language is imaginative and symbolic. A literal reading of the text produces a distorted understanding of John's message. The imagery of *the new Jerusalem* and *the new heaven and the new earth* are symbols of life lived in intimate communion with God.

New Heaven and New Earth, 21:1-8

Not only do earth and heaven give way for a new heaven and new earth (cf. Isa 65:17; 66:22), but the sea no longer exists in John's vision of the new world. The sea is a symbol of chaos, rebellion, and evil. John sees the new Jerusalem coming down out of heaven. This is no human construct. Its origin is from God. The city is *prepared as a bride adorned for her husband* (v. 2). John has earlier painted a graphic picture of another city, "the great city," Rome. The new Jerusalem is in direct contrast to that city. Rome was portrayed as a prostitute; the new city is like a bride. The hallmark of this new city is that God dwells here with God's people. Nothing separates the people from their God, not physical distance, not emotional nor physical pain.

God speaks directly in vv. 5-8, declaring that the re-creation of all things is completed. The end has arrived through the actions of the one who is Alpha and Omega, beginning and end. The faithful (the conquerors) are assured that they will inherit the blessings of God and will be God's children. The wicked, however, are excluded from God's kingdom. The list of those who will be cast into the lake of fire is probably traditional, but some of its elements would have had special significance for John's situation. The cowardly and the faithless are those who did not resist the beast of Rome; the liars are those who confessed the emperor as lord (cf. 14:5).

The Holy City, 21:9-27

An angel comes and takes John up to a high mountain from which he can view the new Jerusalem. The city has *twelve gates* named for the *twelve tribes of Israel* and *twelve foundations* named for the *twelve apostles*. This symbolizes the city as the total people of God. The measurement of the city reveals that it is a cube, symbolizing the perfection of the city. In the Greek text the measurements are multiples of twelve (twelve thousand stadia), symbolizing the enormity and completeness of the city. The city is built of precious metals and jewels (cf. Isa 54:11-12). Much of this description is borrowed from other traditions, including the listing of the precious stones on the breastplate of the high priest (cf. Exod 28:17-20). The presence of these stones support the claims made earlier that the people of God are a priestly people. The gates of the city are made of pearls and the streets are made of gold. The total effect of the description is to overwhelm the reader with the magnificence and glory of this dwelling place for God's people.

No need exists in the city for a temple, symbolic of the presence of God, because in the new Jerusalem God and the Lamb dwell with the people. Likewise no sun or moon are needed because the glory of God and Christ shine throughout the city. The glory of the city is such that it will draw nations and kings into it. It is a place of safety where the gates of the city need never be shut (v. 25). It is also a place of purity and righteousness into which everyone and everything that is unclean are forbidden to enter.

The River of Life, 22:1-5

John's description of the new Jerusalem is heavily dependent on Ezekiel's vision of the restored Jerusalem (chap. 47). In Ezekiel, as well as in other writings (particularly in APOCALYPTIC LITERATURE), future hope is expressed in terms of a restored Garden of Eden. That imagery is prevalent in these verses in the tree of life and in the river that flows through the city. John borrows from Ezekiel the idea that the leaves of the tree will be for healing. The most revealing characteristic of life in the new Jerusalem is that God's servants *will see his face* (v. 4), a feat not possible before (cf. 1 Cor 13:12; Matt 5:8). This act expresses intimacy, fellowship, and complete knowledge. Life in God's new kingdom is eternal, for *they will reign forever and ever* (v. 5).

Epilogue, 22:6-21

The book concludes with a series of warnings, exhortations, and assurances. The identity of the speaker is not clear in all cases. Verses 7, 12, 16, and 20 come from Christ. Verses 6 and 10 may be from Christ or an angel. In v. 6 the speaker declares the message of John to be authentic because its ultimate source is God. Verse 7 presents a blessing for those who hold fast to the message John has revealed in this writing.

Once again (cf. 19:10) John falls down to worship his angelic guide and is strongly rebuked (vv. 8-10). Worship should be directed to God alone. Apocalyptic writings often claim to have been written by venerable figures of the distant past, but their message has only recently come to light. To explain why the works, if ancient, had not been known earlier, a command to secrecy is often included. The works have been sealed up until the last days, which are the present time (cf. Dan 8:26; 12:4, 9). John does not use an ancient pseudonym. He writes in his own name for his own time. There is no need to seal up his message, *for the time is near* (v. 10). In fact the end is so near that little time is left for people to change their ways (v. 11).

Christ declares that he is coming soon to bring punishment and reward (v. 12). He applies to himself the same titles that have been used in the book for God (cf. 1:8; 21:6). The final blessing of the book is pronounced upon *those who wash their robes*, that is, those who have been redeemed by Christ's death (cf. 7:14). While the redeemed may enter the new Jerusalem, the wicked (*dogs* was a derogatory term often applied to the godless) must remain outside. Once more the authenticity of the message is declared (v. 16). In v. 17 the Spirit and the bride (the church) respond to the promise that Christ is coming by issuing their own invitation, *"Come."* (In the Gk. text, *come* is singular, indicating that the invitation is addressed to Christ and not to people in general.) Everyone is urged to join in extending the invitation, and finally the invitation is opened to all who want the water of life to come (cf. John 7:37-38).

Verses 18-19 contain a curse formula to safeguard the accuracy and authenticity of the work. Formulas of this nature, found in many ancient writings, were an attempt to prevent copyists from altering the text. John believes that his message is a true word from God and wants to preserve its integrity. For the third time in this section, Jesus exclaims, *"I am coming soon"* (v. 20). This time John answers in words that are both a shout of jubilation and a prayer for fulfillment: *Amen. Come, Lord Jesus!*

The book ends with an epistolary conclusion similar to those in Paul's letters.

Works Cited

Beasley-Murray, George R. 1974. *The Book of Revelation*, NCB.

Hemer, Colin J. 1986. *The Letters to the Seven Churches of Asia in Their Local Setting.*

Reddish, Mitchell G. 1990. "Antichrist," MDB.

LaVergne, TN USA
28 December 2010
210369LV00007B/32/A